A People and Their Music

A People and Their Music

The Story Behind the Story of Country Music

John Rice Irwin

Schiffer Publishing Ltd

4880 Lower Valley Road, Atglen, PA 19310 USA

Library of Congress Cataloging-in-Publication Data

Irwin, John Rice, 1930-
    A people and their music: the story behind the story of country music/John Rice Irwin.
      p. cm.
    ISBN: 0-7643-0942-0 (pbk.)
    1. Country musicians--United States--Biography.
 I. Title.
 ML394.178 2000
 781.642'0973--dc21   99-049661

Designed by "Sue"
Type set in Winsor BT/Dutch 801

ISBN: 0-7643-0942-0
Printed in China

Published by Schiffer Publishing Ltd.
4880 Lower Valley Road
Atglen, PA 19310
Phone: (610) 593-1777; Fax: (610) 593-2002
E-mail: Schifferbk@aol.com
Please visit our web site catalog at **www.schifferbooks.com**

This book may be purchased from the publisher.
Include $3.95 for shipping.
Please try your bookstore first.
We are interested in hearing from authors
with book ideas on related subjects.
You may write for a free catalog.

In Europe, Schiffer books are distributed by
Bushwood Books
6 Marksbury Ave.
Kew Gardens
Surrey TW9 4JF England
Phone: 44 (0)208 392-8585;
    Fax: 44 (0)208 392-9876
     E-mail: Bushwd@aol.com
Free postage in the UK. Europe: air mail at cost.
Please try your bookstore first.

We are interested in hearing from authors
with book ideas on related subjects.

Acknowledgments

This acknowledgment of gratitude is written not so much because it is customary for an author to do so, but because of a genuine desire to recognize and thank some of those kind folks who contributed to the writing of this book.

First, I should express my indebtedness to the many old-time musicians who excited and inspired me from my childhood days to the present. Some of these were local and unknown outside their small rural communities, and some I knew only through their records and their radio programs. But some were great old-time legendary musical folks, such as Roy Acuff, Bill Monroe, Chet Atkins, and Ralph Stanley. All these groups alluded to here have been inspirational, motivational, and have perhaps inadvertently, nudged me to tell "the story."

I'm most particularly appreciative of the time and patience afforded me by those included in this volume. Janette Carter, one of the warmest and most unpretentious souls I've ever met, never seemed to tire of my many hours of questioning her, nor did her brother Joe. And venerable Bob Douglas, even as he neared 100, could not have been more patient, nor giving, nor more desirous to be helpful. The same can be said for Doug Jackson, who provided me with photographs, papers, and other memorabilia relative to his late father, Jack Jackson. Grandpa Jones allowed me to "pilfer" through his workshop and office where thousands of photographs, awards, celebrity letters, etc. were stored; and he encouraged me to take whatever I needed. He and his wife, Ramona, were kind enough to always invite my wife, Elizabeth, and me to their annual "Christmas-time" get-together at their log home where I met and became acquainted with the "greats" of early country music. Oswald (Beecher [Pete] Kirby) and his wife, Euneta, opened their Nashville home to me, as well as their picture albums and keepsakes. The same is true of Earl and Louise Scruggs, in whose home I spent several hours on two occasions. I'm also indebted to Louise for her meticulous and expert reading of the Earl Scruggs chapter. Mac Wiseman was liberal with his time, both during interviews and during many telephone conversations with him. His ability for accurate and sequential recall is remarkable. Certainly no one was more available than Raymond Fairchild. In addition to his several visits with me here at the Museum of Appalachia, I made three trips to his home in Maggie Valley to talk with him. No one gave me more advice, whether or not I requested it.

I'm indebted also to John Hartford who shared with me his scholarly and insightful knowledge of the subject, and who read a part of the manuscript, as did Bobby Fulcher, another student of the traditional music of our region. And I'm indebted to Dr. Charles Wolfe, the prolific and impeccable writer and authority on old-time music, to whose books I often referred.

I'm grateful to Les Leverett, the noted Nashville photo-journalist, for his generous loan of several photographs for the book. Then there's Frank Hoffman, the master of the darkroom, who has revived and copied virtually every photograph which appears in this book. Additionally, he took several of the pictures included herein.

I must truthfully confess that the book would never have been written were it not for five years of gentle, and sometimes not so gentle, nudging from my dear Yankee friend, Peter Schiffer, the publisher. He thinks we Southerners move slowly—and sometimes we do.

There are others. Dr. Nat Winston of Nashville has provided me with valuable information, especially on Earl Scruggs and Raymond Fairchild. Nat has read portions of the manuscript and has provided encouragement and counsel. Thanks also to Dr. William and Sandra Acuff who spent part of their vacation with us reading portions of the book. I would be remiss if I didn't credit Vicki Langdon of Denison, Texas, for her enthusiastic assistance with regard to the "new" Carter Family, a group she literally adored.

My staff has been helpful. Alene Humphrey has deciphered the hundreds of my handwritten pages, even when I could not do so myself. She's made repeated valid suggestions, and she's typed these pages at least a half dozen times. Misty Yeager has read and re-read every word of the book, several times, for grammatical irregularities and such. And Andrea Fritts, my secretary of 30 years, has had to help keep the office running while we've worked on "the book."

My daughter Elaine Irwin Meyer has carefully read the entire manuscript and has made many valuable suggestions. As Executive Director of the Museum of Appalachia, she has assumed many of my responsibilities, allowing me more time to tinker with this project.

My wife, Elizabeth, deserves much credit for patiently "allowing" me to spend all my spare nights in my office on this project, and for accompanying me on some of the interview trips.

There are many others who have been helpful and supportive of this effort, and to all those I offer my profound thanks.

Contents

Introduction

The use of the term "country music" may be misleading and confusing to some readers. As it is used here, the reference to country music does not apply only to contemporary country music and musicians; but it rather refers in a much broader sense to the music "of and from" the country which has, in the 20th century, been variously called folk music, traditional music, old-time music, hillbilly music, "early" country, and bluegrass music, as well as the country music of the present.

It is most curious that a relatively small, rural region in the Southern Appalachian Mountains has had so much influence on the music listened to by such a large segment of this nation's people, and indeed by people from throughout much of the world. This story is colorful, fascinating and purely American; and it reveals much, not only about how these resourceful and ingenious folk imparted their music to other sections of the country, but it also presents important revelations as to how they have contributed greatly to the general economic, industrial, and agricultural development of a nation.

How was it that people dealt with the isolation of the lonely plains of the Midwest, the drudgery of the coal mines, the tedium of a 72-hour work week in the cotton mills in the South, and the relentlessness of housekeeping, coupled with the sheer poverty endured by so many Americans? I submit that music, singing and playing music, was a powerful and constant companion which served to lend hope, joy, solace, and even exhilaration to these souls, lightening their burden, and spreading happiness along the way. It had inestimable psychological and therapeutic effects. But in order to understand this, one must realize that much old-time music totally *moved* people; it inspired them because they drank it in. It was all consuming, and some people literally would rather hear it than to eat. It carried with it emotion and power that can no more be explained in words than one can convey the feeling one experiences with the birth of a first child. My father sometimes described the effect of hearing an old fiddle tune, expertly played, by saying: "It would make the hair stand up on the back of your neck." People carried it with them in their workplace, they hummed the old tunes or sang fragments of old songs, they "listened" to it in their minds as they toiled, and they were happy. The individual result was a greater work day, and collectively it contributed to a greater nation.

That which started largely with old-time English, Scottish, and Irish ballads being sung and played by the fireside in mountain cabins of Southern Appalachia evolved, in a relatively short time, into the present-day country music phenomenon.

This book began because Peter Schiffer, whose company has published seven books for me, was always suggesting that I do another; and he's offered a variety of topics over the years. But I was determined to complete a few more projects here at the Museum of Appalachia before committing myself to the tedium of such a project, and I always begged for his patience. But when he mentioned a book on "Country Music," a flood of thoughts came rushing to mind, the aggregate of which led me to commence the task with enthusiasm and excitement.

First, I totally love the music and songs of our people, even to the extent that I, early on, learned to play the mandolin, guitar and harmonica, and eventually I formed my own "old-time" country music band, which has remained active for over a quarter century. Secondly, I've always stood in awe and admiration of those colorful, witty, and lovable fiddlers and singers; and the thought of "revisiting" them and re-studying their lives and their music was most pleasing. Additionally, I have collected, over a period of some 30 years, much information and materials on the old-time musicians of the region, including thousands of photographs and hundreds of old-time handmade musical instruments from the Southern Appalachian Mountains. These items constitute a rather large section in the Appalachian Hall of Fame at the Museum of Appalachia in Norris, Tennessee. Further, the annual Museum of Appalachia's Tennessee Fall Homecoming, which I founded in 1980 and have directed since that time, has allowed me to work with and become acquainted with a thousand or so old-time, and not so "old-time," country, folk, bluegrass, and traditional singers and musicians. Also, I should not fail to mention the half century which I have spent periodically visiting in the homes and cabins of so many of these gracious, friendly, and inspiring mountain folk, studying their ways, listening to them sing the plaintive songs and play their fiddles and banjos, and talking with them about their lives, their heritage, and their music.

So it was that I launched into this book. However, I met with a revelation which was very discouraging and disheartening. In looking through my reference books on the subject of country music, I was soon reminded that much had already been written on the subject—voluminous, colorful, and slick productions, some of which contained writings from the leading professional and authoritative writers in the field. I thought to myself: "Boy, what am *I* doing here with paper and pen, writing in longhand and thinking I can compete with the likes of these folks, trying to add to that which seems to need no addition?" I've got to take a different approach, I thought, to present the subject in a fresh and different light, and in a not-done-before manner; or step aside altogether. After all, I'm certainly not interested in writing just another book. It has to be interesting and above all it has to be meaningful. It needs to fill a niche, to make a contribution toward the understanding and meaning of country music—something, too, which has some elements of permanency in a documentary sort of way. Even my daughter and associate, Elaine I. Meyer, questioned the wisdom of such an undertaking.

So, I thought and pondered. It kept occurring to me that the most important aspect of this, or perhaps any music, was the "feel" of it—what there was about it, even in its ever-changing form, which moved people, inspired them, and at times almost consumed them. Then, I thought, there is a need to become acquainted with the friendly, colorful folks who helped to *start* and develop this music. They needed to be presented just as they are, or were: warm, perceptive, sentimental souls who were sometimes somber but more often jovial, and occasionally mischievous, with twinkling eyes and devilish, yet kind, smiles.

So this, then, will be my mission here—to take a personal, people-oriented, human-interest approach to the subject. What better way is there to understand the phenomenal influence this music has had on us than to know and understand the people who nurtured and developed it. Emphasis will be placed on the early years of these musicians, their families, their childhoods, and the lean years as well as their years of success.

It is a people-oriented book. Just as the in-depth study and understanding of a few trees provide an understanding of the total forest in which they stand, it is hoped that a study of a few early and contemporary music folks will help us to understand something of the background and development of traditional, early country, bluegrass, and even modern country music.

In order to accomplish the mission stated above, I've chosen several individuals, and one family, the Carters, to study. No pretense is made that they represent all facets of the development of early country and bluegrass music, or that they are the most appropriate and outstanding, though well they may be. It is believed, however, that they are good representatives of all those who embarked upon a totally unknown future, pioneers as it were, of a profession yet to be defined. The interesting, revealing, and fascinating stories of these folks, herein presented, will, when woven into a single story, present a revealing and realistic understanding of "the story behind the story of country music." Those included herein are from Tennessee, North Carolina, Virginia, Arkansas, and Kentucky, and they have remarkable similarities with regard to their early, rural, and hardship-filled lives, their lack of encouragement, their inward motivation, and their individualism.

Chapter 1

Where It All Started

It was 1965 when I visited Renda Whitaker, a gentle but resolute little lady who lived alone on the Cumberland Mountain Plateau near Monterey, Tennessee, at a place called Lick Skillet. I asked Renda about the old banjo hanging on the wall of her front room; and the mere thought of that old dust-covered instrument evoked a flood of warm and pleasant memories for her.

"Oh, Lord," she said, "that old banjar reminds me of a lot of good times. When me and my husband Vetter got married, we worked hard clearing the land, planting crops and such, trying to get a start. After supper, we'd set on the porch and rest a little until it got dark, and sometimes we'd sing. We'd sing them old songs, and one day Vetter said to me: 'Renda, we need us a banjar. If we had us a banjar we could play a little music while we sing.'

"Well, the very next day we went out here in the woods behind the house and cut a poplar sapling and commenced whittling out the neck for a banjar, and we split a piece of white oak for the rim. In a day or two, Vetter went down there to the corn patch early one morning and he killed a big ground hog. He skinned him and he dug a hole in the ground, put the hide down in it, and covered the hide with hickory ashes from the fireplace to take off the hair. We kept it wet, poured water on it every once in a while for a few days, and then we took it out and rubbed it in corn meal. Just kept working it, pulling and twisting it, until it was good and soft, just like a dish rag. Then we used the hide for the head of the banjo; and when we got it strung up, it sounded pretty good. Law, at the good times me and

Vetter had playing that old banjar!"

Thus the Whitakers were, almost by instinct, following a practice employed by their ancestors, and by thousands of other families throughout the Southern Appalachian Mountain region. They were a people who made their own fiddles, banjos, mouth bows, and such, and they played the tunes and sang the songs their ancestors had carried with them when they settled in this beautiful untamed and isolated countryside.

How could they have known that they were, in such a feeble, modest, and unpretentious way, setting the stage for the development of a music culture which would engulf the country? As I pen these lines, a television program is showing former U. S. President George Bush and his wife, Barbara, celebrating their 50th wedding anniversary in Nashville—at the *Grand Ole Opry*, home of country music. At the same time, almost every person in America could have, if they had chosen, tuned their radio or their television to a station which carried some form of country music. How could the Whitakers have known that their simple and plaintive music would soon become what some scholars describe as "a phenomenon of worldwide appeal"?

Why was this old world music revered, preserved, and practiced in this Southern Appalachian Mountain area, in such pure form? Was it because the people who settled here were more prone to be of the type who loved freedom, independence, and their music? Or was it because the isolation and loneliness itself provided an atmosphere conducive to reflecting on the "old ways" of their kin whom they left behind on the migrating trail?

Opposite page, top:
Renda Whitaker is shown here with the banjo she and her husband made soon after they "started housekeeping" on the Cumberland Plateau at Lick Skillet, near Monterey, Tennessee. "We went to the woods," Renda recalled, "and we cut us a poplar sapling, took us a groundhog hide to make a head, and we made us a banjar. Law, at the good times we had a singing and playing that old banjar." *Photo by the author, 1965*

Opposite page, bottom:
This 1887 photograph, taken in western North Carolina near Morgantown, is one of the earliest I've seen of a string band. The fact that there are three banjo players emphasizes the popularity of the banjo in this area in the latter part of the 1800s. It's also interesting that the guitar and mandolin were present at this early period; however, the mandolin shown here is the rounded back "tater bug" European-style, a type not used in the string bands of the early country and bluegrass era. I think that it is safe to say that it was seldom if ever played in a bluegrass band. *Photo courtesy Steve Shaffer*

Is it true, as is often said, that the people of the isolated coves, hollows, ridges, and valleys of Southern Appalachia retained and preserved the old English, Scottish, and Irish folk music more, perhaps, than anywhere else in the world? Cecil Sharp, the noted English scholar on the subject of early English songs and ballads, came to this region in America to see for himself and to address this question.

He came in July, 1916, directly to the mountainous North Carolina counties of Buncombe and Madison near the Tennessee border. Then he crossed over into Tennessee in August to the communities of Rocky Fork and Flag Pond, two of the region's most picturesque and isolated mountainous areas, located near the upper East Tennessee town of Erwin. He, along with his assistant, Maud Karpeles, visited remote families known by their neighbors to be singers of old songs, and this noted scholar made written records of the words and music to these old ballads.

Cecil Sharp did indeed discover many old Scottish and English songs here in these mountains whose roots sometimes went back 200 years. Dr. Charles Wolfe, the noted scholar on all facets of country music, points out that one such old ballad Sharp heard sung, "The Gypsy Laddie," contained the basic characteristics of the typical modern country music song. It referred to a wife leaving her husband for her lover, and later her lament for having left her faithful mate for the gypsy, Blackjack Davy. The song, in various forms, was known to have existed in England and Scotland as early as 1740, and it was sung in Ireland in the mid-1800s. Sharp now heard it sung by the Coates family in the upper East Tennessee community of Flag Pond. Later on, the Carter Family sang it in a much shorter and abbreviated form, as follows:

The Gypsy Laddie

Blackjack Davy came a riding through the woods
And he sang so loud and gaily
He made the hills around him ring;
And he charmed the heart of a lady;
And he charmed the heart of a lady.

How old are you my pretty little miss?
How old are you my pretty little honey?
She answered him with a gillie smile,
"I'll be 16 next Sunday."
"I'll be 16 next Sunday."

Come go along with me my pretty little miss.
Come go along with me my pretty little honey.
I'll take you across the deep blue sea
Where you never shall want for money,
Where you never shall want for money.

He pulled off her high heel shoes;
They were made of Spanish leather.
He put on those low heel shoes,
And they both rode off together,
And they both rode off together.

Last night I lay on a warm feather bed
Beside my husband and baby.
Tonight I lay on the cold, cold ground
Beside Blackjack Davy,
Beside Blackjack Davy.

Sharp had dedicated his early life to collecting folk songs from the English countryside, and he developed a yearning to know what the life of those English country folk was like 200 or more years before. After visiting and living with the people of this region, he was able to go back in time. Sharp discovered, he said, "The England of my dreams" in the United States of America in the beautiful country of Southern Appalachia.

This English scholar referred to this region as "a paradise," and he was elated with his success in gathering old British ballads. At one point he stated, in regard to his collecting of old songs, "I have never before got such a wonderful lot in such a short time." In a two-week period, he reported that he collected 90 tunes. Maud Karpeles wrote that during his foray in the mountains of Tennessee, North Carolina, Kentucky, and Virginia, he collected 281 songs and 1,612 tunes and that practically all the songs and ballads could have had an historical basis in Lowland Scotland or in England.

In a letter to one John Glenn in 1917, Sharp sets forth a most interesting and intriguing theory as to why the centuries-old songs were preserved in parts of this mountainous region and perhaps nowhere else in the world—not even in their native homeland in the British Isles. He observed that when good wages could be earned and where the valleys were wide and the people more prosperous, they soon dropped their old-fashioned ways, including their ancestral music, choosing more modern and stylish ways, as people almost universally are apt to do. Conversely, one may infer that people living in extremely remote areas clung to the old ways, perhaps not so much by choice or design, but because they did not have occasion to mix and mingle with current vogues and societal trends.

Sharp's main interest was in recording the words and music of the old ballads; and since these were usually sung without musical accompaniment, he expressed little interest in musical instruments. But the fiddle and banjo were well known throughout the region. The fiddle, or violin, whose history goes back at least to the 17th century in Italy, was subsequently introduced in the British Isles; and it was the most universally loved musical instrument in this country in the early years of settlement.

Music making and foxhunting were the two most common forms of entertainment and relaxation in Southern Appalachia during the early part of the 20th century. And when photographer A. M. Porter Feathers of Whitesburg, Tennessee, announced, about 1930, that he was going to photograph the men in the neighborhood, they turned out with their musical instruments, and especially with their fox hounds.
From the author's collection

The fiddle was played by the likes of Thomas Jefferson, Tennessee's famous Governor Bob Taylor, by the late Tennessee Senator Albert Gore, Sr., and by the scholarly Senator Robert Byrd of West Virginia, as well as by those who lived in one-room dirt-floored log cabins. The banjo, which came into existence much later, rapidly took hold in the southern mountains, as well as throughout the South and in other parts of the country. The five-string banjo, in its present form, is attributed to one Joel W. Sweeney of near Appomattox, Virginia. Sweeney, who was born in 1810, likely developed the five-string banjo in stages, perhaps borrowing ideas from instruments used by the slaves with whom he and his brothers worked on the family farm. The five-string banjo was probably completed in the late 1830s by Sweeney and his brothers. They soon found warm acceptance for their music on the courthouse square in Appomattox, and by 1841, they were touring extensively with their minstral-type act.

The banjo, possibly because it was relatively simple to construct, became a popular instrument in the Southern Appalachian region, especially after the Civil War. While the shape, size, and other characteristics of the fiddle remained virtually the same as those made by Amati, Giovanni, and Stradivarius in the 1600s, the banjo took on a multitude of different shapes, forms, and sizes.

But the one characteristic almost always found on the banjo was the 5th drone string. Factories made some banjos without the 5th string (tenor banjos, they're called), but 98% of all the old handmade mountain banjos were "five-string banjars."

So, equipped with these three accouterments—the old-world songs, the fiddle, and the banjo—a musical culture was to be wrought which was destined to develop, grow, change, and to spread in a manner which could not have been imagined at the time. Interestingly, however, these three elements did not develop in concert in the beginning, but separately. (Other musical instruments, such as the harmonica, Jews harp, mouth bow and to a lesser extent the mountain dulcimer, were played by the mountain folk, but the influence of these instruments on the development and promulgation of the music did not rival the fiddle or the banjo, nor in later years the guitar and mandolin.)

The fiddler most often played his instrument without accompaniment, for his own entertainment or for entertaining his family, and sometimes he played for dances, pie suppers, frolics, or for other community gatherings. If there was any singing with a fiddle tune, it was usually sung by the fiddler himself. Sometimes in the middle of a tune, without warning and in what seemed to be an unintended and spontaneous manner, the fiddler would break in with a dozen words or so. An example is: "Shady Grove my little love, Shady Grove my darling, Shady Grove my little love, I'm going back to Harlan." It was as if he became so inspired by his own fiddling, that he just had to add a new dimension of expression. And once done, he seemed satisfied, and played out the remainder of his tune without further interruption. Early singing often emphasized storytelling over singing, and the delivery was more chanting and wailing than it was singing, and almost always without musical accompaniment.

Like the fiddle, the banjo was usually played without the accompaniment of voices, *or* without the benefit of other musical instruments. The banjo gained some acceptance in the latter part of the 19th century as a home instrument, but it was in the early part of the 20th century that the five-string banjo was brought to the fore, and

Tommy Cline, who lived at the foot of the Great Smoky Mountains, "up on" Chestnut Creek in Monroe County, Tennessee, was a logger, trapper, wild-bee hunter, farmer, piddler, and sometimes banjo player. "They's a feller named Kenneth Williams that made me that banjar. He kilt a groundhog and tanned his hide to make the head." *Photo taken 1980 by the author*

combined with the fiddle, and later with the guitar and with singers. The stage was being set for an evolutionary and revolutionary development—the beginning of the string band, and the beginning of country and bluegrass music.

No one knows where or when it happened, but logic would dictate that it *would* happen. An old fiddler and a mountain banjo player, both of whom had always played their instruments solo, got together, likely by chance, and played the fiddle and banjo together. The marriage of the five-string banjo and the fiddle seemed to have been a natural way by which to deliver this old music. Recently, old-time fiddler Charlie Acuff, a member of my band, and the multi-talented John Hartford, recorded several old fiddle tunes with only these two instruments, and in

John Pierson, with fiddle, and his brother Noah, with the banjo, were content to live in a rough board-and-batten cabin in an old field near the town of Church Hill in upper East Tennessee. Neither the little unpainted house nor the surroundings received much care, but John and Noah took the utmost interest and pride in making and playing musical instruments. They dressed in their Sunday clothes and walked down to the public road to have this picture made, about 1951. Tall, straight, and distinguished in appearance, they stood with dignity and with pride with the fiddle and banjo, the two instruments which were the forerunners of the string band in the early part of the 20th century. It is assumed that the automobile belonged to the photographer, and not to John or Noah. *Photo courtesy Charlie Monday and his sister Shirley Monday Williams*

Shown here is the old Pierson homeplace where brothers John and Noah Pierson lived until their deaths, about 1970. John, born about 1884, and Noah, born in 1887, made dulcimers, violas, cellos, and banjos, but their main interest was making fiddles. They studied and tried to apply the techniques of the old masters such as Stradivarius, Guarnerius and Amati. *Photo taken soon after the brothers had passed on, courtesy Charlie Monday and Shirley Monday Williams*

so doing, they illustrated the clean, simplistic beauty which can be produced by the fiddle and the banjo.

The guitar, though an instrument whose history may be traced to the Moors in Spain hundreds of years ago, was nevertheless a latecomer to the southern mountains. Asa Martin, who became well known in the 1920s and 1930s as a purveyor of old-time music, once told me that he never saw a guitar until he was "nearly grown." Several other people from this area also remembered the first guitar they ever saw, most often in the 1920s. Oddly enough, it was the mail-order catalogs, especially *Sears and Roebuck*, which helped to introduce the guitar to rural America. Mother Maybelle Carter of the Carter Family did more to popularize the guitar than perhaps anyone else. The mandolin came to the region even later than the guitar and gained popularity largely through the influence of Bill Monroe, starting in the 1930s.

The mail-order guitar was "seriously" introduced in Southern Appalachia in the late 1920s and especially in the 1930s, heralding the beginning of the old-time string band in this region. Shown here is the interior of the one-room log cabin belonging to the Esco Glandon family located in the community of Bridges Chapel, near old Loyston, some 25 miles north of Knoxville. This photo was taken in 1933 after Esco had returned to Tennessee to work as a sharecropper after having spent three years in the factories in Kokomo, Indiana. *Photo by Louis Hine and courtesy of Tennessee Valley Authority*

So the string band, which we think of as so characteristic of and indigenous to early country music, is a relatively new phenomenon. Edison's talking machine, the radio, and the formation of the string band acted in a synergistic fashion to spread this old-time music like wildfire. It mattered not that there were only one or two phonographs or battery-operated radios in a community; people would walk for miles on the weekends to sit and listen to records of the Carter Family, Riley Puckett, or the Skillet Lickers—or to listen to the *Grand Ole Opry* and to other early radio programs. These two contrivances (the radio and the phonograph) were two-fold in their influence. First, they made it possible for aspiring young musicians to hear what other musicians were singing and playing; and secondly, these media provided an opportunity for early musicians to play and sing on their local radio station themselves, reaching a much wider audience than otherwise would have been possible.

The Gully Jumpers was one of the first and most popular old-time string bands to perform commercially, starting on the *Grand Ole Opry* soon after its beginning in November of 1925. From the left, the members are: Burt Hutcherson, Roy Hardison, Charlie Arrington, and Paul Warmack. *Photo courtesy of Les Leverett*

By the 1940s, the guitar and the mandolin were becoming well-established in Southern Appalachia, sometimes taking the place of the banjo and the fiddle and helping to blend the old-time mountain music with what we call early country. This picture of Rube Dalton, and his sons Dean, at left, and Vernon, taken in the mid-1940s, is illustrative of the popularity that the guitar and mandolin were having during that period. Most youngsters of that era aspired to learn to play those instruments, rather than the fiddle and banjo. Rube still lives in the Coker Creek section of Monroe County. *Photo taken in the 1940s, courtesy Rube Dalton*

The marriage of the old-time singers with musical instruments, so revolutionary in the beginning, and yet so commonplace now, formed the beginning of a new era in "old-time music." This remarkable story may best be told by those who were very much a part of that story. We'll allow them to tell their own stories, and what better folks are there to start with than the members of the inimitable Carter Family.

My long-time friend, Ray King, on the right, owned the once popular Imperial Hotel in Monterey, Tennessee, and after it gradually and finally closed, he continued to live there and to use the cluttered lobby to play music with the neighbors and to "trade." A shrewd and knowledgeable old-time horse trader, he bought and sold everything from musical instruments to old books and used furniture, and he "always softened up the folks with a tune on the banjar," before clinching the deal. He is shown here with another old-time trader, Paul Ault, from down in Sequatchie Valley. Ray is not unmindful of the billfold stuffed with hundred dollar bills visible in Paul's left hand. *Photo taken 1980s by Pulitzer Prize photographer Robin Hood, who often traveled with me to such places*

"The Carters were the most influential singing family in traditional American music." I've suggested this for a quarter century, and no one has ever challenged me. These three individuals comprised the original Carter Family. A.P. stands beside his wife Sara, and her cousin, the truly legendary Mother Maybelle, is shown at left. This photo was taken in Del Rio, Texas, in 1938, the year they started broadcasting across the nation on the 100,000-watt station, XERA. *Photo courtesy Janette Carter*

Chapter 2

The Legendary Carter Family from Poor Valley

"It seemed that even the birds listened when they sang."

There never has been, nor is it likely that there ever will be, a story so colorful, so blessed with success, so fraught with sadness, so influential on the music of a nation, and so totally American as that of the famous singing Carter Family.

The original Carter Family consisted of the legendary A.P. Carter, his wife Sara, and his sister-in-law Maybelle Addington Carter, affectionately known as Mother Maybelle. All three were from that beautiful, rural, isolated mountain area of southwest Virginia, near the Tennessee state line. A.P. and Sara were living in a remote mountain cabin with a dirt floor when their first two children were born. The young couple tried to survive by cutting timber in the surrounding mountains and by raising a little corn on the steep hillsides near the cabin. Within only a few years, they had gained national success,

even adoration, and they left a legacy which continues to influence folk, country, bluegrass, and even popular and rock music to this day.

Although much has been written about how it came to be that this unremarkable family made such a remarkable impact on the music of a nation, the reasons are not at all simplistic. I'm not sure that the Carters knew the answer themselves, or that they ever came close to realizing the extent of their influence. But long, informal talks with Janette and Joe Carter do give insight into the lives of this colorful, imaginative and enigmatic family. Janette and Joe are the children of Sara and A.P., and they shared the stage with the family in the early days; and they continue singing the Carter family songs. A visit with them was a memorable and revealing experience, and an inspirational lesson in modesty and total honesty.

I had spent a night in June of 1991 in Kingsport, Tennessee, and the next morning had driven the twenty miles from there over through historic Moccasin Gap and on up the valley to the community of Maces Springs, once called Hiltons, Virginia. From there I took the back road and followed the railroad tracks some three miles in what Janette unabashedly called "Pore" Valley. I passed the little sign, which was as simple, direct and unpretentious as the Carters themselves. It read: "Carter Fold, 3 miles." At the end of the three miles there sat the old country store, built and operated by A.P. himself, and beside it was the long, rambling, dirt floored, barn-like building which Janette, with Joe's help, had built to carry on the "Carter Music." Janette called it the "Carter Fold."

Directly above these two structures at the top of a steep hill stood a little white farmhouse. A.P. had built this modest structure after he had left the music business, and at a time in his older years when he reverted back to his first trade, that of carpentry. The lumber was sawed on his own mill from trees he cut nearby. He built it for his youngest daughter, Janette, and this is where she continues to live. It was Janette that I had come to visit.

I had known Janette and Joe for several years, mainly as a result of their playing for the annual Museum of Appalachia's Tennessee Fall Homecoming, held each October at the Museum of Appalachia in Norris, Tennessee. But on this particular day, I was not merely talking to old friends, but to the last of the nationally revered and famous Carter Family.

Janette is shown here in her front yard overlooking her beloved Poor Valley, waving at the train engineer as he sounds a greeting whistle. The back of the A.P. Carter Store (now the Carter Museum) is shown at the right. The Carter Fold, not shown, is only a few yards to the right of the store/museum. *Photo courtesy Janette Carter*

The sign at the lower end of Poor Valley, Virginia, near the Tennessee line, is as plain, simple, unpretentious, and effectual as the Carters themselves. *Photo by the author*

"We're just plain country people — I can tell you that all right."

Janette's "front room" was warm and comfortable and informal, and totally characterized with the "lived in" appearance. Some "old" Carter pictures hung on the wall, and some small photographs of her children and grandchildren were scattered around the room, but the large window, and that which it revealed, overshadowed all other aspects of the place. It commanded a view across Poor Valley and to those warm old mountains beyond: Clinch Mountain, Walker Mountain and Mt. Rogers. One could almost see the old graveyard beyond Clinch River and Clinch Mountain where the first pioneer, old Dulaney Carter, settled, lived, and was buried along with his kin; and the silhouette of these ancient ridges, I thought, was little changed from that time.

It was quiet and peaceful here now, not like the last time I came to talk with Janette and Joe—when a crew from *Life* magazine was there to do a major story.

Janette, I believe that your father was born right here in Poor Valley?

(Janette) "He was born right over here in that old log house that you and Joe went to see the other day, in what we call The Little Valley. As you know, it's out in the field, and no road to it. That's where he was born, and all his brothers and sisters was born there. They was eight of them, and Daddy was the oldest. I don't know how ten people could live in that one room, but they was, still is, a little upstairs, and at one time they had built a little lean-to on the old log house."

It was a hot June day in 1991 when I asked Janette and Joe if they would play a couple of songs in Janette's front yard while I photographed them; and it wasn't long before Janette started wiping her brow, a cue that my picture taking time had expired. That's Walker Mountain, Mt. Rogers, and historic Clinch Mountain in the background, the inspiration for A.P. Carter's popular song, "My Old Clinch Mountain Home." *Photo by the author*

Joe Carter stands beside the old log cabin home where his grandmother Molly, age 16, and her husband, Robert, started housekeeping, and where the legendary A.P. Carter and his seven brothers and sisters were born and raised. The photo was taken in June of 1991, after the two barn-like sheds were added for curing tobacco. It is located in Little Valley, next to Poor Valley in Scott County, Virginia, near the Tennessee line. *Photo by the author*

Janette talked in a slow, deliberate manner, with what even the local urban folks called a country accent. She pronounced her words strongly, and her phrases were often almost poetic. The fact that she used quaint words and phrases was an indication of her ties with old English and obsolete speech forms rather than a mark of corruption in her speech, as the town folks thought. She gave the appearance of total honesty, and a complete lack of pretentiousness—but the sense of pride in her family, both expressed and inferred, was evident at every turn. Her voice was lilting and expressive and in total keeping, I thought, with those unadulterated mountains that crept up all around us.

A few weeks earlier Joe and I had visited the little log house where A.P. was born. We had driven down a dirt road until it ended at "Uncle Ermine's" old homeplace. From there we walked through the fields and along fence rows where all traces of any path had long since faded away. The old log house was not unlike a thousand other pioneer homes I'd visited in Southern Appalachia—cabins where the poorest of the poor lived, but the likes of which had produced some of the country's most famous people—such as Cordell Hull, Mark Twain, and Sgt. Alvin C. York.

I was struck, not only by the primitive homestead, but by items found in a trash pile nearby—things that revealed a lifestyle so strikingly similar to all other early mountain homesteads. There was a patched 'possum board, used to stretch 'possum hides to be sold for a nickel at the local store. There was a plow point, worn beyond any redemption. No doubt it had been used by every Carter who had ever lived there to plow the corn patches, the most important of all crops. These simple artifacts, and broken pieces of other tools, intrinsically worthless, revealed much of that early Carter family culture and heritage.

And all eight of the children in your father's family have passed on?

Janette responded: "Yeah, they're all dead now. Aunt Silvey was the youngest, and she died here about two years ago. She played the autoharp and guitar, and sang. She had a pretty voice. She was Silvey Carter Edwards. She married an Edwards."

Your grandfather and grandmother Carter—did they play music? His name was Robert, I believe?

"Yeah, his name was Robert Carter and Grandma Carter's name was Molly Bayes Carter. I remember that Grandma Carter said the first time she seen Grandpa Carter was at a dance. She said she thought he was the handsomest man she ever saw. She told him she'd marry him, and which she did, and she was just sixteen years old."

Mother Maybelle, standing with guitar, is shown here with her three daughters, Anita, June (Mrs. Johnny Cash), and Helen. The fiddler is Maybelle's brother "Little Doc" Addington; the autoharp player is A.P.'s sister "Silvey" Carter Edwards; and the banjo player is "Car" McConnell. *Photo courtesy Janette Carter*

Molly Bays Carter, shown here in Poor Valley, was the mother of A.P. and seven other children. "I believe sincerely that Grandma Carter was the workingest woman in Scott County." *Quote from Janette Carter who provided the photograph*

Do you remember your grandparents?

"Of course I remember them. Joe says Grandpa built barns, cribs, chimneys, and helped at house raisings for other people, but I don't remember seeing him work too much. What I remember most about him and Grandma Carter is that people would send for her to come and help out when they were sick. Or if they were dying, they'd send for Grandpa to come and pray for them. Grandpa was a praying man.

"He'd gather all of us together at night before bedtime, and we'd set on the big warm hearth and Grandpa would read the scripture and pray. He prayed the longest prayers I ever listened to. I would stay on my knees, it seemed, for an hour, but I never moved. I was afraid to.

A.P.'s father, Robert Carter, pictured here, was described by his granddaughter Janette as a praying man. She said: "The neighbors and kinfolks would call on him if they's sick or a-dying, and Grandpa Carter would go and set up with them and pray for them." *Photo courtesy Janette Carter*

"How I loved Ma and Pa Carter! That woman [her grandmother Molly] was a worker. I believe sincerely that she was the workingest woman in Scott County. She never stopped."

I noticed that Janette kept glancing out the window, down to the road as it meandered up Poor Valley and disappeared as it ran over toward Clinch River. She was looking for her brother Joe.

"Let me get Joe over here. He's younger than me and he can remember more, if you can get him awake, and if he gets hisself out here." (Janette chuckled. She dialed the telephone and Joe finally answered, and

"Grandma" (Molly Bays) Carter, on the right, was the mother of A.P., the grandmother of Gladys, at left, and the great-grandmother of Anita Carter, center. *Photo courtesy Janette Carter*

Janette got right to the point.) "Joe, John Rice is out here, and he wants you to come here; he wants to talk to you. Bye, bye.

"I woke him." (She chuckles mischievously.) "That's good for him."

What did he say?

"He said, 'Well.' (more laughter) I tell you that Joe is a mess. He's . . . he's something." (It was obvious how close the two were. Janette always spoke of Joe as a mother speaks of her youngest child—as an older sister speaks of the little brother. After all, he *was* the little baby brother.)

I enjoy talking to Joe. He went with me, you know, all back in these hills—visiting old folks he knew.

"He'll tickle you to death. He will. He has a good memory about people and things in this valley. Well, he got out and run around, and hunted and such, and done a lot of things that girls didn't do. He got more acquainted."

In a few minutes Joe drove up, dressed in his overalls and looking like any other Scott County farmer one would find sitting on the porch of the neighborhood country store. We continued our talk about the Carter family.

We were talking, when Janette called you, about your grandfather being called to visit, assist, and pray with the sick and dying. Did your grandmother accompany him?

(Joe) "She was a midwife. She delivered babies all up and down this valley."

(Janette) "She delivered all three of us, didn't she, Joe? Gladys, Joe, and me."

(Joe) "Yeah. And Early Goode. Early said he'd druther have my grandma to deliver a baby than any doctor. She used to have a little down piller she carried with her—made of down feathers you know. She'd carry her little black satchel and that piller—said it helped if the woman had a good ole soft piller to lay her head on."

(Janette) "Well, I remember that little satchel. I stayed with Grandma so much when I was a child. Every once in a while somebody would come and say 'So and so is going to have a baby,' and Grandma would go. And usually she wouldn't come back 'til daylight. She'd be there all night a' bringing the baby."

(Directed to Janette) **Did you ever go with your grandmother when she went to deliver babies?**

(Janette) "Lord, God, no! They wouldn't let us. They wouldn't let us, would they, Joe?"

(Joe) "No." (He chuckled.)

(Janette) "We never did know nothing about what was going on. And I wondered 'til I was grown what was in that little black satchel." (More laughter)

I don't suppose she got much pay for delivering babies back then?

(Janette) "I don't guess she got anything. They might give her a mess of beans, or something out of the garden."

(Joe) "Cabbage head or something like that."

I think you told me once that your father, A.P. Carter, left home when he was quite young?

(Janette) "He left here and went out, I believe it was, to Indiana. He may have worked in Detroit some, too. He was a carpenter by trade and I reckon that's what he did up there. But he got real sick and he came home, and they said he just about died. He had typhoid fever, and he lay in bed for ever so long, and Grandma nursed him back to health. I heard her talk about it.

"I don't recollect that he took off from home no more. He settled down to farming and selling fruit trees, and he liked to run a sawmill. And one time, I can remember, he had a gristmill. And he had a grocery store back when him and Mother was first married. He worked in a foundry over here in Kingsport, and when it closed down, he bought part of it. So he followed a lot of different trades. He couldn't seem to find exactly what he wanted to do. He was an adventurous person."

Well, I suppose it was hard to make a living, here on the land?

(Janette) "Oh, Lord, yeah. They had a hard time. Right after him and Mother married they used to go in these mountains and cut timber and make crossties. I've heard him talk about cutting timber, and Mother was working right with him—cutting timber with an old crosscut saw. They'd cut timber for paper wood, and peel off the bark. I can remember that. They'd haul it over here to Kingsport and sell it to Mead, the big paper mill."

We were talking earlier about A.P. and Sara, your parents. How and when did they get started in music?

(Janette) "Just about everybody around here played some kind of music—made their own instruments mostly. Daddy learned to play the fiddle. They called him Fiddlin' Doc, and he wanted to do hoedown music, and his mother didn't want him to play hoedown music. [It was said that he acquired the "Doc" title because he would care for and doctor crippled birds, stray cats, and such.] You know they say that the fiddle is the devil's instrument. Grandma was strictly against dancing, though that was where she met Grandpa."

So your father gave up the fiddle because of his mother.

(Janette) "Well, she thought it was all right for him to play hymns—religious music, you know—and he played the fiddle some in churches and at singings."

So when and how did the Carter Family singing group start?

(Janette) "Well, Mother and Daddy started playing together some, in schools, ice cream suppers, pie suppers, and things like that. That was before Maybelle joined them. They wanted Mother and Daddy to put out a record and they wanted to call it 'Fiddlin' Doc.' He wouldn't agree to it, like I said before, because his mother didn't approve of the fiddlin', and he turned them down."

When did "Mother Maybelle" join the group?

(Janette) "Maybelle, she was an Addington, and my

mother, Sara, was raised up side by side over here at Midway, Virginia. They were first cousins, and Maybelle and my mother had played music together, though Maybelle was 10 years younger than my mother. Maybelle married Daddy's brother, Ezra. We called him 'Eck.' So the three of them, Daddy, Mother, and Maybelle, lived close together and they started playing a little around home, after Maybelle married in the family."

I understand that Maybelle came from a musical family. I know Joe and I went to see her oldest brother, Duke, and he played music.

(Janette) "Yeah. Maybelle had nine brothers and sisters, and I believe Maybelle told me once that all her brothers and sisters but one played some kind of a instrument. Yeah, Duke and his brother, Carl, played together for a long time, back in the 1940s, and they were called the 'Virginia Boys.' Duke was one of the best musicians I ever heard in my life. I never heard anyone who could play a guitar like him. He played a lot like Maybelle, but he had a style all his own. He was good on the banjo, too."

Duke, the oldest of Maybelle's brothers and sisters, paradoxically outlived all his younger siblings. Joe and I, along with Frank Hoffman, a photographer, visited him and his wife in their little four-room house on a forlorn and unadorned hill, a few feet off the dirt road. At 92, he was a friendly and witty little fellow, and looked and acted like any other old country man from the area. He had "horse traded" and farmed and was rumored to have "played around" with making and drinking moonshine a good bit. He had, as Janette pointed out, played for local events, and even went "up North" and played.

Joe and I played a few old-time Carter tunes with Duke, and then I bought some old relics from the small smokehouse out back. I bought the worn old chopping block that he had used for years to sit on while splitting kindling for the kitchen stove. This I added to the Carter exhibit in the Appalachian Hall of Fame here at the Museum in Norris.

It was a hot summer day in 1990 that Joe Carter, at right, and I went to see Duke Addington, the oldest and paradoxically the last survivor of Mother Maybelle's nine brothers and sisters. At the age of 92, Duke had no trouble playing the old folk song "Pretty Polly" on his front porch in a rural section of Scott County, Virginia. *Photo by Frank Hoffman*

Maybelle's father, I believe, was named Hugh Jack Addington. I assume that he was a farmer. How did he make his living for so many children?

(Janette) "They lived like everybody else way back then. They had a little farm. They had fruit trees, and they had a cow, a hog, and chickens. They lived off the land, and worked for other people. And they survived."

I knew an old man, John Carrico, from over in that area who said he and Maybelle's father used to make moonshine together. He said they had a still in the upstairs of an old mill, and that Maybelle, when she was just a girl, would serve as the "lookout" for the revenuers. She would sit in the doorway of the millhouse and sing the "Wildwood Flower" and other peaceful old songs as long as no strangers or suspicious people were around. But if she saw anybody she didn't know coming up the road, then she'd sing a certain song like "Run Johnny, Run" or "Up Jumped the Devil," and old John and Hugh Jack would be forewarned.

Janette laughed heartily and long, like a school girl with her hand over her mouth, trying not to laugh too much. I thought that she was not going to respond to my comment; but then she said, in a low, confidential sort of way: "Them was the whiskey makingest bunch you ever saw." (More laughter) "Wasn't they, Joe?"

(Joe grinned broadly and knowingly) "That's what I've heard."

When did your father shift over from the fiddle to the guitar and the singing?

(Janette) "Grandma Carter had a brother named Flanders Bayes and he taught singing schools. Daddy learned a lot from his Uncle Flanders, and the singing schools he taught."

The "singing schools" Janette referred to were common during the last century and well into the 20th century. A "singing master" would travel from one community to another, organizing the singing schools which were usually funded by a small assessment from those who enrolled. In a time when there were few other community gatherings, the singing school, usually held in the local schoolhouse or churchhouse, became quite popular, and the students were taught the rudiments of singing parts and harmony styles. Songbooks were available to the students, and the music was of a gospel, hymn-type nature.

I knew that the old singing schools were held all through this region, but I never heard that they had an influence on the Carters.

(Janette) "Well, they had a great influence on Daddy. He used to sing in the choir down here at Mount Vernon, and of course his mother approved of that." [It is also known that A.P. sang in church quartets and that he participated in the then popular "all-day-singing and dinner-on-the-ground" gatherings. Perhaps the influence of church and gospel music on the Carter Family has not been properly recognized.]

From what I hear, he was a serious minded man.

(Janette) "He was! No foolishness about my daddy. None whatsoever. He was just a serious minded person, and when he told us children to do something, we did it. You didn't talk back, you just obeyed. Now days, you have children who'll stand and argue with their parents—they don't want to do this, and they don't want to do that."

Did your father ever spank you?

(Janette) "He spanked me three times."

Do you remember the reasons?

(Janette) "Yeah. The first time was when I was very small. He told me to go wash the dishes, and I told him I was tired of washing dishes and I wasn't aiming to wash them. So I got a whipping for that with a switch and the blood run down my legs. I never did tell him I wasn't aiming to wash dishes no more. One time me and Joe was fighting and he whipped us. And the other time, well, I needed to be whipped then 'cause I wanted to go and stay all night with a schoolmate and he said no. So I went on anyway and I got whipped for that. Three times is all I ever remember. I don't believe I ever remember my mother spanking me. Of course Mother and Daddy separated when we were small, you know, and I spent very little time with her after that."

I take it that there is no one thing that inspired the Carters to start their singing, their career?

(Janette) "It was a form of entertainment or relaxation for people back then. They worked hard, you know, and it was just—well, it was just something common that they done."

Where was your mother, Sara, born?

(Janette) "She was born in Flat Rock, over around Norton, Virginia, in 1899. Her full name was Sara Elizabeth Dougherty. Her mother died when she was two years old; so she was raised by her uncle and aunt, Milburn and Melinda Nichols, who lived close by. They raised my mother and her sister, Mae."

There were only three children in your family?

(Janette) "Yes. Gladys was the oldest, and you know she died in March, and she would have been seventy-five in April. She lived, you know, just across the road here in our old homeplace. Her daughter went to wake her up one morning—she hadn't heard her stirring, and she had died in her sleep. It was a terrible shock, I'll tell you that. There was about four years difference in our ages. I'm seventy-one, and Joe's sixty-seven."

Were all three of you born near here?

(Janette) "Me and Gladys was born back here in the mountains, in a little log house, but of course it's gone now. But Joe was born in a little two-room house right here at the Museum. [The old A.P. Carter store building is now used as a small museum, containing memorabilia of the Carter family.] Joe, do you remember that little cabin where me and Gladys were born?"

Nottingham Singing School-1909

Old-time singing schools were organized by traveling "singing masters" at community schools and churches; and that's where A. P. Carter first expressed an interest in music and in singing. He is shown here at Nottingham church near his home. He is standing in the third row, third from the left with the black tie, at the age of 18. *Photo courtesy Janette Carter*

(Joe) "It just had a dirt floor. It's been gone for a long time, but I think maybe the old chimney's still standing."

(Janette responded with surprise) "It just had a dirt floor? I didn't know that! Where exactly was it?"

(Joe) "It was just back here in a hole in the mountain. The logs wasn't even hewed—just a little round pole log house. It was right up above where Grandpa's garden used to be; up there where Granny used to feed her chickens. Johnny and June own the place now." [June is Maybelle's daughter and is married to the singer Johnny Cash.]

From the earliest time, log houses made of large well-hewn logs were accepted in this area as adequate living quarters, but the little unhewn log cabins were considered to be adequate only for the poorest of the poor— "little pole cabins" they were derisively called. But even more indicative of the low scale of A.P. and Sara's first abode was that it had no floor, save that which Mother Earth provided. Surely few, if any, of their neighbors fared so poorly.

How did your mother and father meet?

(Joe) "Daddy met our mother when he was out selling fruit trees over here. He'd go plumb through Washington, Russell, and into Scott County. He made a big long circle, selling fruit trees. And he met Mother on one of his selling trips. Dad went up to Copper Creek to see if he could sell some fruit trees to his Uncle Mill [Milburn Nickels] and he heard the beautiful voice of a young girl, singing on the front porch of the cabin. He later said she was the most beautiful woman he ever saw. She was singing 'Engine 143.' when he first heard her. She had a little catalog and she was selling dishes from the catalog—to buy her a autoharp, and Daddy ordered a whole bunch of the dishes. Don't know what use he had for them." (He chuckles.)

A.P. and his wife Sara are shown here soon after their marriage in Poor Valley, Virginia. Janette called it their wedding picture. *Photo courtesy Janette Carter*

Sara Dougherty Carter, shown above, was described by her daughter, Janette, as follows: "Never has anyone had eyes like my mother. They seemed to have gold stars and shone like diamonds. She had long, wavy black hair, and when she cut it years later, my daddy tied it with a ribbon and kept it, even after they divorced. Joe has it now in a trunk. She always reminded me of an Indian maiden, or a queen." *Photo courtesy Janette Carter*

(Janette) "Her brown eyes—never has anyone had eyes like my mother—seemed to have gold stars and shone like diamonds. She had long wavy black hair, and when she cut it years later my daddy tied it with a ribbon and kept it. Joe has it now, kept in a trunk. How he loved her, that 16-year-old girl. She always reminded me of an Indian maiden, or a queen.

"So my daddy kept walking back and forth across Clinch Mountain until he won her heart. She was just 16 when they married, and they moved over here in the valley."

Sevier Dougherty, from the community of Flat Rock in the extreme southwest part of Virginia, was the father of the famous Sara Dougherty Carter, wife of A.P. *Photo courtesy of Janette Carter*

What year was this?

(Janette) "I believe that it was 1914, in the summer, I guess."

Well, it seems that your father tried many different jobs and small businesses. What did he really enjoy?

(Janette) "Daddy loved the land. He loved nature, didn't he, Joe?"

(Joe) "Yeah. He loved dogs—hunting dogs, and tree dogs, like squirrel dogs—and he loved to fish. About every Saturday night he'd go down here and get Jim Goode, and they'd go down here on the [Clinch] river and fish. They had a trot line down there, I think, and they'd take a pine torch for a light. Him and Jim had gone to school together up here at Friendly Grove, in that old log building I showed you."

It seems that your father didn't like the day-to-day drudgery type work.

(Joe) "No. His mind wasn't in it."

(Janette) "No, that certainly was not his calling. It took him a long time to find that out."

(Joe) "He was by no means a farmer. He'd make me do things that, even as a child, I knew better than to do on the farm. He'd put me to plowing in the tobacco patch when it was mud up to your knees, and of course that made the ground as hard as a rock when it dried out."

(Janette, laughing in a sympathetic kind of way, the way folks do about those they love) "He'd take us out in the early morning to the corn field, or hay field, and he'd tell us what to do, when we were kids. He had a way of disappearing, and he'd come back about dark and get us. Wouldn't he, Joe?"

(Joe chuckled) "Yeah."

(Janette) "We'd have to hoe the weeds and crabgrass from the corn and tobacco, and it seemed every row was a mile long. The hoe handle would make a blister on your hands in the spring, then a callus, and by the end of the summer your hands would be rough and you'd have corns.

"Late in the afternoons we'd start looking for Daddy to come and pick us up to go home. Sometimes we thought he'd never come.

"Then after we got home, we'd have the chores to do around the house and barn before we went to bed."

Janette admired, loved and adored both her parents, even to the point of worship, and even when their actions sometimes seemed nonreciprocal to her adoration, her love never wavered. She told the story of how, at age thirteen, her father had so deeply disappointed her.

(Janette) "Gladys had married Milan and moved away taking Joe with her, and that just left me and Daddy at home. I had to run the house, milk and feed the cows and chickens, churn the butter, get the firewood in, and work in the fields and in the gardens. I was saving my money to buy me an autoharp—nickels, dimes, and quarters. I finally got up to thirteen dollars and I gave it to Daddy to buy the autoharp.

"Well, he went off toward town and I kept watching for him to come home. I kept looking down the road for hours. I was so excited. Well, when he finally did come, he had used my thirteen dollars to buy some little baby chickens—that would grow up and lay eggs that we could sell to buy groceries. That was one of the most hurtful days in my life."

When Janette was struggling to get a little money to build the music building (the Carter Fold) and when she worked two jobs in restaurants and in school cafeterias, she wrote Sara, her mother in California, for a little help. But her mother did not choose to assist her in any way.

Janette forgave her father for not buying her the musical instrument by saying, "My daddy was a strange man," and she forgave her mother for not helping her to "save" the old Carter music by saying, "Mother knowed what a crazy idea it was."

Janette said, in later years: "I don't guess any child has ever loved their parents more than I did. Their fame never entered my mind. I loved them because they were my own daddy and mother. I never in all my life heard my mother speak unkindly of anyone." And of her father she said: "I don't believe that his mind was ever off his children."

He was always dreaming, I've heard. He must have had an imaginative, creative mind, didn't he?

(Janette) "He sure did."

(Joe) "He was zeroed in on his thoughts, and that was his main goal in life. He loved to sing, and then when he got started recording, why he just went plumb crazy over it, didn't he?"

(Janette) "Yeah. And, well, they never made anybody that could sing any prettier than my daddy. He had the prettiest bass voice I ever heard. He'd go high, he'd go low, he could. He had a range that was unbelievable. Now, my mother had a pretty voice, too."

(Joe) "They had it together. It was a beautiful sound. But they worked at it."

(Janette) "They worked at it and they didn't play around with it. They was dead serious. And I've heard them say that when they went to make a record, they'd do a song, and when they done it, it was done. They didn't have to keep repeating theirself. Now you take an artist who does an album today; he may work for one week putting out a album, or work I don't know how many times on one song. Now, Mommy and Daddy, when they up and sung the song, it was recorded."

Did your father and mother and Maybelle play very much, just for their own entertainment?

(Janette) "Mother and Maybelle did, in the evenings."

(Joe) "People would come to hear them, and they'd set on the porch in the summertime and play sometimes."

(Janette) "When they had songs that they's going to record, they'd sing them for the neighbors, you know, and let them listen, and they [the neighbors] would say if they thought they's pretty.

"Joe, do you remember the time when all them convicts was working on the road there in front of our house? Using picks and shovels, working on the road? It was time for dinner [lunch] and Daddy invited them over to set under the shade trees in our yard, and on the porch. And I remember that Daddy and Mother come out and sung for them."

And they were prisoners—being guarded?

(Joe) "Yeah, they had shotgun guards guarding them. It was like the old chain gang, but I don't believe these had the balls and chains tied to them."

(Janette is studying and she begins to remember more about the convicts.) "It seems to me like Mommy [She usually said "Mother."] had something cooked, and she brought it out and let them have what she had. Cabbage or something—I don't remember."

(Joe) "I believe she did—peach or berry cobbler, too."

That's very interesting—the way your father and mother, when they were becoming known around the country, becoming very famous, would spend time feeding and playing for convicts. That's the kind of thing I want to bring out. So many people have written about the musical career of the Carter Family, but I've read very little about the human interest aspects of the family.

Milan, Mr. Phipps, Sara, Gladys, A.P. At Homeplace

When the legendary A.P. Carter was not selling fruit trees, operating a country store, running a sawmill, collecting and writing hundreds of songs, or playing music, he worked as a carpenter, and this is the house he bought, renovated, added to and "fixed up" for his family's home. *Photo courtesy Janette Carter*

Mother Maybelle, at left, Sara, and A.P. Carter pose for this photograph in the 1920s in Poor Valley, Virginia, near Clinch Mountain, about the time they made the historic recordings at Bristol, Tennessee/Virginia. *Photo courtesy of Janette Carter*

"The Most Important Event In Country Music History"

A.P. (Doc) Carter was still casting about, coasting along, not knowing whether he should go back to sawmilling, carpentry, farming, opening another country store, or to pursuing a career in music, the love of his life. But no one made a living by playing music in those days. That's what you did for relaxation, for enjoyment, and maybe for a little extra change at schoolhouses and at dances. From all indications, A.P. was not altogether a happy man.

The people in Poor Valley thought Alvin Pleasant (A.P.) Carter to be a bit odd. He'd walk along the railroad tracks, with his hands clasped behind him, they said, and talk to himself. Even his family became dubious when A.P. came up with the idea, in 1927, of going over to Bristol, Tennessee/Virginia, with his wife Sara and his sister-in-law Maybelle to try to record for Victor Records. Ralph Peer, a folklorist and a scout for Victor, had laid plans to record in Bristol on the

first of August, 1927, and he had talked the editor of the Bristol paper into printing a series of stories of his intended recording there, and A.P. doubtless read of Peer's planned visit.

There were problems, however, with A.P.'s plans. He had no automobile in which to drive the 26 miles over the crooked dirt roads to Bristol, and Maybelle was eight-months pregnant. Maybelle's husband (A.P.'s brother Eck) was not at all enthusiastic about loaning A.P. his Model-A Ford and having his pregnant wife go on such a nonsensical venture. Janette remembered that A.P.'s Uncle Lish, upon hearing that he was going to Bristol, said of A.P., "He usually does things right backwards to other people. Send him to Marion." [Marion, Virginia, was the location of the nearest mental hospital.] "He's completely gone this time. His family will starve, no doubt." But A.P. pleaded and even begged, they said, and he even worked with his brother, Eck, for three days plowing and chopping the weeds from Eck's corn field in the hot July sun in exchange for the use of his car to drive to Bristol.

A.P.'s persistence eventually prevailed, and on Sunday, July 31, 1927, the Carter family loaded their instruments and headed across the mountains for the "long" ride to Bristol. Gladys, oldest daughter of A.P. and Sara, went along to help care for baby Joe who was still being breast-fed.

Ralph Peer represented Victor Talking Machine Company of New York City, and he had come to the mountains to find local talent. He had learned, quite by accident, that there might be a market for this type music, but no one would dare to claim that Ralph Peer, nor any of his compatriots, had the slightest idea as to the national phenomenon about to happen.

Peer has been described as having great insight in judging talent, and as being a shrewd businessman as well. He was especially struck by Sara's voice, and though several other local people were there to record, the Carters made more records than anyone else, and all were accepted and released.

No one partaking in those now legendary and famous "Bristol Sessions" (held on the Tennessee/Virginia line) could have dreamed of its importance and impact on the development of country music. Two days after the Carters recorded, Jimmie Rodgers, "the singing brakeman," also recorded for Ralph Peer. His meteoric but short career is legendary and some scholars refer to him as the father of country music. The sessions are generally recognized as being the single most important event in country music history. Dr. Charles Wolfe, one of the most scholarly authorities on the development of early country music in Southern Appalachia, called it "the true dawn of country music." Years later, in 1998, the United States Congress designated Bristol as the official "Birthplace of Country Music," according to the Knoxville Journal.

There were many other groups there who came for Peer's recordings, and they came by train, car, on foot, and some say even in horse-drawn vehicles. The early entertainers who congregated there included the most popular Stoneman Family. There was Alfred Karnes, a preacher and gospel singer from Corbin, Kentucky; Blind Alfred Reed; and B. F. Shelton, also from Kentucky, who sang old ballads such as "Pretty Polly." Then there was the Holiness Preacher, Ernest Phipps, whose family sang with the Carters in later years. But it was the Carters, along with Jimmie Rodgers, that assured this session as an important historic event. Peer's Southern Publishing Company became one of the biggest in the world, and much credit for this is given to the Carter Family and to Jimmie Rodgers.

It is a wonderment that the Carters' songs were so well accepted that day, given the duress and adverse conditions under which the family worked. Janette recalls some of the tribulations: "Joe was just a baby, eight-months old, and he cried all day for his mother's milk, and it was blazing hot there and Gladys had to walk him up and down State Street and him just a bawling." [State Street is that historic street on the Tennessee/Virginia line where the sessions were held.] "Maybelle was expecting Helen in a month or so, and everybody was on edge. Mrs. Peer tried to help with Joe; she saw that Gladys was having such a hard time with him." [It is paradoxical that, going back to Poor Valley from this historic event, A.P. took a short cut and became stranded in the Holston River.]

In 1929, Victor released 12 of the Carter songs including "The Storms Are On the Ocean," "Bury Me Beneath the Weeping Willow," and the "Wildwood Flower" which sold over 100,000 copies. Within a couple of years they had sold over 700,000 copies of their songs, a phenomenal number for that pioneer period of recording. They received only a few hundred dollars in royalties. They started playing in local schools, churches and at public affairs, but it never occurred to them to give up farming, timber cutting and the like.

The local folks said that A.P. became even more of a dreamer after the successful "Bristol Sessions." They said he walked the railroad tracks more, alternating talking to himself, humming some old or new tune, and sometimes chuckling to himself. He spent more time rambling around the mountains looking for songs and did less "worthwhile" chores on and around the farm. When Sara did get him in the cornfield, he would sometimes plow the mule with his necktie on, much to the amusement of his neighbors who often didn't wear a tie even to funerals or to the all-day singings. Joe remembered, "He would leave Mother to cut the firewood, care for the stock, and tend the crops." Janette added, "Daddy always had more than one idea in his head, and you never knowed what he was a'thinking."

Much has been said and written about the Carter music and the Carter songs, and while the music is there for all to hear and analyze, the definition of the Carter songs is quite a different story. A.P. wrote some of those credited to him, but many others he discovered, revised, added to, and changed and arranged to fit the Carter style, with an eye as to what the public wanted to hear—songs about home, mother, love and death. Even so, he should be credited for rescuing scores of old mountain songs, many of English, Irish, and Scots-Irish origin. He is credited with having written or having discovered over 250 songs.

He is said to have written the popular "My Old Clinch Mountain Home," as well as "The Cyclone of Rye Cove," which was about the most catastrophic destruction and death that took place in the schoolhouse in the nearby village of Rye Cove. The school was completely blown away, 12 children and one teacher were killed, and 54 others were injured. It is said that A.P. came upon the scene soon after the cyclone struck, and that he penned the song on the spot.

I knew a kindly old lady, Mary Carter, whose little girl was killed in the storm. I bought a little school bench which had survived the cyclone from Mary for the Carter display here in the Museum of Appalachia. On this bench are the words to "The Cyclone of Rye Cove," sent to me by Janette.

While A.P. either wrote or collected the songs, it was Sara and Maybelle who were the mainstay of the singing. Everyone said that A.P. couldn't be depended on when it came to singing.

Maybelle, in a friendly and non-critical way, once said that if he felt like singing during a show or during a recording session, he would sing, and if he didn't feel like it he'd just walk around and look out the window. She said they got to where they never depended on him. They just let him sing when he got ready. And that's the way it came out on the records which were played around the country. One never knew when he was going to sing a verse in his lonesome shaky but captivating voice.

In 1932, after 18 years of marriage, Sara left A.P., and they said he never got over it. All three of the children, Gladys, Janette, and Joe, emphasized that they never knew why their parents separated. All three children adored both their mother and father. They pointed out that both A.P. and Sara continued on friendly terms, an assertion which seems to be borne out by the fact that they, along with Maybelle, continued to perform together for several years.

Gladys, Joe, Janette
Maybelle's yard

Janette, at right, is shown here with her sister, Gladys Carter, and little brother, Joe. As Janette indicated on the label, the photo was taken in Mother Maybelle's yard. *Photo courtesy Janette Carter.*

This photograph was taken about 1938, when the Carter Family went to Texas for three years to broadcast over radio station XERA, said to be "the most powerful in the world." Sara is holding the autoharp, and Maybelle is shown with her guitar. Her three daughters, from the left, are: Helen, Anita, and June. *Photo courtesy Janette Carter*

Off to Texas and National Broadcasting

In 1938, the Carter Family made their first major attempt to capitalize on their popularity which had resulted largely from the many records which were being sold across the country. They went to Texas to join one of the nation's most powerful radio stations, and it was there that the Carter children started performing with their parents for the first time. They joined an immensely successful, though dubious, purveyor of "snake oil" and other forms of quackery-type medicine, including cures for impotency by transplanting goat glands into the groins of men. He called himself Dr. John Romulus Brinkley, and he lived in what was described as a mansion in Del Rio, Texas. Because Federal law prohibited radio stations in excess of 50,000 watts from broadcasting in the United States, Dr. Brinkley built his own station, XERA, across the border in Mexico. It reportedly was a 100,000-watt station, the most powerful in the world, and capable of covering the entire United States.

The Carters joined this station, thinking they would be promoting a line of hair colors. Sara joined A.P. and Maybelle, and with the exception of Maybelle's daughter, Anita, all the other children were left in Poor Valley. The Carters became immensely popular across the country, and soon Maybelle's other daughters, Helen and June, joined the group, and they each received $15.00 a week, Janette recalled. Janette also joined the group and received $28.00 each week, presumably because she was older. Joe was a mere tyke at the time—too young to perform.

She remembers, with mixed feelings, those days in Texas—the dry, hot country so unlike the verdant hills, valleys and well-watered landscape of Poor Valley. And she missed all her friends. She and Joe stayed with their father in an apartment.

Janette said, "I didn't like Texas at all. I cried my heart out. I was put in school along with Joe, and the school was so large, I kept getting lost. The students there laughed at my southern [mountain] drawl and would say, 'Will you talk?' Then they'd laugh at my accent. For one who always loved school, this was a hurtful ordeal in a strange place. I never felt so alone! I missed my beautiful hills of home. I was in love, too, with Jimmy Jett [back in Poor Valley], which was one of the reasons I had been jerked up [and taken to Texas] in the first place by Daddy.

"I worried him and myself sick with crying; so he finally sent me home to stay with Grandma. I quit school and married.

"Now I look back and realize that I didn't have one lick of sense. All my family was in tears—Grandma, Sib, Gladys. Maybelle said, 'Janette, you are too young. You are a child.' She was sixteen when she was married, as was my mother, but they said *I* was too young!

A.P. is shown here with his wife Sara, with her autoharp, and with their two children, Janette and Joe.
Photo courtesy of Janette Carter

"Well, I found out I was. Just because you can keep house, work, and make your own money doesn't make you grown up. My husband and I moved to Bristol, Virginia. It almost broke my daddy's heart. He said, 'You have had so little happiness, I hope you will be happy.' I endured eighteen years of city life, and I found out why people divorce. If you can't get along, it is the best way. By then I understood a lot, and I only loved my mother and daddy more. To admit failure hurts so very deeply. My divorce left a scar that never will heal.

"I came home [from Bristol] to Daddy. He built me a small house and he moved in with me and my children, Rita and Dale. My Don was sixteen and he decided to stay with his father to continue school. I hold no bitterness or hatred toward their father—my beautiful children were worth it all—and we parted friends.

"After I moved back to Poor Valley, we just had three years with Daddy. He loved his grandchildren, and when I moved back home, they seemed to brighten his life. The most peaceful years of my life were spent with Daddy, Rita, and Dale on 'Happy Hill,' the name we gave our house and the acre of land where it stands."

When Janette returned home from Texas about 1940, the other Carters remained there for two more years. Their influence on the budding "country music" era came about largely through their records and their radio programs. It seems that almost all the entertainers who were starting out at that time were influenced totally or in part by the Carter Family.

As I was writing these lines I received a call from Bill Stewart, of the noted "Stewart Family" band of Mt. Washington, Kentucky. Bill was at one time the youngest fiddler on the *Grand Ole Opry*, and his brother Redd Stewart was a great songwriter, "The Tennessee Waltz" being one of his best known. I said: "**Bill, tell me what influenced you and your family, what inspired 'you all' to take up music?**"

Without hesitation he said, "Well, for one thing, we used to listen to the Carter Family on the radio. I remember that my daddy would get up before daylight, and the first thing he'd do would be to turn on the radio to listen to the Carter Family."

A young Chet Atkins, whose home was a few miles up the road from the Museum here, remembers listening to the Carters on XERA (the Mexican border station) on a battery radio set he had built; and the singer Tom T. Hall, from up in Olive Hill, Kentucky, remembers that he got his start from a Carter songbook. Waylon Jennings recalled that his father would pull his truck up to the open window of their farmhouse in Texas and run a battery cable from the truck to power the radio, so they could hear the Carter Family. Woody Guthrie, the Oklahoma folksinger, was an early Carter Family fan and was greatly influenced by them, and he learned the Maybelle style of guitar playing. Some of his most popular songs were said to be adaptations of those sung by the Carter Family.

Wayne Daniel, who wrote a well-researched book on the influence that the Atlanta area had on country music, said, "The first country song I remember hearing was 'My Old Clinch Mountain Home' by the Carter Family."

And so it was that the nation embraced the Carters, and their popularity and their record sales were growing beyond any dream which even A.P., the dreamer, ever had. In addition to their two daily broadcasts, they made transcriptions which were sent to other radio stations. But troubling matters lay beyond the bright and peaceful horizon. It was 1941, and Dr. Brinkley and his radio station were being sued by countless unhappy clients, and the world's most powerful station, along with the Carters, went off the air. The family went to WBT in Charlotte for a few months, and then they disbanded.

Sara had married one of A.P.'s cousins, Coy Bayes, described as being tall and handsome, and he was not at all keen on his new bride, Sara, continuing to sing with A.P., her former husband. She and Coy soon moved to Angels Camp, California. Mother Maybelle and the girls joined the *Old Dominion Barn Dance* in Richmond, Virginia, and in 1948 they joined the most popular *Mid-Day Merry-Go-Round* in Knoxville, Tennessee.

After Sara remarried and moved to California, she visited her children in Poor Valley each year in this large travel trailer. After crossing the country with it "thirty or forty times," she left it in Janette's yard where it remains to this day, 1999. Her daughter Rita lived in it for a long time, but now it sits vacant. *Photo by the author, ca. 1990*

The station was WNOX, and this noon-day program was the one "everybody" in most of East Tennessee and in parts of other states listened to every day at 12:00 noon for, I believe, an hour and a half. This station, this program, and especially its creator, Lowell Blanchard, started or promulgated the careers of dozens of early country music greats.

I remember that our only rest from a 12- to 14- hour workday on the farm was after the noon meal. We would sit under the shade trees or on our front porch and listen to the *Merry-Go-Round* on our battery-powered radio. Sometimes my father would send me to Nash Copeland's store, a mile and a half away, to buy a plow point, or a hoe, and I'd have to trot most of the way in order to get back in time to return to the fields with the other workers. But I also remember, most fondly, that I never missed hearing a single song on the *Merry-Go-Round*, because the program was belted out from every old house along the way. Just before I would be out of hearing distance from one radio, the same sounds could be heard from the next homestead.

I remember when the Carters joined the *Merry-Go-Round*, and how Lowell Blanchard promoted them and extoled their virtues; and I remember June's wild antics. A.P. played with Maybelle and the girls on occasions, but it wasn't the same as in the old days with Sara. Sunshine Slim Sweet, who was performing on the *Merry-Go-Round* at the time, remembers the Carters and how popular they were. He described A.P. as "real backward," a sort of lonely person who stayed off by himself; but Slim was quick to point out that A.P. was much respected by all the other entertainers.

One of my greatest thrills was when I had a chance to actually visit the WNOX studio on Gay Street in Knoxville where I saw for the first time Mother Maybelle and her daughters, and many other entertainers.

While performing in Knoxville, Mother Maybelle hired the young Chet Atkins (later described as the best known guitar player in the country) to play in the band, and to help drive the band throughout the region, for nightly shows—personal appearances, they called them. Many of the *Merry-Go-Round* stars have told me that they would often leave Knoxville as soon as the noonday show was over and would drive to a little mountain hamlet in Kentucky, Virginia, North Carolina, northern Alabama, Georgia, or somewhere in East Tennessee. After the evening show, they would often have to drive all night, and sometimes they would return only a couple of hours before time for the next *Merry-Go-Round* show. They played to packed schoolhouses, and in this day, long before television, people came to see the performers, whom they had so often heard on radio, but whom they had never seen. Everybody talked about how the entertainers "didn't look like I thought they would."

When Mother Maybelle, along with her three daughters, moved to Nashville in May, 1950, the final death knell of the *old* Carter Family was struck, and the era of the *new* Carter Family commenced. They joined the *Grand Ole Opry* at the old Ryman Auditorium, "the mother church of all country music." They performed there until 1967, when their

After Mother Maybelle and her girls moved to Nashville in 1950, they toured the country and much of the world, made numerous recordings with a half-dozen major record companies, wrote many successful songs, and gained a multitudinous following among the folk music enthusiasts, the college students, and the academia while maintaining their appeal to those who adored the old Carter Family. Anita is the bass player, Helen the accordionist, June holds the autoharp, and Mother Maybelle is shown with her guitar. *Photo courtesy Janette Carter*

international traveling schedule caused them to reluctantly resign from that revered institution, said to be the longest running radio program in the world, and now one of the longest running television programs.

Some insights into the "new" Carters, Mother Maybelle and her daughters, are revealed in an interview Helen gave on October 8, 1987. The person conducting the interview was Vicki Langdon of Denison, Texas, a total convert to the revived Carter Family. Vicki is a former newspaper city editor of the *Denison Herald*, a radio news director in Oklahoma, and presently the Coordinator of Public Information for the Denison School System.

She followed the Carter performances for years and became friends with Helen and Anita. She became a Carter convert when, as a child, she first heard them about 1970 on the *Johnny Cash Show*. It was, she said, "that beautiful, angelic, Carter background harmony" that forever endeared Vicki, even as a child, to Mother Maybelle and the girls. She said, "No one ever has or ever will measure up to them."

Vicki Langdon interviewed Helen when Helen spoke at the Grayson County College in Denison, and Vicki sent me a copy of this taped interview. The interview included human interest type references to the family before they went to Nashville, as well as something of the new success they found during the folk revival. Helen, the reader will recall, joined the original Carter Family during their stay in Texas in the late 1930s. So did her sisters, June and Anita. Helen emphasized that their mother, Maybelle, was first of all a mother to her children: "She did the washing; she did the ironing and cooking; and she made us children mind. She ruled us with a sort of iron hand, but nobody ever loved their mother more than we did.

"We'd travel in a car, day and night sometimes, piled full of all our instruments. Anita always slept in a guitar case when she was little. When she got too big for that, she'd curl up under the neck of the bass fiddle and sleep.

"After the break-up of the original Carter Family, A.P., Sara, and Mother, then she was ready to go back to Poor Valley and give up music. But Daddy [Eck Carter], encouraged her to go out on her own with us girls. Daddy liked classical music, but he encouraged her in every way. He'd say, 'May, I know you can do it if you just go out and try it.'

"Mother had never done anything on her own [in a leadership way] but she brought us all down to Nashville, and a whole new career began. I'm very, very proud of my mother. She was quiet and dignified, but we never realized how much the world loved her until she died. I remember that someone wrote in the Atlanta paper that 'this little lady very quietly became a superstar'."

After the renaissance of Maybelle and the girls, they could hardly satisfy the demand for personal appearances, and the schedule became reminiscent of the old days. Helen gave an example:

"We had been touring Europe—Poland, Switzerland, Czechoslovakia, Norway, eight different countries—and we were all exhausted when we got back to Nashville. Well, we just spent one night at home, and then we were off to Nova Scotia where we played for four days, and then back home again for one night, and then we were off to Texas."

CARTER

Although Mother Maybelle Carter was best known for her phenomenal influence as a guitar player, she often played the autoharp, as this photo of her would suggest. She was an integral part of the three-member original Carter Family, and she became the leader of the new Carter Family which gained national and international acclaim. *Photo courtesy Janette Carter*

It was in this building, which A.P. Carter built, that he operated a country store for many years in Poor Valley. Located adjacent to the Carter Fold building, Janette turned this old store into The Carter Museum. A.P. poses on the store porch with Sara, his wife, and their daughter Janette. *Photo courtesy Janette Carter*

In the meantime, A.P. went back for a short time to a radio station in Bristol, the place of his beginning. But soon a tired and dejected A.P. Carter was back in Poor Valley working as a carpenter, bent on building each of his three children a house. It was during this time that he opened the A.P. Carter Country Store.

According to Chet Atkins, who continued to play with Maybelle and the girls in Nashville, Hank Williams was always wooing Anita and offering her expensive gifts. Elvis Presley, who started working with the Carters in 1955, was reportedly much taken with the family and especially loved Mother Maybelle. The girls remembered that Elvis often popped a button from his jacket during a show and that Mother Maybelle would borrow a button from one of their skirts and sew it on Elvis' garment. "He'd go on stage looking good," they laughed, "and we'd go on stage with safety pins."

It is paradoxical that the new, exciting, and provocative music which Elvis and others of his style introduced, was the beginning (at least for a time) of the end of the old-time Carter-type music which had become so popular. The Carters continued for a while to travel throughout the country, appearing at county fairs, auditoriums, theaters and the like. But eventually, "rock and roll" engulfed the country like a winter sage-grass fire in Poor Valley. The girls were mostly home with their children, A.P. was building houses in Poor Valley, and Mother Maybelle was working as a part-time nurse in Nashville.

Sometimes, it was oft told, when Maybelle and her girls were playing in northeast Tennessee or southwest Virginia, they would see a lonely, but familiar, face, usually in the back of the auditorium—that of A.P. It was a sad sight for Maybelle and the girls.

With the advent of the outdoor festivals in the 1960s, however, and when the folk music craze permeated the coffee houses and the college campuses, it was suddenly and surprisingly apparent that the old-fashioned, "obsolete" country music of the Carters was now in vogue again.

Johnny Cash had been an early and avid fan of the Carters, and when he hosted his popular prime-time *Johnny Cash Show* on national television (ABC), starting in 1969, he often featured Mother Maybelle, June, to whom he was married, and sometimes Anita and Helen as well.

Mother Maybelle and her three daughters appeared on other national television shows, and they appeared with Johnny Cash on stage in various parts of the country. But the meteoric rise in the popularity of Mother Maybelle and her daughters was by no means dependent upon the popularity of the famous Johnny Cash, although June did accompany him as an entertainer throughout much of the world. Carlene Carter, June's daughter by an earlier marriage to country star Carl Smith, became an entertainer in her own right. She did quite well in the country-rock field in the late seventies and early eighties, but seems to have gravitated back toward her music roots.

In the spring of 1998, I started corresponding with Anita in Nashville, and we had several telephone conversations in an endeavor to more accurately summarize the "new" Carter Family—Mother Maybelle and the girls. She was most cordial and helpful, but she was in frail health, and she was caring for a son who was, I believe, hospitalized during that time. Additionally her beloved sister Helen was, and had been for weeks, hospitalized with what proved to be a fatal malady. Anita visited Helen at the hospital almost daily until Helen's death on June 2, 1998, at the age of 70.

Despite the difficult circumstances of the time, Anita did provide important information relevant to the renaissance of the Carters. This information forms the basis for the following brief review of the advent of the second Carter Family.

The career of Mother Maybelle and "her girls," really started after they moved to Nashville in the spring of 1950. First they joined the *Grand Ole Opry* and performed there every week until 1967, when their popularity was ever increasing and their world-wide schedule forced them to reluctantly resign from this hallowed institution.

No attempt beyond a mere mention of some of the more notable accomplishments will be attempted here. The popularity of Mother Maybelle and her daughters increased over the years, and it was especially notable with the increased popularity of folk music during the 1960s. The mere enumeration of some high points of their success may provide a hint of their doings during these years, and as such may titillate the reader to pursue in a more substantive fashion the story of Mother Maybelle and the Carter girls.

They recorded many songs for RCA Victor, Columbia, Okeh, Mercury, Republic, Hickory, Capital and for several other recording companies. And they wrote songs, many of which became "hits," such as June's "Ring of Fire," recorded by her husband, Johnny Cash. Helen wrote songs which were recorded by the most popular country artists of the day, including: Ray Price, Willie Nelson, Wayland Jennings, Jean Shepard, and Ann Margret. Mother Maybelle's historic recordings with the Nitty Gritty Dirt Band in 1972 of "Will The Circle Be Unbroken" was followed by a second award winning volume by the same name in 1989 featuring Helen, June, and Anita, also with the Nitty Gritty Dirt Band.

Those who recorded the 30 songs on these historic recordings included some of the most popular old-time country music stars of the era: Earl Scruggs, Doc Watson, Roy Acuff, Merle Travis, Jimmy Martin, as well as the previously mentioned Nitty Gritty Dirt Band, and many others. Interestingly and significantly, the first person whose name appeared on this impressive album was that of Mother Maybelle Carter.

As has been stated earlier, Chet Atkins was their guitarist for many years, and they made major tours with Elvis Presley, Hank Snow, and Hank Williams. They performed on the *Kraft Music Hall* several times, played at the White House, the Kennedy Center, and at the Newport Folk Festival. They worked as a group or individually in television and movie productions with Kris Kristofferson, Robert Duvall, Jack Linkletter, Zsa Zsa Gabor, and of course many times with Johnny Cash. They performed throughout the United States and in numerous foreign countries.

They were reputed to have been the first country music show to be aired on network television when they appeared on the popular Kate Smith shows, and they were credited with having been the first country music show to have performed behind the Iron Curtain in Czechoslovakia. The Czech audience was apparently familiar with their music, and Anita recalled that they joined in and helped to sing "The Wabash Cannon Ball" and many old-time Carter songs.

After their mother Maybelle died in 1976, the new "Carter Family" continued to perform in this and other countries, even into the 1990s. The sisters, from the left, Anita, June (Mrs. Johnny Cash), and Helen, are shown here in this formal publicity photograph. *Photo courtesy Janette Carter*

The Carters continued to tour the country and the world, primarily with the most popular *Johnny Cash Show*. Mother Maybelle was beset with a terminal illness, similar to Parkinson's disease, and died in 1978. The girls continued and remained active with Johnny Cash until the mid-1990s when he became afflicted with the same rare degenerative (but not contagious) disease as that which ended the life of Mother Maybelle.

Mention should be made of the third generation Carters who have followed in the footsteps of their parents and grandparents. They include Helen's sons, Danny, David and Kevin; June's daughters Carlene (mentioned earlier) and Rosie; and Anita's daughter Lorrie. The son of June and Johnny Cash, John Carter Cash, has appeared on his father's shows, and is a performer in his own right.

Although some of the younger Carters have strayed a bit from the original Carter-style music, they revert back to the old style occasionally, and they seem not to have forgotten their roots. A.P. would be proud of this.

A.P.'s last admonishment to his daughter, Janette, was that she keep their old-style music alive. Janette later said, "He tried the hardest of any man I ever knew to keep his music going. He told me, after I moved back to the valley, 'There needs to be one of my children to carry on my work—will you try?' How could I ever do that? I had no income, no money and I had two babies to raise. But I said, 'Daddy, I will try.' For all Daddy, Mother, and Maybelle had done for me, I decided that I'd try to keep their old-time music alive, if I had to work night and day, 'til I fell over dead.

"I worked in restaurants, in factories, in fields, in school cafeterias. I cooked and washed dishes to be near my children; I cleaned houses. I had to work to raise my family. Daddy helped, but soon he was gone. So I prayed for strength, for health, and for work to give them what they needed. I wanted them to have much more than I ever had, but it was very hard to even keep food on the table! I hung on. I prayed and cried hundreds of times. I kept charging along like old Custer. I worked harder at being a good mother than I had at any other job I'd ever done. My beautiful children were mine; no one but God could take them. I was their world; just like my daddy was to me, I am to them."

As mentioned earlier, Janette chose, as a means of perpetuating the old Carter Family music, the establishment of what she called "The Carter Fold."

Janette's first effort to revive and perpetuate the old Carter Family music after A.P. died was on this little make-shift stage at the back of the A.P. Carter store in 1974. The reader will note the logs and planks for seating, and the conveniently located outdoor toilet. *Photo courtesy Janette Carter*

The Carter Family Fold Music Barn was built by the hands of A.P.'s three children, Janette, Joe and Gladys, with the help of neighbors and other family members, in accordance with A.P.'s dying charge: "Keep my old-time music alive if you can." It is located in Poor Valley, on part of the Carter farm. Janette, left, Joe and Gladys pose proudly in front of "The Fold." *Photo taken by the author, ca. 1990*

In the beginning, (late 1960s), "The Fold" consisted of a Saturday night gathering at the little country store building which A.P. had built and operated, across the road from his home. Later, Janette, Gladys, and Joe built a crude dirt-floored shed adjacent to the old Carter Store, and in front of Janette's house. A few years later, this hillside "theater" was enlarged extensively. It is clearly a labor of love, and both the building and the weekly shows are totally consistent with the Carter Family: plain, utilitarian, and totally non-pretentious.

In the summer of 1988, I attended the Saturday night Carter Fold gathering in Poor Valley. Interestingly, the structure looked strikingly like the unpainted tobacco curing barns of the region. It was built up the side of the steep hill, and followed exactly the contours of the land so that no excavation was necessary. The result was a kind of amphitheater effect. It was what Joe called an "ample" theater. It was supported by locust poles set upright. These poles were unhewn and unpeeled, so that they resembled the growing trees themselves. The structure was listing north-eastwardly, and it was propped on the outside by several other long locust poles, similar to those used for support inside.

The featured music for the evening was Ramona Jones, wife of the legendary Grandpa Jones, their son Mark, and their son-in-law Ron Wall. They all rode from our house with my wife Elizabeth and me, and we were met there by Chris and Dale Ballinger, a husband and wife music and singing duo from Cookeville, Tennessee.

Janette had prepared sandwiches and other victuals for us; but unfortunately, we had eaten at the nearby country store at Hiltons, at the lower end of Poor Valley.

The most impressive and characteristic aspects of the entire Carter Fold was the complete lack of commercialism, and the informality of it all. First there was no designated parking area, although crowds of several hundred, I am told, sometimes congregate there. Some kindly old man, who apparently recognized Ramona, motioned for us to park on the grassy area near the front of the building.

We carried our instruments inside to a small room which was adjacent to the stage. It was apparently intended as a dressing room, but people entered from either door, and there was little privacy. It contained an old sofa and a few odd chairs.

In a few minutes, Janette came down the hill from her house. She carried a bucket of what I later learned was potato soup that she made to sell by the cup in a corner of the building, near the stage. She also sold coffee, popcorn, and a few other knickknacks. She had two wood burning "stoves" made, as I recall, from old oil drums; and she encouraged people to use these heaters to roast their potatoes, which they could eat during the intermission.

The Carter Fold building was built of rough-sawn lumber by Joe, Janette, and Gladys, and followed the slope of the hillside, and the bare ground serves as the floor. It was completed in 1974 and remains in use every Saturday night, as of 1999. *Photo by the author in 1990*

While we were waiting to go on stage, we went next door, to A.P.'s little store, which now contained a good deal of the Carter Family memorabilia. Janette called it her Museum. Although several people had assembled outside by 6:00 p.m., and the show wasn't scheduled to start until 7:30, only one person, other than our group, came to the Museum.

Janette prided herself on being prompt, and at exactly 7:30 she opened the program. The building could seat over four hundred, and it was filled to about half of its capacity. Janette called off the names of several states, and if there were visitors from a particular state, they would wave, whistle, and applaud. Several states were represented, but the vast majority of those in attendance were local folk, people she called "regulars." Many of the men sat with their hats or caps on, and several were dressed in overalls or other work clothes. There was not a single necktie in the crowd.

The seats were bleacher-like, made of discarded railroad crossties and without backs. I wondered if any of these crossties had been cut and hewn by A.P. and Sara over a half century earlier. The seats were covered with scraps of carpet of every conceivable variation and color. But the regulars were allowed to bring old chairs of myriad forms, shapes and sizes, and to actually nail them to the crossties so that they couldn't be removed, and so they could be occupied only by those people who placed them there.

Janette and Joe sang a few of the old Carter songs; the same ones, I imagine, which they sang every Saturday night. Then she introduced Ramona, and as she and her group played, many of those in the audience danced in front of the stage. It was a kind of buck dance, and although both men and women danced, they did so singularly and not as couples. I played a couple of pieces on the mandolin with Ramona, mainly just to have the satisfaction of having played "at The Fold."

During Ramona's portion of the evening's entertainment, a group of a half dozen young men came in the dressing room carrying their instruments. They were largely unshaven, and dressed in well-worn work clothes. They seemed courteous and kindly, but shy, and they talked little. Janette came in and asked: "Now what did you say you called yourselves?" The apparent leader, a tall, dark-haired man in his thirties said meekly: "The Horse Creek Mountain Boys." Janette couldn't understand him because he spoke in a soft muffled voice. She asked him a couple of times to repeat himself, and each time he repeated, in precisely the same manner as before: "The Horse Creek Mountain Boys."

Janette admonished them that they were to sing only two songs. "Now, boys, we've got a lot of folks to go on tonight," she said, "Joe and Mr. Johnson, the Hensley Brothers, Ramona and her folks, and John Rice—and we've just got time for two numbers." They nodded politely.

I don't think Janette ever got their name straight, because when she introduced them a few minutes later she said: "And now we have a new group and they're called the Horse Creek Boys or the Boys from Horse Creek, or something like that. You boys come on out."

If anyone ever questioned the genuine rural, mountain background of the Carter Family, this apprehension would be quickly allayed if he visited the Saturday night Carter Fold in Poor Valley. Janette and Joe are an extension, a reflection, of the old Carters, an indication that the lives of the members of the singing Carter Family were as simple and honest as the songs they sang and the music they played, and maybe that's why the Carter Family was doubtless the most influential singing family in the history of country music.

They developed, or perhaps more accurately, emulated, a type and style of music that was dominant in the community from which they came. They somewhat formalized their style in the mid to late 1920s, and they never changed that style throughout their career (although Maybelle and her girls, and other members of the clan did make some changes after going to Nashville). But when the old Carter Family style became un-stylish, they didn't (perhaps couldn't) change to accommodate the honky-tonk, or bluegrass, or other country offshoots. The influence, however, of the "original" Carter Family has not faded, and though its influence may be more difficult to trace, its multitudinous ramifications go on and on and permeate virtually all present-day, traditional, bluegrass, and contemporary country music.

Chet Atkins, who at last count had won 10 Grammy Awards, said that the greatest experience of his life was working with the Carter Family. Jerry Garcia of the Grateful Dead said that Maybelle's guitar playing influenced three generations of country guitar players in a serious way. Others who were influenced by the Carters include Joan Baez and Emmylou Harris, who once said, "The first time I heard the Carters sing the 'Gold Watch and Chain,' I thought about my grandparents and I cried." Jeff Hanna of The Nitty Gritty Dirt Band went so far as to call the Carters ". . . a great American family, like the Kennedys or the Rockefellers."

Don Reid, a member of the popular Statler Brothers said that the Carters "were the basis of everything in country music"; and Arlo Guthrie described the Carter Family music as " . . . the last real music before commercialization." Dr. Bill Malone, respected country music scholar, pointed out that their music never changed—it just got better.

I asked Earl Scruggs, the country's best known banjo player and "co-father" of bluegrass music, who inspired him to start playing music. He replied forthrightly and without hesitation: "Mother Maybelle."

One of the most encompassing tributes ever paid to the Carter Family came from a premier authority on early country music, Dr. Charles Wolfe, in a sort of inadvertent backhanded way. In extoling the contributions of the inimitable Uncle Dave Macon, Dr. Wolfe said: "With the exception of the Carter Family, Uncle Dave Macon preserved more valuable American folklore . . . than any other folk or country music performer."

During most of my childhood and teenage years, in the 1930s and 1940s, we had no electricity, but we heard the Carter Family nonetheless on a hand-cranked Victrola, and I always looked forward to visiting with my Uncle Frank and Aunt Sophia because they had a similar record player, but with many more Carter records. In reflecting back, I don't recall a single record that Uncle Frank and Aunt Sophia had that *wasn't* by the Carter Family.

My father bought a battery-operated radio, and sometimes we heard them on it. I was inspired by them, as were half the farm boys of the country, it seemed, to learn to play music, especially the guitar. I saved enough money to buy a $4.00 Stella guitar from my cousin, Amos Stooksbury; then I took it to a neighbor, Fiddlin' Bob Coxe, who showed me how to tune it. The first song I learned was Mother Maybelle's most famous "Wildwood Flower" which I thought was the most beautiful piece I ever heard. It was the first song that virtually every guitar player learned to play from the 1930s through the 1940s, and even later. Archie Campbell had learned it from Maybelle and it became his most requested piece. Tom T. Hall, musician, songwriter, and author, called it "the national anthem of country music."

Cormac McCarthy is considered to be one of the most respected writers in the nation, and he was winner of the National Book Award of 1992. *The New York Times* Book Review section in the June 12, 1994 edition, compared him to William Faulkner, Mark Twain, Herman Melville and Shakespeare. The noted historian, Shelby Foote, described him as "America's greatest living author." Cormac is a native of Knoxville, Tennessee, and a longtime resident of El Paso, Texas. With all his profoundly and highly respected literary skills, Cormac is a devoted Carter Family fan, and knows, I think, every song they ever recorded, and when he comes by the Museum here, he even plays some of their music on the guitar.

The late Elmer Byrd of Turkey Creek, West Virginia, was a classic example of those influenced by the Carter Family. Elmer played for me here at the Tennessee Fall Homecoming every October, and he traveled the entire country playing the old time claw-hammer type banjo music. He was voted the nation's best old-time banjo player by Bluegrass Music Awards. I asked him why and how he got started playing music and he told me the following story, almost identical to that I've heard from most every other early country entertainer with whom I've talked:

"We didn't have a radio way back here in the mountains of West Virginia. We didn't even have a record player, and we'd walk to one of the neighbors to hear the Carter Family records. We heard the same songs over and over again and that made me want to play myself. I soon learned to play the banjo and guitar and so did my cousin, George Byrd.

"We thought we were pretty good, and when I was 19 and George was 17, we started walking from Turkey Creek, West Virginia, to Nashville, Tennessee, to see if we could get on the *Grand Ole Opry*. That was in 1939.

"We carried a banjo, guitar, and fiddle with us, and when we got to Ashland, Kentucky, we got a room at a rooming house for $1.00. We was wore out, and we went right to sleep. In a few minutes the landlady came knocking on our door, wanting to know if we'd come down and play for her family, and maybe a few customers— said she'd give us our dollar back if we would. We jumped up and played for her and we ended up playing around Ashland for five or six months. We entered a big fiddle contest. There were over a thousand people there, and we won first place."

George Byrd was later killed in WWII, and Elmer went on to a career in old-time music, and he later played with the Carter Family, and with many of the other outstanding folks in the traditional and early country field. He came to be known as "The Banjo Man from Turkey Creek," and he played here at the annual Tennessee Fall Homecoming until he passed away in July, 1997.

An important part of the Museum of Appalachia's Hall of Fame is a large section dealing with the people and their music, a portion of which is devoted to the Carter Family. Among the items I have displayed there is an open Bible I found among the effects of my mother's cousin, Sally Rice. When I opened the Bible I could hardly believe what I saw: a picture of the Carter Family pasted to the fly leaf. No one, I thought, would ever desecrate the Holy Bible by pasting any kind of a picture in it—unless, of course, it was of the Carter Family.

Before concluding this chapter on the Carters, I wanted to once again talk with Joe and Janette. I had thought of a few more questions.

Well, Janette, your father, as well as your mother and Maybelle, would be proud of the way the Carter music has survived, and how it is still talked about and sung today.

(Janette) "Yes, even though Mother and her husband Coy moved to California, she kept an interest in the music, and she came back, you know, and recorded with the family in New York, Chicago and other places. She came back here in 1975 for my A.P. Carter Memorial Day and I almost broke down in tears trying to introduce her and Maybelle. It seemed that even the birds listened to them sing that day. I never heard no prettier singing in my life."

Janette is shown here with her mother, Sara Carter, in front of the A.P. Carter store building after it had been closed and converted into a dwelling. This picture was made when Sara came from her California home to visit her children and other relatives in Poor Valley. *Photo courtesy Janette Carter*

And your father spent his last days here in Poor Valley.

"Yeah, but he couldn't carry on the music without Mother and Maybelle. Mother was in California and Maybelle was in Nashville, touring the country with her girls. And he couldn't play much, you know, •because of his trembling."

(Joe) "No, no, not much at all. He had this nervous condition from birth. It really hampered his music."

(Janette) "His hands just went like this, all the time." (Janette gestured with her own trembling hands.)

I asked Janette the cause of his nervous condition, his trembling hands. She explained that he was "marked" before he was born, a belief commonly held here in Southern Appalachia, and elsewhere perhaps, that a traumatic experience by the expectant mother could "mark" the child for life, in a manner associated with the trauma. For example, I had a distant cousin, Caney Stooksbury, who had only the semblance of one of his ears. It was almost non-existent—just two or three little ragged protrusions. Everyone said that his mother saw one of her sheep whose ear was mutilated, chewed off, by a dog just before Caney was born; and that's why he had no ear. Janette had a similar reason for her father's lifelong nervous condition, but Joe was more than skeptical of the explanation of how their father was "marked" before birth.

Janette explained: "Grandma was out in the apple orchard gathering apples. I guess it was late fall, and she was with child, our daddy, who was born in December. Well, it came up an awful storm and the lightning struck the tree she was under and it liked to have scared her to death. Didn't it, Joe?"

(Joe mutters an unenthusiastic answer.) "I've heard that."

(Janette) "Well, the lightning run down the tree trunk and played around under her feet, and she claimed that the child, our daddy, was marked by that. That's why he had this nervous condition all his life. He had that tremor in his hands."

(Joe) "I don't think so. Some people swear to that, but I don't much believe it."

He never got over it?

(Janette) "No, he was that way all his life. By the fall of 1960, Daddy was in bad health. He was getting old and he was tired, and his heart bothered him a lot. On November 7, he called me to his bedside, and he told me again that he wanted me to keep this old-time music a'goin', if I could. I told him I'd do my very best to do so, and I took his hand. I said, 'Why, Daddy, you're not nervous any more. You're not shaking.' He said, 'I know. I've been this way all day.' And in just a little while he was dead."

A.P. Carter lies in the lonely Mount Vernon churchyard above Poor Valley, where he first started singing. The record embossed on the tombstone is that of one of A.P.'s favorite songs, "Keep on the Sunny Side." Johnny Cash described how he was moved the first time he visited A.P.'s grave and read the title of this familiar Carter song. *Photo by the author, spring, 1991*

Jack Jackson is shown here at the age of 16 playing on the famous WSM radio station in Nashville in 1925, the year the *Grand Ole Opry* was started there. At this time, his family recalls, Jack had taught himself to play the guitar, banjo, and harmonica, instruments he bought with his own money. *Photo courtesy Doug and John Jackson*

Chapter 3

Jack Jackson, Nashville's
First Country Recording "Artist"

"Perhaps the Most Popular Radio Entertainer in the South"

It is paradoxical that the story of Jack Jackson (1909-1994), one of the very first stars in country music, and one of the most interesting, is now all but totally unknown, even to the most avid students of the subject. I learned of the fascinating and unlikely story of Jonas Asa (Jack) Jackson, The Strolling Yodeler, quite by accident and in a most circuitous manner.

I received a telephone call in 1994 from Patsy Weiler, a friend and free-lance newspaper reporter from Murfreesboro in Middle Tennessee. She told me of the passing of 85-year-old Jack Jackson of Lebanon, a few miles east of Nashville. Dr. Charles K. Wolfe, also a friend of mine, had gone to Jackson's home, Patsy informed me, to examine some of the songs Jackson had written in his youth and to look at other music-related Jackson memorabilia. (Wolfe is the only country music researcher I know who has even mentioned Jack Jackson in his writings.) While at the Jackson homeplace, Dr. Wolfe noticed a most unusual relic in Jackson's large workshop located in the back yard. It was part of a "perpetual motion machine" made before the Civil War by Jack's great-grandfather, Asa Jackson.

Both Charles and Patsy opined that I'd be interested in this most unusual piece for the Museum of Appalachia. I contacted Jack Jackson's sons, Doug and John, and purchased this most fascinating, all wooden contraption which, according to legend, old Asa Jackson kept hidden in a cave, especially during those destructive years of the Civil War. (The story, along with a photograph, of Asa Jackson's device, with its hundreds of mysterious wooden parts, was carried nationwide by the Associated Press after I assembled it and permanently displayed it here at the Museum of Appalachia.)

It was during my visits with the Jackson brothers that I began to learn of the fabulous musical career of their father, Jack Jackson. I talked with them and together we looked through old letters, newspapers, magazine articles, and such.

This photo of Jack's father, Jonas Asa Jackson, on their farm in Middle Tennessee, suggests the nature of the rural and farm background from which Jack came. *Photo courtesy Doug and John Jackson*

He was born June 14, 1909, on a farm in the community of Leeville in Wilson County, some 20 miles east of Nashville. He must have been a precocious and driven little lad, and he seemed to have mastered whatever task he tackled. Family members said that he started collecting tools at the age of seven, and that he had built his own blacksmith shop by the time he was ten. When he was twelve, he had become an avid trapper. He rode a horse to school, his son Doug related, and he had a string of traps along the way which he checked every morning. In the afternoon, he brought the varmints home and skinned them. At that time fur hides were bringing high prices and an innovative and persevering person could make "good" money running trap lines. It is likely that he used some of his trapping money to purchase various musical instruments. Totally self-taught, he is reputed to have learned to play the guitar, banjo, harmonica and the dobro as a teenager.

A precocious lad, Jack was said to have had his own blacksmith shop when he was ten, and at the age of 12 he was an active hunter and trapper. He is shown here with the "tools of the trade": a 22 caliber rifle, a kerosene lantern for night hunting and for running the trap lines before daylight, and his dog. Tacked to the side of the house is a prized mink skin, at left, a 'possum hide, and a mole skin. *Photo ca. 1921, courtesy of Jack's sons Doug and John Jackson*

Few full-time adult trappers could boast of so many prime fox skins as young Jack displays here. *Courtesy Doug and John Jackson*

Young Jackson started playing music, usually the guitar, with old-time fiddlers and banjo players of the area, where such musicians were the heroes of the day, and they were doubtless held in awe by the young, would-be musicians, such as Jack Jackson. Perhaps the person who most inspired and influenced Jackson's early musical career was his older cousin, Tom Guthrie. Jack later recalled that Tom, whom he described as an old bachelor, had been a champion fiddler, both in Tennessee and in Texas. Jack bought a banjo from him and learned to play, and soon the two were playing together—Jack, the banjo, and Tom, the fiddle.

In 1926, when Jack was but 17, he wrote a song called "Peay's Walkover" for Austin Peay, a candidate for Governor of Tennessee. It became popular throughout the state and was reportedly adopted as Peay's campaign theme song. Peay won the election and Jack was invited to the capitol by the new governor to sing this, and other songs, as a sort of victory celebration. The local (Lebanon) paper proudly reported the event of their young hero, and the headline was: "Governor Listens While Boy Sings 'Peay's Walkover'."

Dr. Wolfe states that the first professional job Jack Jackson had was playing the banjo with an old harmonica player named George Jenkins from Lebanon, Tennessee. In a May 4, 1952, article by Hugh Walker in *The Nashville Tennessean Magazine*, Walker described Jenkins as a "seven-foot harness maker." Jackson and Jenkins played such instrumental pieces as "When You and I Were Young, Maggie" and "Silver Threads Among the Gold." They played for dances and at various local gatherings. George Jenkins and Jack started playing on Nashville's WLAC station in 1926, and according to *The Nashville Banner*, Jack sang the first song that went over the 5000-watt transmitter. It was, again based on an article from the Nashville paper, heard as far away as Sydney, Australia. Jack later recalled that he received a good bit of fan mail from Australia. He told of how he was given his first "single act" slot on the radio:

One night somebody ahead of us failed to show up, and they wanted us to take up their time, and old George was afraid he couldn't make it, said he hadn't practiced for the extra time, and kid-like I thought I could pick and sing. . . so they turned me loose and from then on they gave me a spot by myself.

Jack also played with an old-time fiddler, the legendary Arthur Smith, described by country music scholar Professor Bill C. Malone as being generally acknowledged as the best of all the Southeast fiddlers; and at another time, Malone described Smith as "the greatest fiddler of them all." Smith, a native of the Middle Tennessee county of Humphreys, became an early *Grand Ole Opry* star, a respected songwriter, and he appeared with cowboy singer Jimmy Wakely in movies in the mid-1940's. Jack had this to say about his association with the famous fiddler, Arthur Smith:

I played with Arthur Smith before I went close to a radio station. Arthur was a railroad construction man and he had a floating gang that would go to a place that needed a bridge built or something, and he happened to locate in Mt. Juliet where I went to school and he stayed there several months. When I found out that he was a fiddler—he lived in railroad cars fixed up for living quarters—I'd stay 'til he got in and pick with him until he got ready to go to bed. Then I'd walk home.

A yodeler from rural Tennessee sounds somewhat incongruent, but it demonstrates the constant influx of outside influences to the "pure" old-time music. A singer named Jimmy Franklin, from nearby Murfreesboro, had served in WWI and had reportedly spent time in Switzerland where he learned to yodel. Jack, apparently impressed with the new sound, also learned to yodel. Walker, *The Nashville Tennessean* writer, wrote that "he yodeled high, low, early and late, and radio listeners never suspected that the popular singer was only 17 years old."

At an early age, Jack sensed that many of the "cultural" folk in Nashville (then called the Athens of the South) looked "way down" on anyone who played a guitar, and other stringed instruments. He tried to dispel this stereotypical view by his dress, the songs he wrote and sang, and by his "non-hillbilly" demeanor. He is shown here with his fiddle, guitar, and banjo, dressed in a three-piece suit, tie, and the straw hat, which was in vogue at the time. *Photo courtesy Doug and John Jackson*

It is said that Jack was impatient, perhaps a little nervous, while waiting to perform on radio programs. "I was always pacing the floor," Jack later said about his early days. One night one of the announcers noticed Jack's impatient pacing and said: "Well, there's the yodeler strolling around," hence the name, Jack Jackson the Strolling Yodeler, which stuck with him throughout his meteoric, but short-lived musical career.

It may be parenthetically observed here that Nashville was called the "Athens of the South" because of its several colleges and because of other cultural manifestations. Many of the socially elite citizens did not welcome this "hillbilly" music with open arms, but looked upon it with disdain, even contempt. Jack, even at his young age, sensed this attitude. In an interview with Dr. Wolfe, a half century later, Jack said: "The union musicians in Nashville then, they looked way down upon a guitar. That was just the bottom of the barrel: a guitar player, he was just like a blind man sittin' on the street making a noise to attract people. They didn't

Jack Jackson
THE STROLLING YODLER
OF W-L-A-C
VICTOR RECORD ARTIST
LEBANON, TENNESSEE
ROUTE 6, BOX 3B

In 1926, when Jack was but 17 years old, he was featured on Nashville's powerful WLAC radio station, heard across the nation and even in Australia. By this time Jack had become known as the "Strolling Yodeler," and the reader will note that he signed his photos: "Best wishes and a yodel for all. Jack" *Photo courtesy Doug and John Jackson*

even recognize guitar players and fiddlers as musicians." This attitude toward the country music folks may have been responsible for Jack Jackson's decision to learn to read music, which, of course, he did. He once stated: "I took lessons from everybody I could."

Interestingly, the early radio stations often did not pay the performers. The incentive for the musicians, in addition to "being on the radio," was to promote their personal appearance shows and perhaps to sell a few records and autobiographical pamphlets. When Jack was appearing on the Hopkinsville, Kentucky, station, for example, he was selling a booklet with "simplified courses in reading, writing, harmonizing and transposing music" which also contained 25 popular old-time songs "as sung by Jack Jackson."

Jack was 19 years old in 1928, and he was playing music in Georgia when he heard that the two powerful radio stations in Nashville, WSM and WLAC, had started to pay the musicians for their performances. Jack immediately wrote both stations, offering his services.

Both stations offered to hire him, and he chose to go with WLAC where he worked for about two years. His popularity began to grow, and he fondly remembered he'd sometimes get "a tub full" of mail in a single day. His radio programs were not pre-planned, and the station took requests even as Jack was on the air. One night, he recalled, "a boy [at the station] took 90 calls in 15 minutes, over the two telephone lines. I tried to do what they called for, and if I didn't know it, I tried to learn it."

Jack's son Doug gave me a copy of a weekly periodical published by the Life and Casualty Insurance Co. in Nashville, dated May 16, 1929. It was among the personal effects and memorabilia found in Jack's home after his death. This small publication contained an article on Jack Jackson, and it stated that WLAC had the distinction of having "an artist who is proving to be an outstanding radio entertainer—none other than Jack Jackson, the Strolling Yodeler." The article went on to read: "The telephone lines are in constant use when Jack Jackson broadcasts and his popularity is growing by leaps and bounds." It was stated that when Jack offered to send his photograph to interested listeners he, almost overnight, received 3000 requests. During his short career, Jack played on 15 different radio stations, including the most popular WSM where the *Grand Ole Opry* started in 1925 and continues to this day. Jack himself played on the *Grand Ole Opry* "off and on" from 1928 until his retirement in 1934.

Dr. Wolfe's impeccable research indicates that Jack Jackson was indeed the first country singer to record in Nashville, which was later dubbed the "Recording Capital of the World." The Victor recording people offered to record a group known as the Binkley Brothers' Dixie Clodhoppers, an established and respected group of instrumentalists. They had to have a singer in their group, and they asked Jack to join them. Although he had never

sung with them before, he agreed to do so for that first recording session. The accepted date of this recording was September 28, 1928, and Jack said it took place at the WSM studios in Nashville.

I asked Doug and John Jackson one night the name of the song which their father, Jack, sang on that first historic Nashville record. "It was a song that you never heard of—nobody ever heard of it," Doug told me. "It's called, 'I'll Rise When the Rooster Crows'." Incredibly, the song was, purely by chance, *most* familiar to me.

"That's amazing," I said. "We had an old hand-cranked Victrola, and one of my favorite songs was, 'I'll Rise When the Rooster Crows.' My mother still has that old Victrola, and I'll bet that record is also there. I'll check as soon as I get home."

Well, Doug and John looked a little skeptical—after all, the song had been recorded 65 years before, and even then only a few copies were sold. So, to verify my claim, I sang a few lines, which for some reason I still remembered:

I'll rise when the rooster crows
Oh, I'll rise when the rooster crows
I'm goin' down south
Where the sun shines bright
Down where the sugarcane grows.

When I returned home, I did find the old well-worn record in the storage section of my mother's tall, hand-cranked Victrola, and listening to it brought back many fond memories. I was most impressed with the fine quality and distinctive sound of Jack's voice. It was just a delightful old song, and I could now understand why it had stayed with me for those many years.

The Binkley Brothers group was apparently satisfied with young Jackson, for he continued to play and record with them. The band, along with other well-known groups, entered an old-time music contest in Chattanooga. The Binkley Brothers, with Jack singing, won second place among contestants from 13 states. Then Jack entered in the individual category, competing with 125 other acts, and to his great surprise won first place. *The Nashville Banner* reported that "he had the distinguished record of winning every one-man entertainer contest he ever entered, and there were many."

In addition to recording for Victor, Jack recorded four songs in 1930 for Columbia Record Company in Johnson City, in upper East Tennessee. The songs included "I'm Just a Black Sheep" which was written by a prisoner, a man named Dawson. He had heard Jack sing and sent him the words and music. The other songs he recorded in Johnson City were "Flat Tire Blues," which Jack himself wrote; "My Alabama Home," for which Jack wrote the music; and "In Our Little Home Sweet Home." Jack was paid $100 for the recordings with no provisions for royalty payments. (Johnson City is only 30 miles from Bristol, where the historic recordings of the Carter Family, Jimmie Rodgers, and other early performers took place, only three years before.)

It was while playing with the Dixie Clodhoppers that Jack sang the first country song ever recorded in Nashville, a city now considered to be the recording capital of the world. The date was September 28, 1928, and the recording took place in the WSM studios. The name of the song was "I'll Rise When the Rooster Crows." In the photograph, the members of the popular Dixie Clodhoppers, from the left, are: Tom Andrews with guitar; Gale Binkley with cigar box fiddle; Jack Jackson with guitar; and Amos Binkley with the banjo. *Photo courtesy Doug and John Jackson*

Doug and John Jackson indicated that their father seldom talked about his musical career and that he didn't dwell too much on the past. But they did remember him describing, in some detail, his awful experience during the recording session in Johnson City. As long as he lived, he never forgot the disgust associated with those sessions, and Doug felt that this event contributed to Jack's early resignation from his career as a professional musician.

Dr. Wolfe, in an interview with Jack Jackson, recorded Jack's account of the 1929 Johnson City recording session. It provides a graphic and revealing comparison between those pioneer recording sessions, and the sophisticated and highly technical methods of present day recording. Jack's account of the session follows:

"That was the most miserable day . . . I was supposed to be the first one on the list [to record], at 8:00 Monday morning. But for some reason they didn't get their equipment in. It was just a vacated store building. I think it had probably been used for a cream station. It rained all day and the whole front was jammed with people. More of them were curious than [those who] wanted to make records; I didn't recognize many groups; in fact, some of them left, and I wish I had, and had come back rested. I stood there without as much as a cup of coffee from 8:00 in the morning until 4:00 in the evening. And every few minutes a man would run and stick his head out and say, 'Don't you leave; we'll be ready in a minute.'

"You can imagine how I felt standing there for eight hours, and soaking wet, too." When they finally called Jack in, he remained less than pleased. "They had one carbon mike sitting on a stand, bouncing every time you breathed at it — the crudest outfit you could think of . . . I just wish I'd never made those records. They didn't come through right, and were a mess. I went back the next day, and the next day, and the next day to try to get 'em to let me make 'em over, but they would not do it."

Despite the bad experience in Johnson City, Jack's success as a singer continued to grow, and *The Nashville Banner* later referred to Jack Jackson as "perhaps the most popular radio entertainer in the South." But his pay was certainly not commensurate with his popularity, and in 1930 he left the Nashville area for a radio station in Hopkinsville, Kentucky. Here his salary was $30.00 a week, double that which he had been receiving in Nashville. The Hopkinsville station, WFIW, broadcast 24 hours a day and was heard throughout Kentucky and surrounding states, and at times, when they ostensibly illegally increased the station's power, it could reportedly be heard throughout the country.

Jack later played on radio station WBOW in Terre Haute, Indiana; and he was apparently well received. An article from *The Terre Haute Star* stated that he received a "wild reception," and that the switchboard was swamped with calls regarding what the paper called the "Yodel King."

In 1930, while performing at the Cedar Grove School near Gallatin, Tennessee, Jack met a "sweet-faced" school teacher named Nellie Sue Bivins who also played the guitar and sang. They were soon married, and for a while they performed as a radio team known as Jack and Jill.

In 1934, when Jack Jackson was only 25 years of age, and seemingly an ever rising star among his radio fans, he quit—suddenly and without apparent reason. When pressed for an answer years later, the quiet and reserved singer said merely, "I wanted to stay home." When Walker of the *Tennessean*, asked him in 1952 why he gave up the promising musical career, Jack pointed to his 16-year-old daughter, Mary Ann, and said, "That! Singing didn't pay much in the 1930s."

I visited one of Jack's longtime friends, a former legislator and former member of the Interstate Commerce Commission, Alfred T. MacFarland, at his home in nearby Castilian Springs, in the hope of learning a bit more about the taciturn Jack Jackson. But apparently Jack had, in typical fashion, talked little to his old friend about his short-lived career in music. "I asked Jack once why he quit the *Grand Ole Opry*," MacFarland recalled. "Asked him why he quit the radio and the touring, and Jack just said: 'I got hungry'."

Jack learned to accompany himself on the guitar while playing the harmonica. *Photo courtesy Doug and John Jackson*

In 1934, when Jack was only 25 years old and riding an ever increasing crest of popularity, he suddenly quit the music business, traded his three-piece suit for a pair of overalls, and opened up a blacksmith and fix-it shop near his home in Lebanon, Tennessee. At the time, the *Nashville Banner* described him as "perhaps the most popular radio entertainer in the South." *Photo courtesy Doug and John Jackson*

Jack Jackson, the Strolling Yodeler, opened a combination blacksmith, fix-it, and welding shop on "The Square" in Lebanon. He had the reputation of being able to make or repair anything. Eventually he built a larger shop, literally in his back yard on the outskirts of Lebanon, and after expansions, it was more like a little factory. He became an inventor, displaying an ingenuity suggestive of the *old* Asa Jack Jackson, his great-grandfather who had built the "perpetual motion" machine. Jack's most notable invention was a machine for transplanting tobacco and other plants. Jack called it the "Jackson Transplanter," which he eventually patented and manufactured by the thousands. Among his other inventions was a machine for McDowell Tire Company, used in the process of vulcanizing automobile tires.

Jack Jackson was truly one of the pioneers in what came to be the country music phenomenon. He came early, achieved unprecedented success, and left soon thereafter. One might say that he was a dropout, but few people, indeed, ever contributed so much in such a short time. And he's the type of person the likes of which needs to be recorded if one is to form a somewhat "total" picture of the country music story.

He represents so many good musicians and singers who, for one reason or another, did give up their music for more permanent, predictable, and less stressful careers. Some returned to their first love, music; and some, perhaps most, like Jack Jackson, never did. A reporter, Michelle Williams of *The Nashville Banner*, asked The Strolling Yodeler in 1986 if he ever thought of performing again. He said, "Gal, I retired in 1934. That was for good."

When Jack gave up his popular career as a musician/singer, he built this modest house near Lebanon where he reared his family and where he spent the remainder of his life. (His machine shop in back of this house grew into a small factory where he invented and produced farm equipment and other mechanical devices.) *Photo by the author*

"I'd a little druther keep my hat on. My hair is getting thin and a little gray, but I guess we can try it." That's what 96-year-old Bob Douglas told me when I asked him if he could remove his hat for this 1996 photograph. *Photo taken January, 1996, by the author*

Standing on the cluttered little porch of his sister Nellie's house, near Dayton, Tennessee, Bob feels at home back in the mountains where he was reared. He lives in a "little den" in a corner of her house, which he insists is "all in the world I need." *Photo taken January, 1996, by the author*

Chapter 4

Bob Douglas, Portrait of an Old-Time Fiddler

"I played my three tunes, and the crowd, they just went wild."

He lived on rugged Walden's Ridge, sometimes with his father, sometimes with his mother, but more often with relatives. He was nine years old before he had his first pair of shoes, and he thought nothing of hunting rabbits in foot-deep snow, barefoot and coatless. He became an old-time fiddler and won hundreds of contests, including first place at the Festival of American Folklife in Washington, D.C., in 1975, competing with dozens of noted contestants from throughout the world. Bob Douglas, who has just celebrated his 99th birthday, is looking forward to his next public appearance.

Although he won an important fiddle contest a few months after he started playing, and although he has played consistently for dances, parties, schools, store openings, and on radio since his youth, he spent most of his life working at menial and manual labor jobs. That's the way it was with most of the country musicians and singers of that period; and to know the life of the legendary Bob Douglas is to know something about most of the entertainers of our region in the late 19th and early 20th centuries, especially the respected, admired, and celebrated old-time fiddler.

On one of my earlier visits with Bob in his modest two-room apartment on the outskirts of Chattanooga, I listened to him play the fiddle (and guitar); but mostly I asked questions and listened as he talked. He was then in his 89th year but acting very much like a man 20 or 30 years younger. Some seven years later, on January 13, 1996, I interviewed Bob again, this time at the home of his sister, Nellie, who lived at the foot of Walden's Ridge near where Bob was raised.

He had moved from his little apartment in Chattanooga when he was 94 years old because his girlfriend, who lived nearby, had died. "I come back up here in the mountains to live with my sister, Nellie. I have this little den—this little room here in the back of the house, and that's all I need."

There was a small bed, a chest of drawers, a little television set, a chair with four cushions, a tape player, records and tapes stacked everywhere, and boxes filled with letters and papers. There were notes and pens which suggested that he kept busy corresponding with old friends and admirers. Then, of course, there was his fiddle, and a guitar.

The most unusual item in the tiny room was an exercise bicycle which he used on a regular basis. He had a big thermometer hanging on the bicycle so he could keep the room at the "right" temperature. He had an electric heater next to his bed.

The trip to Nellie's place was most interesting. It was a narrow, winding dirt road, alongside which sat many homes, mostly older trailers with homemade additions, or which were in the process of being added onto. There were other small houses within a few feet of the road, and many, many cars, some of which were jacked up for repair. I later learned that Nellie had 11 living children, 25 grandchildren, scores of great-grandchildren, and two great-great-grandchildren. Amazingly, they all lived nearby, and almost all of those houses on Coulter Road were Nellie Coulter's offspring, and their spouses.

While my wife, Elizabeth, and I were at Nellie's home, a steady stream of her folks came, had coffee and desserts, and several ate some of Nellie's great bean soup, and almost all of them brought bread, milk, or some other foodstuff. They were a most friendly and affable lot, and they apparently took good care of Nellie.

The name of this little isolated community is Cranmore's Cove, located at the foot of Walden's Ridge near an abandoned coal mine. Nellie's house was the very last one on the road that literally ended at her front door. It was located three miles from Dayton, the Tennessee town where the nationally famous Scopes "Monkey Trial" took place; and Nellie's house was also three miles from the community of Graysville, the home of the legendary Curly Fox, a world champion fiddler.

Bob was 20 years old when Nellie was born to Bob's mother and stepfather. I asked Nellie about Bob. "I think he's a pretty good feller," she laughed. "I never did hear tell of him smoking, drinking or anything bad. Mommy never did have anything bad to say about him." One could quickly discern the love and pride she felt for her older brother who early on had become a local celebrity.

Nellie said, "I never did see him very much when I was growing up. He'd come by, maybe, two or three times a year. We used to listen to him on the radio. We didn't have a radio ourselves, didn't even have no 'lectricity. But a neighbor down the road here had a radio and we'd go down there every night at five o'clock and listen to Bob on the radio, out of Chattanooga."

The following is an account of my extended talks with Bob, in November of 1988 in Chattanooga and again on January 13, 1996, at Nellie's home and at other times and places. At the time of the 1996 interview, Bob was a few months shy of his 96th birthday.

Bob, tell me a little about your early life.

"Well, I was born in Sequatchie Valley at the foot of Cumberland Mountain, about eight miles down from Pikeville—that's about 40 miles north of Chattanooga."

That was Walden's Ridge?

"Walden's Ridge, yes. We moved into a little two room log house, and then we moved around a right smart, from one little cabin to another."

Did your father own any property, and what kind of work did he follow?

"No, he never owned any land. Dad worked anywhere he could find a day's work. He farmed a little and he worked in the timber a lot, and he worked at sawmills. He'd cut timber, and snake it off that mountain with mules. My daddy and my mother separated when I was little."

And you lived with . . .?

"Well, I stayed with my mother some, and sometimes I stayed with my dad, but I stayed with other people, too. I lived most of the time with Aunt Lucy Stewart. She had two boys about my age, Charlie and Velt

Stewart. They was my first cousins, but they was just like brothers to me. We worked together, cutting timber for crossties."

What kind of house did your Aunt Lucy have?

"It was just a little log cabin."

I suppose that the living conditions were pretty difficult back then.

"I run a trap line when I was just a boy—catching 'possums, skunks, 'coons, foxes, and I'd skin them and sell the hides, you know. There was fur buyers that would come around every once in a while during the winter. I started work on the mountain when I was just a child snaking crossties. I could do a man's work, and I got 50 cents a day. I got my first pair of shoes when I was eight or nine years old. My mother got a little money somewhere and she bought me a pair of old brogan shoes, and my two cousins got new shoes at the same time.

"I remember that we started to the store the next morning and there was four or five inches of snow on the ground. They told us to wear our new shoes. They was so stiff that we had to grease them with mutton tallow before we could get them on. We hadn't hardly got out of sight from the house before them shoes started hurting our feet. We had never wore shoes before, you know, and they felt awful funny and they hurt our feet so bad that we took them off and hid them in a big hollow chestnut stump. We walked on to the store—it was eight miles away. Of course it took us about all day to go there and back. Just before we got back home, we got our shoes and put them on again. We'd gone barefooted all our lives and we was used to it."

I take it that you liked the woods, the outdoors, and the mountains.

"Oh, I loved that mountain. We hunted a lot, and we roamed the mountains for wild things—muscadines, chestnuts, chinquapins, haws and so forth. We'd go out and fox hunt all night, and get home at daylight, and go to work and work all day.

"My Grandpa Harvey lived way back up above us, and he had hogs all over that mountain. They run wild. They fattened on acorns and things, and he'd call them up once in a while—just to keep a check on them. Any time we needed fresh meat, he'd let us go out and kill one of his hogs.

"Grandpa was an old Civil War veteran and I remember that he said the Army paid him off in gold and he drawed a pension. He'd go down here to Soddy and put his money in the bank there. Well, that bank went busted, and he lost every cent of it."

I suppose that you didn't have a chance to attend school very much.

"No. There was a little one-room school over at a place they called Flat Top, out on the mountain from Soddy, and it was seven miles away. We had to walk barefooted, seven miles each way to attend school."

And this was mainly during the winter months.

"Yeah, and we had a awful lot of snow on the mountain back in them days, you know, so lots of days I'd have to walk through snow to get to where I went to school."

How far did you get in school?

"I got about through the fourth grade, I think. We'd just go a few months out of the year, and I just didn't get any kind of an education."

You learned a great deal in the school of life.

"Yeah, a lot more than I ever learned in school."

Well, Bob, how did you get started as a musician?

"My daddy was a good old-time fiddler and I always wanted to learn to play. He lived about 10 miles up Walden's Ridge from where my Aunt Lucy lived, with his second wife. Lived near a place they called Hickory Grove. You might know where it's at. Well, I'd go up there every week or two to see him and I got to playing the guitar. Sometimes when he'd lay his fiddle down, I'd slip and get it, but that wasn't often. When I was 16, me and him went down to Chattanooga to Uncle Sam's pawn shop on Fourth and Market Street, and he bought me an old Stella guitar. I didn't have no pick, so I went out in the woods and cut me a hickory bush and skinned the bark off, and whittled it down right thin, and scraped it. Hickory's tough, you know. That's the way I commenced playing the guitar. Dad liked for me to second for him, and he sort of kept me away from the fiddle because he wanted me to back him up on the guitar. When he'd catch me with his fiddle, he'd say, 'Put that fiddle down, Bob'." (Bob laughed as he mimicked his father.)

Bob, on the right, is shown here playing the guitar in front of his aunt Lucy's primitive log cabin on Walden's Ridge where he was "mostly raised." His father, "Fiddlin'" Tom Douglas, is on the left, and banjo player Joe Varnes is in the center. Bob recalls when this picture was made. "The three of us had been roaming the mountains for about two weeks playing music, and we stopped here at Aunt Lucy's home. You might say that there's where I was raised—there in that little log cabin. That's my cousin Lena Stewart, standing barefoot in the doorway. I think that picture was made about 1922." *Photo courtesy of Bob Douglas*

I believe you told me once that you and your father played for dances in the community.

"There was an old man by the name of Ab Ferguson who lived above us on top of a big rock cliff. He played the five-string banjo and we got to playing with him—formed a little band and played at people's houses for dances.

"When Uncle Ab would get a dance lined up, his wife Sarah would come out on top of that bluff and holler. You could hear her for miles." (Bob chuckled when he recalled that little mountain woman standing there on top of the mountain hollering for all to hear.) "She'd holler 'til we answered her. Then she'd tell us where we were supposed to play. There was just a little hog trail up to their place—no roads that you could get even a wagon over.

"Dad didn't have no case for his fiddle and he carried it in an old flour sack, and Ab carried his banjar in a meal sack, and I just carried my guitar on my shoulder. We played all over them mountains—walked wherever we needed to go. We didn't think nothing about walking 15 or 20 miles to play. We each had a little suitcase if we's going to be gone a week or so—carried a change of clothes. Back then folks didn't change clothes too much anyway."

You were telling me once about the time your father went down to Dayton, or somewhere, to hear a violinist.

(Laughing) "Yeah." (More laughter) "Yeah, that's so. He did. We didn't know what a violinist was, you know. And, so, one day Dad says, 'Bob,' says, 'I wanna go down to Hendron Chapel. They's gonna be a violinist down there,' says, 'I never have heared of a violinist.' Says, 'I wanna go down there and see him—see what a violin looks like'."

How far was it?

"'Bout ten miles. One mornin' he started walkin' down there, left me at the house, says, 'Now you take care of ever thing, Bob,' and he left me there with his wife. He's livin' with his wife then. And he went down there, and was gone all day.

"Sometime after night he come back, got back home, went to bed. I didn't say nothin' to him that night. And got up the next morning, I said, 'Dad,' I said, 'did you see that violin?' He said, 'Yeah,' says, 'I seen the durn ol' thing.' I said, 'Well, what did it look like?' He says, 'It wasn't nothing in the world but a durned old fiddle.' (Laughing) I 'member him sayin' that. 'Wasn't a durn thing but an old fiddle'."

During this time, when you were very young, you were working as a lumberjack, or as a farm hand.

"Yeah, we'd cut timber with a crosscut saw, and then we'd hew out crossties, you know for the railroads, with a broad axe."

Fiddling Tom Douglas, is shown in the ca. 1910 photograph with his banjo-playing cousin, A. B. Ferguson. "This is how Dad always played the fiddle," Bob remembers, "propping his left foot on the bottom chair rung and resting his fiddle on his knee. See, that way there was no strain on him. He could play in that position all night, and I've seen him playing many a time when I thought he was asleep." *Photo courtesy of Bob Douglas*

You and your father worked together?

"When I stayed with him we'd work together. We'd go down to Sequatchie Valley after I was grown and work for Riley Hutchison who had a big farm. We couldn't get but 50 cents a day apiece. Worked from sun-up to sundown— 50 cents a day apiece. Hoover was in there, you know, and he liked to have let people starve to death.

"Sometimes, when the weekends came, Mr. Hutchison would say, 'Sorry Mr. Douglas, I ain't got no cash. I've got plenty of meat and corn, milk and butter, anything you want besides money.' So, sometimes we'd take our pay in milk or corn that we'd take to the mill and have ground into meal for our bread."

Herbert Hoover was President from 1929-33, hence Bob, having been born in 1900, would have been about 30 years of age when he and his father worked on the "big farm." It is interesting that Bob, with all his musical talents, having won a major fiddle championship and having played regularly on the radio, was still working 12 or more hours a day as a common farm hand for 50 cents a day—and even so he and his father often had to take their pay in foodstuff. But then the depression was not kind to anyone.

The radio stations, realizing that young, ambitious musicians were eager to "play on the radio," paid them nothing for their services, even though they played daily. The only compensation was that they were allowed to announce the location of their night-time engagements, usually in some small mountain school miles from town.

Bob and his father, Tom Douglas, are shown in this ca. 1930 photograph. "I was living in Chattanooga, working and playing on the radio," Bob remembers. "I come home one day to visit Dad when he lived over on Back Valley Road, at the foot of Walden's Ridge in a cove about six or seven miles down from Pikeville. That's when this picture was made. That was Dad's old dog shaking hands with him. He called him Pup."
Photo courtesy of Bob Douglas

Bob is shown here wearing his stage regalia, posing proudly with his father, Tom Douglas, in this ca. 1928 photograph taken on Walden's Ridge. "Dad's full name was Thomas William Douglas. He couldn't read and write, and we never knowed when he was born. I sorta figured it out by talking to some of the old folks around. He said that he remembered certain things about the Civil War, and that helped to establish his age. The best I could come up with was that he was born in 1860. That would have made him 97 years old when he died in 1957." *Photo courtesy of Bob Douglas*

What else did you do to survive during the depression?

"Well," and here Bob paused for a long while, trying to decide, I thought, whether or not he should answer. Then he continued: "I used to make whiskey, but I never did tell anybody. Me and my cousins had us a little pot down on the creek and we made pure corn whiskey—no sugar. And we made some brandy, apple brandy and peach brandy, but the best we ever made was crab apple brandy. It had a great smell and you could smell it a half mile away. Now, we never made much, just a little for our own use. [As if this justified the illegal operation.] Of course, if some old man came by with his fruit jar in his overall bib, we'd sell him some." Bob paused again and then he said, "I used to take a little drink—on the weekend."

I could see that he wasn't anxious to pursue his moonshining days; so we went on to a subject more pleasing to him.

You always wanted to play the fiddle didn't you? When did you start in earnest, playing the fiddle?

"In 1928 my daddy give me his fiddle and said: 'Now, you've always wanted to play the fiddle, so here—get at it'."

And you followed his advice?

"I started playing and three months later I entered a big contest [the All Southern Fiddlers' Convention] at the Memorial Auditorium in Chattanooga and won first place. They was some fine fiddlers there: Sawmill Tom Smith; Arthur Smith; Clayton McMichen; Jess Young, and a whole lot more. Jess Young had been winning about every year, and I beat him out that time. It surprised all of 'em so bad, and Clayton McMichen, he like to have blowed up when I won. You know he was awful high tempered anyhow. He thought he had it, and he got mad, and me and him liked to have had a fight."

I've heard of most of those you mentioned, and they were considered to be among the best in the South—maybe some of the best in the nation. Let's see, you had already started playing on the radio, hadn't you?

"I started playing on WDOD radio [in Chattanooga] in the late 1920s, and they have always said I was the first person to play old-time music on the radio in this area. I played on the radio with a lot of people—five days a week: Archie Campbell; Homer and Jethro; and the Louvin Brothers. I hired the Louvin Brothers when they first came down off Sand Mountain."

Fiddlin' Bob Douglas is shown here in the 1930s playing on Chattanooga radio station WDOD with a group called Jack Savage's Texas Farm Boys and Girls. Kneeling in front, from the left, are: Hammerhandle and Jack Savage. Standing, from the left, are: Slim Tuttom, Joe Powell, Bob Douglas, Cousin Ida and Charlie Savage. *Photo courtesy of Bob Douglas*

Bob Douglas and His Foggy Mountain Boys are shown here in Chattanooga's famous Reed House Hotel in this ca. 1940 photograph. (Later, Lester Flatt and Earl Scruggs formed their legendary band by the same name.) The Louvin Brothers, standing at right, whom Bob is credited with discovering, gained national fame a few years later. Bob's band, from the left, included: Charlie Bell; Bob; the program announcer (Bob thinks his name was McDonald); Ira Louvin; Charlie Louvin; and kneeling, Uncle Ben. *Photo courtesy of Bob Douglas*

Bob has been playing old-time Appalachian music for over 80 years, and his influence on countless other musicians during that long period of time is immeasurable. Dr. Charles Wolfe stated: "Bob Douglas, a national champion fiddler, . . . has led bands in Chattanooga from 1928 to the present . . . and has discovered later country music greats like the Louvin Brothers."

This writer is prudent enough not to attempt to document the extent of Bob's influence on other musicians, but mention should perhaps be made of some notable folks he inspired and assisted in their respective careers. Certainly the "discovery" of the Louvin Brothers was among Bob's most noteworthy.

Bill Malone, in his highly acclaimed book, *Country Music USA*, states: "With the Louvin Brothers, country music found its greatest duet." He further states, "No one in country music before or since achieved the kind of crisp, precise, and yet sky-high style of harmony heard in their music." They recorded many country gospel songs as well as such highly popular songs as "When I Stop Dreaming," and "The Knoxville Girl," and they became popular *Grand Ole Opry* stars.

Dr. Wolfe, in his well-researched book about the Louvin Brothers, points out that a young Elvis Presley toured with the brothers and that he preferred their music to the rock and roll for which he was to gain such worldwide fame. They were Elvis's favorite duo and he once pointed out that his mother had every record the Louvin Brothers made.

Bill Monroe, the father of bluegrass music and who sang at Ira's funeral, declared that he, Ira Louvin, was one of the two greatest tenor singers. (The other, it was inferred, was Bill Monroe himself.)

The Grove Dictionary of American Music states that the Louvin Brothers were "probably the greatest country duo in history." They had a strong influence on "almost all" rock-and-roll singers and country singers from the Everly Brothers to Emmylou Harris, to Johnny Cash, who sought their autographs when he was a lad of 12.

Bob, they give you credit for discovering the Louvin Brothers, I hear.

"Well, yeah. Did I ever tell you how I got with them?"

I don't think so. I've heard it, but I haven't heard it from you.

"Well, me and my wife was living down there on Long Street below Main Street [in Chattanooga] and we always went up on Friday night to the amateur programs, up at the American Theatre on Main Street.

"So, we went up there one night, and we was setting there and here come Charlie and Ira out on the stage. First time I ever seen them, you know."

They weren't called the Louvin Brothers at that time, were they?

"No, their name was Loudermilk. But they didn't go by that name. They changed their name to Louvin. And so, they come out on stage and commenced singing. I told my wife, I said, 'There's two boys right there I want on my show.' At that time I had a program on WAPO and we's doing shows, you know, schools and theaters and things."

As soon as you heard them, you knew . . .?

"Yeah. And, so, I went backstage after the show and talked to them, and they agreed to go to work with me. And they played with me a long time, and finally, Charlie had to go to the war [World War II].

"They never had played nowhere before they started with me. Nowhere only just out there on Sand Mountain [in Alabama] and around, you know. After Charlie got back from the war, they went to Knoxville, I believe, and played on the *Mid-Day Merry-Go-Round*, then they went to Memphis, it seems, and finally back to Nashville. And they became famous, you know, all over the country."

Another person whose early career was greatly influenced by Bob was the nationally popular Curly Fox. Curly grew up in the village of Graysville, near where Bob lived. Curly's career was a long and varied one, and he won countless old-time fiddle contests, including first place in the National Fiddle contest for 10 years straight—from 1936 through 1946 when he stopped entering the contest.

He had his own band when he was only 13, in 1923, and he eventually gained national exposure during his 36 years on the *Grand Ole Opry*. Some of his most popular fiddle tunes were "Listen to the Mocking Bird," "Orange Blossom Special," and his most popular "Johnson's Old Gray Mule." I recall as a child listening to him every Saturday night on the *Grand Ole Opry* over WSM's

powerful station. We didn't have electricity, but we did have a battery powered radio, and neighbors would sometimes come to our house on Saturday night to listen to this famous radio program.

Curly played in such places as Carnegie Hall in New York, Constitution Hall in Washington, D.C., and according to his hometown paper, in most of the great concert halls in America and Europe. He played for King Paul and Queen Frederika of Greece and it is said that the King loved Curly's fiddling so much that he would only allow Curly to quit after he had played over 50 tunes. Bill C. Malone in his voluminous book, *Country Music USA* called Curly "the greatest showman of all fiddlers."

In 1959 Curly married the most popular "Texas Ruby," the "original yodeling cowgirl," and the duo achieved national acclaim, and were commonly referred to as "Curly Fox and Texas Ruby, the most popular country singing duet in America."

Curly's beloved Texas Ruby died tragically in a house fire in 1963 while Curly was playing on the *Grand Ole Opry*, and he never seemed to be able to display the enthusiasm of his earlier years. He eventually moved back to Graysville and suffered poor health the remainder of his life. He had no home of his own, and he lived in a trailer with a friend for a while, and then he moved in with his sister, Helen Cofer. It was a big "come down" for one who had enjoyed the national limelight for so long.

I hired Curly to perform here at the Tennessee Fall Homecoming for several years, the last time being in 1991. He was enthusiastically received, both by the audience and by many other old-time musicians; and he reciprocated in kind, and the old showman, the super star, was back again. He later told me that that was the last time he ever did a stage show. He died in November, 1995, at the age of 85 in the little community of Graysville near where he was born.

Bob, I understand that you had an important influence on Curly Fox.

"Well, Curly lived right here at Graysville, and I lived there for a while myself. He was several years younger than me, and I remember when he first started to learn to play the fiddle. He was having trouble with his bowing—he couldn't use the bow right. I worked with him some, and he soon caught on. And when he started, Buddy, he just kept a'going."

I'm sure you knew of his death a few weeks ago?

"Oh, yes. I went down to the funeral home, over here at Dayton. Yeah, he passed on, and I shore hated to hear about it."

You once told me about taking Curly with you up north where you worked with a medicine show.

"Yeah, that was with Dr. White Owl. I got Curly down here, and a boy named Jimmy Brown, and I took them up to Indiana to join Dr. White Owl's Medicine Show. That was about 1929 and Curly was just a young feller—maybe 18 or 19 years old. [He was 19.]

"Well, none of us had any money, and we got a ride to Louisville on the back of a truck. I had a suitcase and a fiddle, and Curly had his guitar. He played a guitar then.

"Well, we caught a freight train out of Louisville. Them railroad cops, they didn't like hoboes you know, and they found us about 40 miles from where we's going, and they put us off the train, and we had to hitchhike the rest of the way."

Bob didn't indicate what punishment, if any, resulted from their apprehension for hoboing on the freight train. But, according to Tom Morgan, a close friend and neighbor to both Bob and Curly, the three "railroad bums" had to spend the night in jail. Tom recalled that they all became heavily infected with lice, but that didn't dampen their enthusiasm to join the medicine show.

(Bob) "We joined up with old White Owl, and we played all over that country. We'd stay two weeks in one place, then we'd move on. Curly was just learning the fiddle, so he mostly played the guitar for me, and Jimmy, he played the part of a black face comedian. We had all kinds of acts, and old White Owl would come out between acts and sell his medicine. I made the medicine for him, from some sort of powder he'd get, and I'd mix it all up and it was supposed to be some kind of herbal medicine that cured everything. Old White Owl, he wasn't no Indian, but he dressed up like one, and put on all them feathers, you know. We worked with him a long time, and when he went out of business, we caught a ride back to Graysville, and I believe Curly got his own band soon after that."

Bob, during all those years you played in and around Chattanooga, you held down a regular job, I understand.

"I worked during the day and played music at night. I played 12 years at a dance hall up near Cleveland [Tennessee], and I played seven years at a place down in Lake Howard, Georgia. We'd play for parties, dances, political rallies and for anybody who wanted us."

Bob is shown here, with cigarette, at Lake Howard Dance Hall near LaFayette, Georgia, where he played shows nightly for seven years, during which time he worked during the day, every day, as a laborer. *Photo ca. 1950, from Bob Douglas' collection*

What type work did you follow—other than your music?

"Well, I've dug a lot of ditches, by hand, all over Chattanooga. I worked as a day laborer. I worked in a mattress factory for a while, and in a glass plant. I guess the first job I got there in Chattanooga was working as a water boy for them glass blowers. They blowed glass by mouth, and they required a lot of water. I worked as a welder during the war, and that's where I ruint my eyes. Got where I couldn't hardly see, and I had to quit. And I worked as a carpenter's helper for a long time. I passed a house out here the other day that me and an old man built. I worked so many places I can't think of all of them. I worked for 18 years in the textile mills—made thread and yarn."

So you really had two jobs most of the time?

"Most of the time. I'd work eight or ten hours during the day, and then maybe drive an hour or two and play 'til past midnight. Sometimes we played four or five nights a week. Sometimes we'd play nearly all night. Most of what sleep I got, I got in the car."

You were also entering fiddling contests during this time I believe. I noticed that the *Chattanooga Free Press* stated that you had won first place in more fiddle contests than anyone in Tennessee.

"I won a lot of contests. I have no idea how many contests I won before this trophy business started. If I'd got a trophy for every contest I won, I'd have a room full."

As a child, I remember going to some of those fiddle contests, and there were thousands of people, it seemed to me, who would turn out for them. They were very popular, weren't they?

"They were about the only entertainment they was back then, and just about everybody would come out. There was always a lot of excitement.

"One time I entered a big contest and there were a lot of great fiddlers there. They finally narrowed it down to just me and Carl Cotner. Now, he was a great violinist, as well as a fiddler. We played one old-time piece after another, and we always ended up in a tie—according to the judges. I finally said to my guitar player, I said, 'I'm going to try something different,' and I played the 'St. Louis Blues.' There's where I made my big mistake."

It was like throwing the rabbit in the briar patch?

"Yeah, that's right. That kind of music was right up his alley, him being a violinist, you know. Carl got up after me and played the same piece—the 'St. Louis Blues,' and John Rice, I ain't never heard nobody play it so pretty in my life. Man, I'm telling you. That was more his kind of music. He beat me. I ought to have stayed with the old fiddle tunes, and I might have won.

"He left here soon after that and went with Gene Autry [in California], and done all of Gene's arranging. I noticed in the papers just a few days ago where he had died."

I imagine that you got to know your competitors pretty well—those who entered the contests?

"Oh, yeah. We were all pretty close friends. I told you about beating out Jess Young in my first contest. He was a great fiddler and we got to be close friends. We often played against one another, but that didn't affect our friendship. He was the first man I ever heard play the fiddle, other than my dad. We went down there to see him once, me and Dad did. They were good friends. He lived down here at Whitwell and he played the fiddle for us—I never will forget that.

"When I finally moved down to Chattanooga, why Jess, he moved down there, too. He wasn't well. He was a coal miner and he got that black lung. Well, he moved back to Sequatchie Valley—back to Whitwell—and he died over there.

"I went over there and his widow wanted me to play at his funeral. I first turned her down, but she really wanted me to play and I couldn't say no to her. I stood right over him in the little church with the coffin open, and I played some hymns for him and that was the hardest thing I ever done in my life. I said I'd never play at the funeral for an old friend again—and I haven't." (Bob paused, reflecting on that sad scene, and it took him a while to gain his composure.)

Bob, for as long as we've known one another, we've never talked much about your immediate family, your wife and your children.

"They was a family named Casteel that bought Uncle Taylor Harbett's place up there on the mountain. The Casteels had a girl named Julia, and she got growed up pretty fast, you know, and I was sweet on her. We started going together a little—going to church together once in a while."

Did she ever go with you to the dances?

"One night I heard they's going to be a dance over at Lewis's Chapel—at Frank Shadwick's place. So I talked Julia into the notion of going. She had got to where she could rap on the banjar pretty good—pick a little bit."

So, Julia agreed to go with you to the square dance?

"Yeah, and as soon as we got there the old fiddler says: 'Bob,' he says, 'I hear you've been playing the fiddle.' I said, 'Well, I practice on it whenever I can get a hold of one.' I didn't have no fiddle, and I'd play Dad's when I could get a chance, but I hadn't never played at a square dance. He said, 'I want you to rest me,' and he handed me the fiddle.

"They all lined up on the floor and took up a collection, you know, like they do—so much a couple (10 cents apiece) and I started playing. And I only knowed two tunes at that time. One was 'Corn in the Crib' and the other, I believe, was 'Shake the Acorns Down.' Just old country tunes.

"Man, they liked it so much that I just kept playing them two tunes over and over, and I finally quit. And they said, 'Come on. Play some more. That sounded good.' I said, 'Them's the only tunes I know,' and I said, 'Where'd the fiddler go?' And somebody said, 'He's done gone home.' He'd had a little too much to drink, and he had just give his fiddle to me and left.

"Well, I kept playing them two tunes the biggest part of the night and they kept a dancing—and that's the first time me and Julia went out to a dance together."

So, you and Julia were soon married?

"Yeah, we was married about five or six years before we separated."

And there were children. Three, I believe.

"We had two boys and a girl. The girl's name was Virginia, and she lived out in California, and she died just recently. I'll tell you when she died. She died when I had them shingles so bad, and I couldn't go to her funeral. And now her mother's dead, too, I hear."

And the two boys?

"One I named Robert, Jr., and we called him 'Buddy.' He lives in Indianapolis. The other boy is named Howard and he lives in Nevada. You've met Buddy. He came up there with me to your Museum one time."

Yes, I remember. Do you have grandchildren?

"I've got a couple of grandchildren that I didn't know I had 'til right here lately. My daughter, Virginia, I knowed she had a grown boy, but she also had two girls that I didn't know about. They found out where I's at just recently, and they've been calling me here lately, sending me cards and letters. One of them lives in California, and one lives somewhere in Utah."

And you've never seen them?

"No. Never seen them."

And your second wife also passed on?

Bob and his longtime accompanist Ray "Georgia Boy" Brown enjoy the applause after playing an old-time fiddle breakdown. *Photo taken ca. 1990 at a place called "The Coke Ovens" at Dunlap, Tennessee, near where Bob grew up on Walden's Ridge*

"I didn't remarry for a long time—in the 1940s, and she died in 1973."

Bob Douglas played in and around Chattanooga— on the radio stations, at dance halls, picnics, store openings, parties, and at hundreds of other events. He had won hundreds of fiddle contests; and he was the old master in that area. When the fiddle contests and the outdoor festivals were revived in the 1960s and '70s, Bob was ready and waiting, and he was rediscovered by the neophytes.

In 1975, the Smithsonian Institution's Festival of American Folklife sponsored the National Fiddle Contest in Washington, D.C. Some of the premier old-time fiddlers from throughout the country were invited, among them Bob Douglas. He took his favorite guitar accompanist, Roy "Georgia Boy" Brown with him and headed for the capitol.

Bob, tell me about the first time you played in Washington, D.C., in the National Fiddle Contest.

"Yeah, I've played in Washington, D.C., two or three times, about three times I think. The first time I went up there was in '75. I was invited up there to an old-time fiddlers' contest to represent Tennessee, and they invited the champion fiddle players from everywhere. They come from California, and they was a Chinese there, and they was a Japanese there. They's all kind of fiddle players, and they's a girl from India with long, slick, shiny black hair. They was old-time fiddle players and they's bluegrass fiddle players. They was just all kinds of them there. And they had it out there in that big park, not far from the Monument.

"Big woodland, you know? That's where it was, in that woodland, and they had a big old stage. Boy, it was a great long thing. And they had it settin' full of microphones. And people, you never seen such a crowd, John Rice, in your life. Them trees, people was even all up in them trees. Me and my buddy, we went up there, me and Georgie Boy. He played the guitar for me, you know.

"And, so, we stood around all day there at the end of the stage and watched fiddle players come in and play. And they's just everywhere, all types of 'em. And we stood there 'til late in the evenin'. It was almost over with. Georgie Boy said, 'Bob,' said, 'We just as well go home. I'm worn out.' He says, 'We ain't gonna do no good up here.' I said, 'No, sir, I come up here to play and,' I says, 'I'm gonna play in this contest.'

"So I had me some good breakdown pieces picked out, you know, and waltzes. And so, I think we's about the last ones who played. We went on the stage, and they had microphones standing all the way across it. You could hear a pin drop. We went out there and we cut loose on them ol' breakdowns. I played 'Leather Britches' and the 'Carroll County Blues,' and boy, the people just went wild. Just tore the whole place up. It was somethin' different, you see. They'd been listenin' to that other stuff all day.

"And so I played my three tunes, just supposed to play three tunes, and so, they wouldn't let me leave. The crowd just raised cane. Man, they's up in the trees pattin' their hands and ever thing. So, after I played my three tunes, why, this here announcer, he run out there and he says, 'Bob,' says, 'I don't know what to do.' Says, 'You're just supposed to play three tunes [for the contest].' Says, 'I don't know what to do. They won't let you leave the stage.'

"Says, 'I guess you'll just have to play three more tunes. Do you know some more tunes?' I said, 'I know plenty of 'em.' So, we cut loose on some of them good ol' breakdowns you know, and I played 'em a pretty waltz, and man, they still just tore the place down.

"The judges was down there in a closed-up wagon. They could see out of a little winder and see us playin' but the only way they could hear us was over the microphones. And one of the women, she was one of the judges, she come runnin' up there, come on the stage and come to me, says, 'Are you Bob Douglas?' I said, 'Yes, ma'am.' She said, 'Well, you've got it won,' says, 'they ain't no doubt about that.' Says, 'You've got it.' So I did."

You won first place?

"Yeah. I got three hundred dollars and a great big trophy. You got the trophy in your Museum."

Yes, it's there for all to see. How many people entered the contest?

"Oh, they's over a hundred of them. They's over a hundred from all over the world, and they played all kinds of styles. I played that old country style, and buddy, that's what they wanted. Yeah, I won first place, me and old Georgie Boy, a backing me up on the guitar."

I know that you were invited recently to perform at the Festival of American Fiddle Tunes in Port Townsend, Washington. That was quite an honor, too, and I'm sure that you were the oldest person ever to participate in the event. You were 92 at the time, I believe. Tell me a little about that trip.

"Let's see, that was four years ago in July. It was held in an abandoned Army post about 75 miles down the coast from Seattle."

Was that the first time you were on the West Coast?

"Yeah, and it was the first time I ever rode an airplane. I was a little scared at first, but after we once got started I was all right."

What exactly did you do out there?

"When I got out there, I asked the boss man, I said, 'Well, what am I gonna be doing?' and he said, 'You're gonna be teaching a bunch of teenagers to play the old-time fiddle'."

Bob goes into great detail of how he taught his first workshop, "feeling his way along." Before the week was out, these young violin students, mostly girls I believe, learned old-time fiddling from Bob, playing such pieces as "Going to Chattanooga." There were many other groups being taught by other masters, and a competition was held at the end of the two-week period, and Bob was more than pleased with the progress his band had made.

"Boy, when my band came out there and played, they sounded like a young orchestra. I mean they was good. And you know what? We won first place—over all them other bands! My students, they's tickled to death."

I had spent a good part of the afternoon in Bob's little den, as he aptly called it. I was putting the tape recorder away, but Bob was just getting wound up, and the fond recollections of long ago seemed to have rejuvenated him. He started talking again.

"You know what I done the other day? Let me show you." At this point Bob got up and started rummaging through neat stacks of papers on a little table, and he came out with a long white envelope someone had sent him, and the back was totally filled with Bob's scribbling. Then he continued. "I got to studying about the songs and the tunes that I'd wrote myself, you know, and I sat down and started writing them down."

Is this a list of the ones you wrote?

"Yeah, and I thought to myself, 'I've got enough there to make a tape.' And I made a tape just of the songs I wrote, and I'll make you a copy."

That would be great! Let's see here: "Fall Creek Waltz," "Walden's Ridge," "Bob's Special," "Cockle Burr," "Indian River," "Mountain City Stomp," and what's this "Skiddy Bob?"

"Yeah, 'Skiddy Bob'." He repeats, laughing. "That's one of them."

One of the tunes was "Sequatchie Valley," reputed to have been written by Bob and his father about 1923. This piece has been described by the old-time fiddle connoisseur Bobby Fulcher, a friend and an admirer of Bob Douglas, as a "remarkable piece of music."

Forty years after it was written, Bob got around to recording it, in a studio in Nashville. Fulcher described the piece as having the "feel of the old Appalachian solo fiddle music: six unequal parts, a patch of droning whole notes, and odd melodic turns and surprises, and both original and archaic."

Whatever technical and analytical phraseology one may employ to describe the tune, it is a moving one. As I penned these lines I dug out some of the old tapes Bob had made for me, and I played "Sequatchie Valley." It alternately inspires one to tears by its lonesome beauty and then makes one want to jump for joy with the happy galloping effect of precise and hard driving parts of the tune. I played it for the ladies in my office the next day, including my daughter,

Elaine—young folks who aren't particularly appreciative of old-time fiddling. But they were most impressed. Elaine said, "You just can't listen to it and sit still." Andrea said that we ought to have Bob for all four days of the Homecoming.

A few days after returning home with the list of tunes Bob had given me, I received a letter from him, which read in part: "About that list of tunes I give you that I said I wrote—I have been checking and they's two tunes on the list I didn't write, 'Going Back to Chattanooga,' and 'I Love You So Much It Hurts.' All the others I wrote. John Rice, I'm sorry I get all mixed up sometimes. Bye, bye—God bless you all."

My observations indicate that Bob Douglas gets "mixed up" very, very little. While writing this piece, on March 7, 1998, I noticed in my notes that Bob's birthday was only two days away, and that he would be 98 years old. I had not heard from him for a few months, and I decided to call him, but with some anxiety; for I had concern for his state of health.

Nellie answered the phone and said that Bob had been having a "terrible time" with his back. "He can get in the bed, but he can't get out." (She laughed.) "I have to pull him out of a morning."

I asked her about his birthday, and she again laughed heartily. "Tom Morgan and some other folks around here have planned a big 'to-do' down here at the courthouse [in Dayton] for Bob tomorrow—for his birthday. Well, it was all supposed to be a big surprise to him—nobody supposed to name it to him, you know. Well, he got a hold of a newspaper the other day and read all about it, and he come in here out of his den and said, 'Look here Nellie, they're planning a big celebration for me down at the courthouse.' I said, 'Yes I know but it was supposed to be a big surprise to you.'

"You can't keep nothing from him," Nellie laughed. "Well, here talk to him, he'll be tickled to hear from you. He was a talkin' about you yesterday."

Bob was in a talkative mood, about the 98th birthday celebration they were having for him, and about a new fiddle tune he had just heard, and learned.

"Steve Goforth sent me a tape the other day and they was a tune on there that I liked so well that I got my fiddle out, and I learned to play it. It's called 'Charleston Number One.' Oh, hits a pretty tune, and I just set down here and listened to it over and over and then I'd play and I've got it down pretty good."

Simply amazing, I thought. Here this 98-year-old man sits up there in his one little room and his zest for living, for life, and for his music is as great, it seemed, as it was when he was just learning to play as a teenager. Maybe this enthusiasm and his futuristic outlook is responsible for his longevity, and for his happy and cheerful countenance.

Bob is shown here, fiddle in hand, with the author. After visiting with Bob for several hours in January, 1996, he followed me to the front porch, fiddle in hand, where my wife Elizabeth took this picture of him and me, when Bob was almost 96. *Photo by Elizabeth Irwin*

I had a few questions for him.

Bob, I'm working on writing the captions for some of the pictures I got from you. Do you happen to remember the name of the big dog shown in one of those old photographs of you and your father? The dog was standing on his hind legs against your father "shaking hands." There was silence on the phone and I thought that he had not understood my questions.

"Let me study," he finally said. "Yeah, I remember Dad's old dog. He called him 'Pup.' I think. Yeah, that was his name, old Pup. I don't know what breed he was—all mixed up I think. He was just a dog, but he was smart. I remember that."

Well, you're sounding great, and it looks like you're going to make it to one hundred, and then some.

"The Lord knows more about that than I do. Whatever he says is all right with me."

I don't know which I admire more about Bob Douglas: his great old-time fiddling, so beautiful that it seems to flow from those grand old mountains and verdant valleys of which he is so much a part; or the warm, friendly, gentle, and empathetic qualities of Bob Douglas, the man. He has a countenance of love and compassion which sort of flows from him and settles over those who take the time to talk with him. Either way, he is a man worth knowing, and an inspiration to all who *do* get to know him. One could hardly hope to find another soul who more accurately portrays the old-time mountain fiddler.

Bobby Fulcher, mentioned earlier, has an insightful ability to analyze and compare the various attributes and characteristics of old-time fiddlers—Bob Douglas included. In a recent telephone conversation with Bobby, we discussed the career of Bob Douglas at length, and just as we were ending the protracted conversation he said: "Bob Douglas is an example of a country fiddler who ran the distance between the oldest mountain-style fiddling to the slickest, most urban style which was in vogue and demand during the 1940s and 1950s."

For various reasons, Bob did not go to Nashville in his prime nor try passionately for the big time like so many other musicians had successfully done; and he remained largely unknown except in the greater Chattanooga area. He didn't like to travel and he was content to work as a laborer by day and to play music by night, in his old haunts in Southeast Tennessee and Northern Georgia and Alabama. I'm sorry to say that I had not even heard of this great fiddler, this endearing man, until about 1985. I invited him to play in the annual Museum of Appalachia Tennessee Fall Homecoming.

Bob plays an old tune in the doorway of the Arnwine Cabin at the Museum of Appalachia in Norris, Tennessee. *Photo ca. 1989 by Frank Hoffman*

I remember the first time I saw him. He was small of stature, thin, and with an air of total serenity. He carried his fiddle and bow with him, waiting patiently to go on stage, and he seemed to be bothered not one whit that there were dozens of other performers ahead of him. He's the kind of person who can mingle through a crowd for hours and never be seen. He was, and is, soft spoken and responds to the other person's comments and questions, rarely initiating the conversation himself. He seems like an old friend a few minutes after one meets him. And he is wont to start his statements and comments by using the first name of the person with whom he is talking. For example, he says, "Jim, I tell you, he is a great fiddler"; or "Jim, I want you all to come down and see me." And he looks you in the eye, and he often places his hand on the shoulder of the person he's addressing.

Bob was most warmly received here at the Homecoming, by the tens of thousands of people from around the world. Many people were not particularly familiar with or appreciative of traditional, old-time, or fiddle music, but they were much impressed by the rich and clear sounds of those classic old tunes, some of which are traceable to old England, Ireland, and Scotland.

He's been attending the Homecoming every year for the past 12 years, joining such early country music greats as Bill Monroe, Roy Acuff's Smoky Mountain Boys, John Hartford, Mac Wiseman, Raymond Fairchild, and Grandpa Jones. Bobby Fulcher drives down each year and fetches Bob and his sister Nellie, and Bobby accompanies the old fiddler on the guitar. (I should point out here that Bob still drives his car around Dayton and Graysville, but he's a little reluctant to take on long trips.) The last time Bob played at the Homecoming was on October 8 and 9, 1998. He was past the age of 98, but he was as enthusiastic and as exuberant as ever, and so were those who heard him. I called him on December 7, 1998, and he said he wanted to come to see us "during Christmas." Then he went on to tell me with an air of excitement, about a show he was scheduled to play in April, 1999. "Bobby [Fulcher] called me up the other day and said we had a job up in Knoxville in April."

Well, Bob did indeed show up for the engagement on April 3, 1999, at the Laurel Theater near the University of Tennessee campus. Not only was the theater filled to capacity, but many stood in the outside hallways, straining to hear the old-time fiddler. Bob, who had just turned 99, stood and played for over half an hour, and he received several standing ovations. He was elated, but he had little time to receive accolades because he wanted to get to bed so he could arise early the next morning for the trip home to "see a man" who wanted to buy Bob's car. "I just don't drive it enough to make it worth while to keep it up," Bob explained.

A few years ago, during all the din at the Homecoming, Bob indicated that he wanted to talk with me. As soon as I could find a spare minute, I met him in front of the big fireplace in the auditorium. He had a worn old scrapbook with him and its pages were filled with pictures of the ribbons, plaques and trophies he had won over the years. They were presented to him as the first place winner at fiddle contests conducted throughout the region. "I want you to have all these awards if you want them," he said. "Maybe you can find a place to put them. Now, that is, if you want them. They're down there at my little place, in that closet, and nobody ever sees them. Maybe you could put them on display at the Museum somewhere."

I was moved by the old man's willingness to part with what he apparently considered to be some of his most precious possessions. A few weeks later I got the trophies, along with several of his 78 RPM records, and some other Bob Douglas memorabilia. I made copies of numerous photographs, and I built an exhibit area here in the Museum of Appalachia's Hall of Fame, especially for Bob's items. While attending the Homecoming in more recent years, he'll slip over to his display and take some of his special friends. He brought his sister Nellie a couple of times, and one time he brought his son Buddy over, proudly pointing out his exhibit.

Bob had told me on more than one occasion that he wanted me to have his fiddle—that much talked about and oft praised old instrument his father had given him in the 1920s. It was easily his most cherished and valuable possession, and I always suggested that he give the matter more consideration. First, I seldom accept gifts for the Museum, preferring to pay a fair price for all items; and secondly, I was concerned that his children or grandchildren may want this great old heirloom. But Bob kept raising the subject. Then on September 13, 1996, I received a message: "Bob Douglas is coming to see you."

He was agile in mind and body, notwithstanding the fact that he was recovering from his second recent bout with pneumonia. He came with his sister, Nellie, and he got right to the point.

"I've studied and studied about what I wanted to do with my fiddle, John Rice, and I've decided that I want you to have it. I know you'll take good care of it, and that you'll put it here in my display for everybody to see."

He thereupon took the beautiful instrument from its case and handed it to me, and I still don't know which of us was the most overcome with the emotional drama of the moment. His voice broke and I, too, was unable to respond. The fiddle had been his life from the time he sat as a child over 90 years ago in the one room log cabin on cold nights and listened to his father play.

Several people had noticed the old gentleman, and curiosity had drawn them to listen to him as we stood there in the Hall of Fame Building by his exhibit; and ironically, a crew from a Chattanooga television station was also there, purely by happenstance.

A woman from Minneapolis asked for Bob's autograph, and a dozen cameras clicked as Bob recalled the many fiddle contests he had won. He was asked to play and he did indeed; first the old tune "Fishers Hornpipe" and when he finished more people had gathered 'round, and the applause lasted half as long as the tune itself. Then Bob said: "Now I ain't giving up fiddling altogether. I wanted this one to have a special home here, but I've got another one at the house that I'll play here in October at the Tennessee Fall Homecoming and at other gatherings." The small group applauded again, and all the while the television camera was rolling, capturing the colorful old fiddler for a spot on the evening news.

"I've winned all these trophies you see here with this fiddle," Bob said, waving in the direction of his exhibit. "I've played all kinds of fiddles but I ain't never played one that sounded as good as this one. My daddy give it to me in 1928, when his left hand got sick and he couldn't note it no more. Poor old feller, he never could afford a case for it, and he carried it all over them mountains in an old flour sack to protect it.

"I can see him now," Bob recalled. "He was 97 when he died, and I'll soon be 97, too". Bob handed me the fiddle for one last time and as he started to leave, the group of visitors applauded the little man once again, and I heard him say, barely audible: "Thank you so much."

Bob retires his fiddle, but not himself. He poses here in front of his display at the Museum of Appalachia's Hall of Fame Building in Norris, Tennessee, where his many plaques and trophies are exhibited. He is holding the fiddle his father gave him in 1928, and which he retired to the Museum in 1996 when he was 96 years old. Bob was quick to add, however, that he had another fiddle at home and that he would continue to play. *Photo in the fall of 1996 by the author*

Chapter 5
Grandpa Jones

"A great musician and one of the funniest souls that God ever created."

On February 20, 1998, the bold headlines on the front page of Nashville's daily paper, *The Tennessean*, read: "Everybody's Grandpa Dies," and there was scarcely a soul in Nashville who didn't know that the story was about the inimitable and legendary Grandpa Jones. The *Associated Press* quickly spread the word across the nation, and for those who didn't read newspapers, the news of Grandpa's passing was broadcast on television and radio stations throughout the country. The account of his passing appeared in Europe, and doubtless in other foreign countries.

Three days later memorial services were held in the *Grand Ole Opry House*, and it was appropriate that this was the first time that a funeral had ever been held in this large auditorium from which the *Grand Ole Opry* is broadcast. Grandpa's parking space, reserved there for him for so many years, was draped in black; and a wreath hung backstage on the door of his dressing room.

When his millions of fans hear the name, "Grandpa Jones," this is likely the image which comes to their minds. He is shown here with Tennessee Ernie Ford while waiting to perform on the popular *Hee Haw* television program. *Photo courtesy Grandpa Jones*

I commented at the time, and I continue to believe, that the service was the most impressive and inspirational ceremony of any kind I had ever attended. Almost everyone with whom I talked expressed the same or similar feelings. There was proper solemnity, homage, prayers, and scripture readings; but there was mirth, also, and several "Grandpa" stories, and laughter. His wife, Ramona, and their children, Eloise, Alisa, and Mark, were pleased; and I think Grandpa would have heartily approved. Ramona later told me that the hardest part for her and the children was their arrival at the *Opry House*, just as Grandpa's coffin was being carried inside.

Marty Stuart introduced the various participants, and he played some incredibly beautiful mandolin pieces. Sam Lovello, who started and produced the *Hee Haw* show, had flown from California weeks earlier and had stayed by Grandpa's bedside much of the time prior to Grandpa's passing. In his eulogy, or "reflections" as he called it, Sam referred to Grandpa as his second father, his mentor, his close, close friend, and the one who taught him to love and respect country music.

Recalling Grandpa's wit and humor, Sam told of a time when he played a tape of a new, modern group which he was considering putting on the nationally popular program. He asked Grandpa what he thought of the group, with all the electrical instruments, drums, loud music and such. He said he wanted Grandpa's honest opinion, and after hearing the tape, Grandpa said: "It sounds like the static on an old Philco radio I used to have."

He told another story which happened there at Opryland. It had been a busy and hectic day, filming for several television programs, and Sam and Grandpa walked out in the warm, spring sunshine to rest on a tree-shaded bench. They wanted to just sit and relax, but soon they were surrounded by a crowd of people, wanting autographs from Grandpa and wanting to have their picture taken with him.

Some woman who happened to be passing sensed that there was some celebrity at bay, but she didn't know who it was. She forced her way through the crowd and looked at Grandpa questioningly. Finally she said: "I know you!" Grandpa stared back at her and said nothing. She repeated, "I know you," thinking she'd get help. But instead Grandpa said, "Well, who am I?" She replied, "You're Grandpa Moses."

George Lindsey, remembered best for his appearances on the *Andy Griffith Show* and *Hee Haw*, recalled a time that he and Grandpa were performing in the state of Oregon. After the show, Grandpa asked George if he liked Chinese food; and thinking that Grandpa knew of some outstanding Chinese restaurant, George answered an enthusiastic "Yes." They went to Grandpa's van and he opened a can of Chun King. When George complained, Grandpa said, "Well, it's Chinese, ain't it?"

There were sad parts to the funeral also, as when Ricky Skaggs, The Whites, Larry Sledge, and Ruth McLain sang, "Come and Dine," one of Grandpa's favorite songs, and one he had sung so often.

Then Jim and Jessie and the Virginia Boys sang "Falling Leaves," a beautiful and popular song Grandpa had written many years ago and which he often sang. There were few indeed who did not shed a tear as the familiar words and melody were sent forth, especially so when the last two lines were sung: "When you leave this earth for a better home someday, the only thing you take, is what you gave away."

There were dozens of celebrities and country music greats there, and many hundreds of friends and admirers. Among the mourners were scores of entertainers who had known Grandpa for so many years, and who had admired him so much—such stars as Ray Stevens, Porter Wagoner, John Conlee, Earl Scruggs, Jim Ed Brown, Charlie Louvin, Connie Smith, George Jones, Jeanne Pruett, and his dear old friend, 88-year-old Bill Carlisle. There were entertainment executives, including *Grand Ole Opry* president, Bob Whittaker; and the popular Gary Chapman, host of TNN's *Prime Time Country* show, took part in the eulogy. Dr. Charles Wolfe, the eminent scholar of early country music who advised Grandpa in the writing of his autobiography, *Everybody's Grandpa*, was there looking solemn and reflective.

On the stage in front of a large color portrait of Grandpa, there was, on a spotlighted chair, his old hat, his suspenders, his banjo, and his famous boots, now over 100 years old. Garth Brooks, in noting the boots, said: "There's this thing about 'who's going to fill their shoes?' You just as well put Grandpa's shoes in a trophy case because nobody will ever fill them."

Ricky Skaggs said, "He was probably the most natural comedian I've ever known"; and Jerry Strobel, the manager of the *Grand Ole Opry*, described him as "a great entertainer and musician and one of the funniest souls that God ever created."

Grandpa was low keyed and witty, and he possessed a dry sense of humor. He was funny without ever trying to be so. He played his last show on the *Grand Ole Opry* on January 3, 1998, pretty much as he had done for the past 60 years. The name of the last song he sang was "Any Old Time You Want to Come Back Home," and he left the stage waving his banjo and hopping sprightly back stage. He was stopped by a lady who wanted his autograph, and as he was laying his banjo aside and reaching for a pen, he seemed to feel faint, and just before he became totally incapacitated he said, as if apologizing to the lady: "I think I've struck a snag."

It was not surprising that the last words Grandpa uttered were short, concise, tinted with a bit of subtle humor, and most expressive—especially for country folk who knew what it meant to strike a stump or snag while plowing. He was rushed to the hospital, and after

"Me and Bill Carlisle, one of my best friends." That's what Grandpa had scribbled on the back of this photograph taken by Les Leverett at the WSM studio in Nashville. *Photo courtesy Grandpa Jones*

suffering another stroke, he lingered for a few weeks and then passed away on February 19, 1998. Ramona called us the next morning with the terse message: "Grandpa passed away last night."

The family had received friends at the funeral home in Goodlettsville for three days prior to the funeral, and even so, the large facility could hardly accommodate all those thousands who came in a continuous stream to pay their last respects. At times it took five policemen to direct traffic in and around the funeral home. My wife, Elizabeth, and I, along with Dr. Nat Winston and his wife, Martha, spent a few hours there, mostly in an anteroom with Ramona and the family, and we were as impressed with the throng of unknown admirers as we were with the celebrities—such folks as Eddy Arnold, Boots Randolph . . .

How did it come about that this quiet, unpretentious man from a poor farm family in Kentucky was able to command the attention and admiration of people from every strata of society, from presidents, to the country greats, to the academia of the nation's colleges, and especially to the rural and working class people of America? Who was this Grandpa Jones fellow and how was it that he gained such popularity, first in the Boston area, of all places, and then continuing to enthral audiences with his music, his songs, and his humor for the next 60 years? It is indeed an understatement to suggest that the life of Grandpa Jones was an interesting, colorful, and fascinating one.

The last of 10 children, he was born October 20, 1913, in an old log house near the village of Niagara, in northwest Kentucky. His father, David, was a tenant farmer, often moving from one farmhouse to another, and his mother, Kate, was a kind and loving housewife, doing the best she could in bringing up 10 children in conditions totally lacking in modern, even essential, conveniences. They named him Louis Marshall Jones, but the country would know him simply as Grandpa Jones.

He was an observant little tyke and he especially noted and remembered those incidents of a humorous nature, true and honest happenings about people in that rural and impoverished farming area. The fact, even at an early age, that he was impressed by and remembered these stories, gives insight into Grandpa's innate ability to judge that which *was* funny, and to whom it would so appear. The humorous happenings which occurred in a drab and sometimes desolate setting, with people laughing at themselves, provided fodder for the humorous stories and anecdotes for which he would become famous. When he told of the rifle that was accidently fired by his brothers while they tinkered with it as the family sat before the fireplace one cold night, there was no intrinsic humor. But when he went on to tell about the bullet passing through the closet door and breaking "14 good quart jars of blackberries" and how his outraged mother threw the boys and the gun out of the house, then country folks could all visualize the incident and relate to the story.

As most good humorists know, self-deriding stories are often better accepted than those which ridicule others. For example, Grandpa told of his early days in a new school, and how he was totally and adamantly set against attending class. Every day his brother had to drag him to the schoolhouse. He later said: "I kicked and screamed and fought all the way to the schoolhouse every day until it got to where it was a show for the neighbors. When it came time for school to start of a morning, the women would sit at their windows just to watch."

A young and resolute Grandpa is shown here, at right, in his baby dress and button shoes at the "old Smith place" near Smith Mills, Kentucky. His little friend is Barry Smith. *Photo courtesy Grandpa Jones*

This family portrait of the Jones family, lacking in formal dress, realistically portrays the poor tenant farm family as it was. David and his wife Kate Jones sit among six of their ten children, along with some extended family members. Sitting on the ground, from the left, are: Spurgeon Jones, Grandpa, Eugene Jones and Lucian Vickers; seated: Grandpa's parents; standing, from the left: Louise Jones, Bessie Vickers Jones (Homer's wife and Grandpa's sister-in-law), Homer Jones, Gordon Jones, and Uncle Lofton. *Photo courtesy Grandpa Jones*

He had the ability to convey strong, poignant feelings in a short, concise manner—simple little statements which had unbounded meaning. In recalling his earliest memories about his grandparents, he said: "My grandpa was a carpenter, and when Grandma died, he made her a coffin and lined it with silk." His ability to compose short, gripping little lines such as this, no doubt, contributed to his ability to write expressive songs, many of which are still sung after half a century. He had a bent toward poetry, and many of the songs written by Grandpa, the comedian, were paradoxically sad, philosophical, and thought provoking.

In August, 1920, when Grandpa was six years old, the family moved a few miles north to the city of Evansville, Indiana, in search of work. His father and older brothers never found employment in the ironworks there as they expected, and they survived by taking odd jobs, mowing yards, and such. Grandpa hated every minute of the city, and he thought his schoolmates made light of his country manner and funny speech.

The countenance of total pleasure on young Grandpa's face tells the story of his exhilaration with the large toy car he's "driving." It was bought for him by his sister Velma after she left home and started working in Evansville, Indiana. *Photo courtesy Grandpa Jones*

After a few months, the family moved back to Kentucky to a farm owned by an acquaintance to whom the family referred as Uncle Billy Todd. They moved into the house late at night with scant chattels, and no conveniences. They built a fire in the fireplace, his mother made coffee and heated some food on the hot coals, and the family bedded down wherever they could find a corner. The next morning Grandpa could see old familiar fields, fences, cattle, and trees, instead of asphalt streets, and it was good. He later said: "And to this day I've never wanted to live in town." Remarkably, he was able to find a little farm on which to live throughout much of his career, whether he was playing in Nashville or Washington, D. C.

Grandpa remembered the stay there as the leanest years his family ever experienced. "Things got so bad," he often recalled, "that Mother would get corn from the old crib, shell it, parch it in the oven, and then grind it in the hand-cranked coffee mill and make it into meal. Then she'd pour on it a little milk from the one old cow we had—and for three weeks we ate that and nothing else."

During his career, Grandpa would use his recollections of these stark and pathetic conditions to weave in a funny, but non-condescending story about poverty and the humorous side of it. "There was an old boy," he would say, "who worked on a sawmill gang, and his lunch bucket never contained more than a small piece of corn bread with a little homemade jelly spread on it. Every day at noon he watched the other workers open their old dinner buckets and bring out ham and biscuits, baked potatoes, boiled eggs, cake, pie, and such, and every day old Jake would sneak off to himself and eat his lowly piece of corn bread, because he was ashamed for the other men to see how little he had. Jake was an honest feller," Grandpa would say, "but he was hungry, always hungry, and he decided that he'd find the heaviest bucket there and he'd get it for himself.

"Well, while the men were out working, he picked up each dinner pail to see how heavy it was, and finally he came to one that was the heaviest of all. He took it and ran back up in the woods to have himself one good meal; and when he opened it up there was nothing in it but eight black walnuts and a clawhammer to crack them with."

This was the type story to which most Americans could relate, especially those who remembered the Depression Era, and it also contained a not-too-subtle moral. This boded well with those who knew that it was wrong to steal—and that nothing good would result therefrom. No matter that his audience had heard Grandpa tell this story half a dozen times before—no matter at all; they would always laugh boisterously and applaud. He was a truly superb storyteller, and his timing and his emphasis were perfectly orchestrated. As Roy Clark once said, "Grandpa could make people laugh by just saying 'Hello'."

Grandpa and his brothers, during their brief stay in Evansville, had become acquainted with the Lindersmitt

This photograph of Grandpa's sister Louise plowing the tobacco patch dramatizes the stark, poverty ridden background of the Jones family. The old mule's name, Grandpa vividly recalled, was "Preacher." *Photo courtesy Grandpa Jones*

boys who would come to visit the Jones family on Sundays and eat dinner with them. They would bring a mandolin and a fiddle, and this was one of the first exposures Grandpa had to musical instruments.

Uncle Willie sold the timber on the farm and a sawmill crew moved in to cut, snake, and saw the logs into lumber. Grandpa used to go down to the campsite at the sawmill in the evenings and talk to some of these old sawmillers. Two members of the crew, Wilbert and Joe Lee Howard, had a guitar, and that greatly intrigued the young Grandpa. The Howard boys would leave the guitar at Grandpa's house during the day for safe keeping and because of the dampness in the tent. Grandpa would slip it out and play it every time he had a chance. With no one to teach him the chords, he first used a small bottle instead of a steel bar and would play it Dobro, or steel-guitar, style. He later described the sound of that cheap guitar, played by Wilbert Howard, as "the finest sounding thing I ever heard."

Soon the Howard boys and the Lindersmitt boys were coming to the Jones' front porch almost every night during the summer to make music. The first song Grandpa learned from them was "Sweet Dreams of Kentucky."

One characteristic of tenant farmers, or sharecroppers, was their tendency to move often. I once wrote of such a family in East Tennessee, and we calculated that they had moved 21 times during a period of 23 years—always looking, hoping, and expecting that the next move would provide something better—but it never did. In fact, they often returned to the same little tenant houses where they had lived previously.

So it wasn't unexpected that the Jones family soon moved from Uncle Billy Todd's place—when Grandpa was about seven years old. They moved into a big log house on the old Shepherd place near the community of Posey Chapel. It was a cold house, with large cracks, and Grandpa said he could sit by the fire and look through the large openings around the chimney and see the chickens running around the yard. He attended a two-room school at Posey Chapel where the students either walked or rode horses or mules to class, and near the school was a shed and a manger for sheltering and feeding the mounts.

A young barefoot Grandpa and his niece Eleanor pose with his dog Joe for the camera, while his other niece Frances looks on. *Photo taken at the old Smith place near Smith Mills where the Jones family lived at the time; courtesy Grandpa Jones*

Grandpa, on the right, is shown here with his boyhood friend Randall Sellers, Jr., on the Green River in Henderson County, Kentucky. *Photo taken ca. 1925 when Grandpa was about 12 years old, courtesy Grandpa Jones*

Grandpa's dinner at school usually consisted of a biscuit with a piece of home-cured bacon and another one with blackberry jam. He remembers that one boy brought fancy food—even a piece of celery once in a while.

When Grandpa graduated from the 8th grade, he still had not been able to accumulate enough money to buy himself a guitar, but he had never stopped wanting one. His daddy played an old-time fiddle and his mother sang old ballads, some of which Grandpa later recorded himself.

Grandpa's sister, Velma, had bought a record player and some records of opera singers and bands which she and their mother liked; but Grandpa and his brother Gordon especially liked such early pioneer country singers as Jimmie Rodgers, the singing brakeman, and Grandpa was particularly taken by the yodeling for which Rodgers became so famous.

A great moment in Grandpa's life occurred when he was about 14. His brother Aubry had a job working in a garage in nearby Henderson, Kentucky, and when he came in from work one day, he told Grandpa to go look in the cab of the truck. Grandpa remembered that day for the remainder of his life, with clarity and with great joy: "I expected to find some candy or maybe some oranges, but instead there lay a guitar. It was old, warped a little, and the label was worn off, but it looked like gold to me. Aubry had bought it in Henderson at a second-hand place called 'Cheap John's' for 75 cents."

Grandpa remembered that his mother had cooked a big supper that night, and he also remembered that he ate not a bite, but instead played on that old guitar until bedtime. From that time on, he listened to other guitar players, learning chords and songs wherever he had the chance. He even watched the blind singers as they performed on the streets in Henderson.

He'd go to square dances at Posey School, and one night some musicians asked him to join them. It was with great trepidation that Grandpa joined that little rag-tag group of young musicians there at the little two-room school at Posey Chapel. That may have been his very first experience of performing before an audience, small as it doubtlessly was.

He kept listening to the records of the great singer-yodeler Jimmie Rodgers, and he kept practicing when no one else was nearby. He finally built up enough confidence to allow others to hear him, the family members at first, and then the boys with whom he played.

He enrolled in Barrett Manual Training High School in Henderson, but soon thereafter the family moved to Akron, Ohio, where the oldest boy in the family, Wilmer, worked for the telephone company. Wilmer thought he could help his father and the other boys gain employment there.

Grandpa didn't like big city life in Akron any more than he had liked his short stay in Evansville years earlier. When he went to enroll as a sophomore there, he was informed that the credits he had earned in the trade school in Kentucky were not acceptable, and he had to back up and start over as a freshman. It was during this time that he started playing at community gatherings and at dance halls. He even played guitar with an orchestra for several months.

Perhaps the most exciting and important event in Grandpa's young life took place there in Akron in March of 1929 when he was only 16 years old. A family friend, whom they referred to as Aunt Polly, had heard that a week-long talent contest was to be held in Akron, and she persuaded her young, shy friend to enter.

Many years later Grandpa told me the story, which remained fresh in his mind after the passage of some 64 years. He was nervous from the start, he said, because of the nature and importance of the event and because of his inexperience and most especially because of all the contestants—450 from throughout the region.

To his utter amazement, he won in the preliminary judging, and he found himself in a wing of the stage, about to compete for first place. The longer he waited the more nervous he became, and when he glanced down at his guitar he saw that he had literally gnawed the end of the neck to where it looked like rats had been chewing on it. He was, as he said, "as nervous as a one-eyed cat in a dog pound."

Finally his time came, and somehow he managed to reach center stage. He sang one of Jimmie Rodgers yodeling songs, "Dear Old Sunny South by the Sea," and his second number was "Going Back to Texas."

When he finished his two songs he was so tense and "keyed up" that he didn't wait for the final results of the contest. He just took off home, before it was announced that he had won first place. When a friend came and told him the news, he didn't believe him, but, finally convinced, Grandpa went back to claim the prize—five ten-dollar gold coins. He added a little more to the $50 and went immediately and bought a guitar which he described as "a little green Gibson."

"That was the first good guitar I ever had," Grandpa told me in 1993, "and boy, was I proud. I've played it all over the country—even took it with me to Europe during the War. Now, I want you to have it, to put there in your Museum, in the Hall of Fame with my other stuff."

I was honored and most pleased, not just because of the intrinsic and historical value of the guitar, but because Grandpa Jones wanted me to have it, and as they say, "that says volumes."

It wasn't long until the industrious teenager had a job on radio station WJW in Akron, sponsored by a Dr. Pennington, who described himself as "Akron's Leading Dentist" and who proudly announced that he was open Monday through Saturday, from nine o'clock in the morning until eight o'clock at night, and on Sunday morning from ten o'clock until one o'clock in the afternoon. The charge for pulling teeth was 50 cents each. While at WJW, Grandpa got $14 per week, and he gave his mother $11, keeping only $3 for his school and personal expenses.

He continued to play, often with other musicians, on the radio in Akron and also in Cleveland. He played with a singer named Warren Caplinger and another musician named Andy Patterson from Petros, Tennessee. These two were known as Cap and Andy. When Grandpa graduated from high school in 1932 in the very depths of the Great Depression, he fondly recalled that he was able to afford a two-toned pair of shoes, white pants, and a black coat.

At the age of 16, Grandpa won first place in a talent contest in which 450 other contestants participated, and he bought this "little green guitar" with his prize money. He is shown here in 1930 at age 20 playing that guitar on radio station WADO in Akron, Ohio. *Photo courtesy Grandpa Jones*

In 1932 Grandpa, along with Cap and Andy, joined the most popular Lum and Abner road-show band called The Pine Ridge String Band. The *Lum and Abner Show*, set in Pine Ridge, Arkansas, was soon to become one of the most popular radio shows in the country. I can remember when people bought battery-operated radios in the late 1930s, mainly so they could hear *The Lone Ranger* and *The Lum and Abner Show*.

I also recall listening to a popular singer of folk songs and old ballads, on the *Grand Ole Opry*. His name was Bradley Kincaid, and he had a beautiful, clear tenor voice and made songs come alive. I was thoroughly taken by his singing and by the type songs he sang. Apparently millions of other people agreed; for he became one of the most popular ballad singers in the country.

Many years later I became acquainted with Bradley Kincaid when we both served on a committee at Berea College for the furtherance of traditional music of the region. He was an impressive and courtly southern gentleman whose appearance belied his rough mountain upbringing. For example, he never attended school until he was 19 years old, at which time he entered the 4th grade. He eventually worked his way through high school, and afterwards he received a degree from the respected Berea College in Berea, Kentucky, by waiting on tables.

In 1932, Grandpa, back row second from the right, joined the popular Lum and Abner Pine Ridge String Band. The *Lum and Abner Radio Show*, set in Pine Ridge, Arkansas, was soon to become one of the most popular radio programs in the country. The members of the group include, on the front row, from the left: Lum, The Three Milkmaids, and Abner; back row: (?) Coleman, Harmonica Joe, Davey West, Andy Patterson, Grandpa Jones, and Warren Caplinger. *Photo courtesy Grandpa Jones*

It happened that Grandpa and an entertainer known as Bashful Harmonica Joe performed at a charity benefit in Akron in February of 1935, the same night that Bradley Kincaid was performing on the program. He heard the two young musicians, and after the show, the popular Kincaid, who was one of Grandpa's idols, offered Joe and him a job. As excited as they were, the two teenagers felt obliged to consult with their parents before committing themselves to join Kincaid for their first real job in the entertainment business.

They drove all night to meet Bradley in Huntington, West Virginia, and when they finally found their designated meeting place, a theater called the RKO Palace, they could hardly believe their eyes. The marquee read: "Bradley Kincaid with Marshall Jones and Harmonica Joe from the Lum and Abner Show." That was the first time Grandpa saw his name "in lights" and he never forgot his exhilaration at that sight.

They traveled with Bradley in West Virginia, Ohio, and Kentucky—on a day-and-night schedule for audiences hungry for their kind of music. Grandpa recalled that they were scheduled to play a midnight show in the small town of East Rainelle, West Virginia, but because of a severe storm they didn't arrive until two o'clock in the morning. Instead of finding an empty theater as they expected, they found the theater full of people, most of whom were sound asleep, but waiting for the show. "We made an extra special effort to please them and put on a good show," Grandpa later recalled.

In the spring of 1935, Bradley had made arrangements to broadcast from Boston, Massachusetts. Interestingly, Grandpa and Joe again consulted with and received the blessings from their respective families before they agreed.

The three rented a tiny apartment and did their own cooking. The two young men found the life in Boston to be totally foreign to them, and they were homesick for more familiar haunts. But at the same time, Grandpa was intrigued by all the interesting and historical places, and he visited and studied the sights, unlike so many musicians who see all towns and cities as merely places with stages and auditoriums from which to perform.

They knew that New England was not accustomed to their kind of music; so they had not planned to schedule personal appearances in the beginning, not until they introduced their kind of music to the region. But their reception was so positive that after only two weeks on the radio they made their first personal appearance in the town of Gardner, Massachusetts. The crowd was so great that they had to play three shows that one night, and even then they couldn't accommodate everyone.

Bradley, Grandpa, and Joe couldn't believe how friendly, gracious and kind those northern folks were—often inviting the trio to dine with them in their homes, and bringing them pies and cakes and such. Grandpa later described them as "just good old-timey people."

The band played throughout New England, from Rhode Island to northern Maine, always having to drive back after the shows for the next radio program on WBZ. Sometimes the only sleep they got was in their car, and often they would be dog tired when time came for the broadcast. One morning, after driving all night, young Jones was moving slowly, not quite fully awake. Bradley admonished the 22-year-old Marshall Jones to get up to the mike, and then he added six words which were to change the entire life of this young entertainer. He said: "You're just like an old grandpa."

Boston, Massachusetts, seems an unlikely place for Grandpa to get his "real" start in old-time country music, but it happened nevertheless. Pictured here are: Grandpa, on the right; Bradley Kincaid, center, the popular ballad singer from Kentucky; and Bashful Harmonica Joe Troyan during the time they played New England and Canada, ca. 1935. *Photo courtesy Grandpa Jones*

Hence, Louis Marshall Jones donned an old man's clothing, applied a false mustache, pencil-lined his face, got an old hat, a pair of suspenders, put on a pair of "small-rimmed" glasses, and accentuated what Grandpa himself characterized as his naturally "whiny" voice, and he became Grandpa Jones. It strikes one as being odd that the "character" of Grandpa Jones was "born" in Boston, and not in Henderson, Kentucky, or Petros, Tennessee, or in some other rural setting.

Left: The formal photograph of Louis Marshall Jones, at age 23, was taken about the same time Bradley Kincaid dubbed him "Grandpa" Jones in Boston, Massachusetts. He was billed as "the young singer of old songs." The photo above shows Grandpa a few years later with his "Grandpa" regalia. *Photo courtesy Grandpa Jones*

Bradley gave him a pair of his discarded boots, which Grandpa said were 50 years old at the time; and he wore this same pair for sixty years. He had them re-soled many times, just from the wear of walking to and from the dressing rooms and the stages. (These boots and other items of "Grandpa" regalia were presented to the Country Music Hall of Fame on Friday, February 19, 1999, amid much fanfare and press coverage.) Grandpa and Joe were each making $50 per week, good wages for those Depression years.

Grandpa gives much credit to Bradley for teaching him about entertainment, stage manners, and about personal matters, such as not to eat bacon in restaurants with his fingers. But Joe was leaving the trio, and Grandpa was becoming weary with the constant traveling. More than anything else, he just wanted to be on his own; and Bradley's friendly beseeching could not change Grandpa's mind.

In 1937 he went to WWVA in Wheeling, West Virginia, and without notice, walked in off the street, auditioned and got a job, and soon had his own program on this station which was heard across the country. He had saved his money parsimoniously and bought two houses in Akron, renting one and letting his folks move into the other—and he visited his family every chance he got. As in Boston, he roamed around Wheeling and was intrigued with the history and sites—but this coal-based town was quite different from the historic and cultural city of Boston.

There was a plethora of musicians in the Wheeling area at that time, including the popular Cousin Emmy who played old-time drop-thumb banjo. Grandpa was much taken with her playing, and he bought himself a banjo. With her tutelage, he learned to play the "frailing" style which was to become his trademark. He first learned such songs as "Little Birdie," "Ground Hog," and "Cripple Creek."

In 1938, Grandpa went back to join Bradley for a series of engagements, this time in and around Hartford, Connecticut. After a few weeks, he went to Charleston,

Grandpa and His Grandsons, a group which Grandpa formed ca. 1938, gained considerable popularity on radio stations in West Virginia and surrounding states, and they became "one of the heaviest mail-drawing attractions on the air." From the left are: Pete Hendsler, Grandpa, Lennie Aleshire, and Biff Bledsoe.
Photo courtesy Grandpa Jones

West Virginia, and started playing on radio station WCHS, on the *Old Farm Hour*. Here he met Eulalia Losier, the niece of his old friend, Andy Patterson, from Petros, Tennessee, and in the fall of 1938 Grandpa and Eulalia were married. A few months later Grandpa was playing on a radio station in Fairmont, West Virginia, where he put together his first band called Grandpa Jones and his Grandsons.

During this time, Grandpa sang old ballads such as "Barbara Allen," and songs from Jimmie Rodgers, The Carter Family, and Bradley Kincaid; and he continued to write songs and to print and sell little songbooks. One of the more popular songs he wrote was "The Tragic Romance," which I had so often heard as a youngster, never realizing until recently that Grandpa had written it.

From Fairmont, he was back in Wheeling for a while, in 1941, then later to WLW in Cincinnati, a 500,000-watt station said to be the most powerful in the country. There he worked with the most popular people in the business including Curly Fox and Texas Ruby, the Delmore Brothers, and Merle Travis with whom he would later develop a close friendship.

One would think that Grandpa would be doing well financially by the early 1940s—with the songbooks he had written, the personal appearances, and the records he had made. But World War II had started and times were changing, competition keen, and the personal appearances lagging; so he got a job at the loading dock, as a laborer.

He and his wife, Eulalia, were apparently not getting along too well, and Uncle Sam was constantly reminding the country's men: "I Need You"; so at age 31, Grandpa joined the Army to "see what all the fighting was about."

Grandpa and his older brother, Dr. Eugene Jones, both soldiers in WWII, "got together" in Nuremburg, Germany, in 1945. *Photo courtesy Grandpa Jones*

He reached Europe in early 1945 and, while never encountering any front line fighting, spent some time trying to control some of the Russian soldiers who were our allies, but who were pillaging the countryside and murdering German civilians. On one occasion, he came upon a German woman who had just been shot multiple times in the head, presumably by the Russians. He sat with the body until German civilians came by, and they summoned an ambulance. He remained in the Aachen and Cologne area, guarding bridges and patrolling the area until the War ended a few months later; then he was sent to Munich in the southern part of Germany.

Grandpa carried his guitar with him and while in the Munich area, other soldiers would join him singing and playing. Before long a little band was formed, and they called themselves The Munich Mountaineers. They soon started playing on the Armed Forces Network, heard throughout Europe. They even made personal appearances, much as Grandpa had done in the states.

He was discharged in January, 1946. The reuniting with Eulalia did little to mend their strained relationship, and soon they were divorced. He returned to Cincinnati with the idea of resuming his old job on WLW. In discussing his return, the officials reminded him that they were bound by law to take him back, since he had been away serving his country. This infuriated Grandpa—the idea that they would infer that they were re-hiring him only for obligatory reasons and not because of merit.

His quick temper came into play and he stormed out of the office. He soon joined Merle Travis to make some records for Syd Nathan, who was trying to start a record company. Grandpa and Merle Travis made the first recordings for what was the beginning of King Records.

They first recorded under the name of the Shepherd Brothers, and Grandpa later formed a gospel quartet with the popular Delmore Brothers and Merle, and they named themselves the Brown's Ferry Four. This group became quite popular. Dr. Charles Wolfe, writing in *Bluegrass Unlimited* in 1998, called the group: "The first great country gospel quartet." They sang songs such as "Just a Little Talk with Jesus" and "Will The Circle Be Unbroken." The little record company was also selling records which featured Grandpa alone.

Then it was to Los Angeles [Burbank] where King recorded some of the songs Grandpa had written, including what was to become one of his greatest hits and one with which he came to be so closely associated: "Eight More Miles To Louisville." His records were becoming popular nationwide, and he was recording "right and left," as he put it.

Prior to this time, Grandpa renewed his acquaintance with a pretty, young fiddle and mandolin player, Ramona Riggins, who was playing in a trio called Sunshine Sue and the Rock Creek Rangers. Grandpa heard that the group was playing on a radio station in Keene, New Hampshire, and he drove there to see her. By the time he arrived, the temperature was 28 degrees below zero. He told her that he was going down to Nashville to audition for WSM, and he invited her to come down and work with him if he got the job. He didn't get an affirmative answer, but neither did he get a definite "no."

Grandpa's old friend Bradley Kincaid was now in Nashville, and he introduced Grandpa to Pee Wee King, who was very popular at the time, and who later co-wrote with Redd Stewart the famous "Tennessee Waltz." Grandpa played for the first time on the stage of the *Grand Ole Opry* with Pee Wee King on March 16, 1946, and he would continue to do so off and on for the next 51 years.

When Grandpa took the stage, he literally took the audience, with his bold and boisterous demeanor, his fine singing, his expert banjo playing, and his "honest" and subtle humor. *Photo courtesy Country Music Foundation, Nashville*

Ramona did eventually come to Nashville, after Bradley invited her to work with him and Grandpa, and she started playing on the *Grand Ole Opry* with them, as well as performing at tent shows with them during the week. Grandpa and Ramona and the band toured during the spring and summer of 1946, and that fall they were married.

In March of 1947, Grandpa recorded several songs for King, one of which became one of his most famous songs, "Mountain Dew." It was his first recording with Ramona (and Cowboy Copas), and it was the first time he had played his five-string banjo on a record. The record sold 40,000 copies in a few months (impressive then, though not by today's standards), and more people began to talk about Grandpa Jones.

This was followed by another hit, a song about a faithful hunting dog, "Old Rattler." It was even more popular than "Mountain Dew," and became and remained one of his most requested songs.

The *Grand Ole Opry* enabled Grandpa to make personal appearances throughout the South and into the Pennsylvania, Maryland, and Washington, D. C., areas. He became so popular that in 1948 he and Ramona moved to a small farm near Lorton, Virginia, to be near radio station WARL in Arlington. Through the management efforts of Connie B. Gay, they made personal appearances throughout the Washington area and in the New England states, and even in Nova Scotia and other Canadian provinces.

When the *Grand Ole Opry* celebrated its 50th anniversary in October, 1975, Grandpa was featured as one of the star performers.
Photo by Les Leveret

It was while a young Louis Marshall Jones was performing in the Boston, Massachusetts, area that he was given the name "Grandpa," after which he started "dressing and acting like an old Grandpa." He is shown here in this 1946-47 photo with "Old Rattler," the inspiration for Grandpa's popular song by the same name. *Photo courtesy Grandpa Jones*

In March of 1951, Grandpa, Ramona, and Mary Klick, from the Johnson City area in upper East Tennessee, were asked to entertain the troops during the Korean War. They first arrived in Tokyo and performed 15 shows (in a single day) for wounded American soldiers in the hospitals there, and then to Korea where they played 34 shows in two weeks for combat troops, sometimes within 200 yards of the front lines—in earshot of the fighting. During this relatively short tour, they played for an estimated 38,000 troops.

Grandpa and Ramona both told me that performing in that cold, damp area in the rice paddies and devastated countryside was the most tiring, uncomfortable, and exhausting tour they ever made.

Both emphasized, however, that donating their services for these "boys" was the most satisfying and rewarding tour they ever made, because the troops were so kind, receptive, and grateful.

After returning home from the Korean tour, Grandpa switched from King Records, which he had helped start with their first recordings, to RCA Victor where he recorded a number of songs, many of which he wrote. The RCA executives kept trying to nudge him over into a style which would have wider appeal—for an emerging new audience. But Grandpa finally decided that he should stay with his old, original songs he knew and loved, and let the chips fall where they may. The passage of time vindicated the wisdom of his decision.

Ramona and Grandpa Jones are shown here with Mary Click, at right, at the Command Post on the Central Front while entertaining the troops during the Korean War. *Photo taken March, 1951—courtesy of Grandpa and Ramona Jones*

Ramona, left, Mary Click, and Grandpa played 34 shows in 14 days for an estimated 38,000 soldiers during the Korean War, often within 200 yards of the front lines, and within earshot of the fighting. *Photo courtesy Grandpa and Ramona Jones*

In 1952, Grandpa and Ramona again volunteered their services and talents to entertain American troops, this time in Europe, sponsored by the United Service Organizations (U.S.O.). They toured for four weeks through Italy, Austria, and Germany without any compensation. [In 1961, Grandpa returned to Europe with the Gatlin Brothers and performed with a commercially sponsored tour.]

The 1950s were not good for old-time traditional musicians, and Grandpa and Ramona, like so many of these type musicians, became victims of the "new" country sound and the rock-and-roll music. Radio stations had stopped playing the fiddle, banjo, non-acoustic type songs, and record companies had largely given up recording them. Without air play and records, the

personal appearances also dissipated. This not-too-rosy outlook may have prompted Grandpa and Ramona to buy a little farm some 20 miles north of Nashville in the community of Ridgetop, near Goodlettsville. It is interesting that they moved into a log house, reflective of the old log houses where Grandpa had lived as a child. But this one was larger, and while retaining the aura of the abodes of his childhood, it was warm and much more spacious and contained all the amenities of a modern home—a beautiful place set at the very end of a meandering dirt and gravel road, which wound through a tree shrouded lane and by a little creek. When they first moved there, the lane, in wet and wintry months, would become muddy; and the ruts held water, prompting Grandpa to say that he couldn't decide whether to have the road graveled, or to stock it with catfish. But it was "way back in the country"—just what Grandpa wanted. Grandpa could raise a large garden and keep some cattle on the 15-acre tract.

By this time, they had two children, Eloise, born in 1948 and Mark, born in 1955. Grandpa's daughter Marsha, by his first wife, was also living with them. [Alisa, the youngest daughter, had not come on the scene yet. She was born November 17, 1960.]

Grandpa always remembered the great acceptance that he had received in Canada, and he turned his thoughts in that direction. He found the reception there as good as ever, better than he anticipated, and he began making more appearances in Canada than in the United States, sometimes with Ramona, but more often with other entertainers.

Then he, like so many other purveyors of the traditional music of the country, cast an inquisitive eye toward new phenomena which started to appear on the landscape—the folk festival and a revival of interest in the old-time music and songs. These outdoor events fitted Grandpa's style of performing perfectly, perhaps more so for him than for any other entertainer of the day. He was exhilarating and energetic, and he commanded the attention of an audience as few could. His natural antics, his boisterous though well-orchestrated "frailing" on the banjo, and his Grandpa outfit captivated the audience. How could any audience not be impressed? He took two old-time Middle Tennessee musicians, Sam and Kirk McGee, with him to play at a festival in Maryland in 1955. These brothers had played on the *Grand Ole Opry* for as far back as I could remember, in the mid-1930s, and they were always introduced by George D. Hay, The Solemn Ole Judge, as "Sam and Kirk McGee from Sunny Tennessee." Like most old-time *Opry* stars, they made their living by farming and such, even when they became well known across the country. Their time had come and passed, they thought, but when they played for a new, younger crowd with Grandpa in Maryland, they were all astounded by their great reception.

Interestingly and ironically, Grandpa drew more enthusiastic audiences and had a more ardent following in the Northeast than in the Southeast. Ramona recently reminded me that Grandpa often said that "he made more money in Pennsylvania than in any other state."

As Grandpa so wisely observed, these college-type folks looked upon them, not as old-time, old-fashioned, out-of-date musicians, but as folk musicians—a discovery, these youngsters thought they themselves had made.

Even though Grandpa had played throughout this country, Canada, and in other foreign countries for over 40 years, and had written dozens of songs and recorded many more, it was a new, different, and not altogether sophisticated show in Nashville for which he became most famous. It was called *Hee Haw*, and when Grandpa first heard about it, he allowed that the name alone would kill it. Of course many others shared his feeling. He was persuaded, however, to join *Hee Haw*, and it soon became one of the most popular shows in the nation, and was viewed by some thirty million viewers each week for almost 25 years, from 1969 until 1993. It was said to be the longest running television show in the country. Even after it was discontinued as a network program, it continued to be played as re-runs and on cable televison.

Longtime friends and regular performers on the *Grand Ole Opry* and *Hee Haw*, Grandpa and Minnie Pearl are shown here with their stage regalia. *Photo courtesy Grandpa Jones*

Grandpa played and sang on the program, but his role was largely as a comedian, and it was his first significant encounter with television. He harkened back to his country upbringing, and borrowed jokes and one liners from his long career, and he soon became a favorite. The hour-long program was fast paced and featured a large cast of entertainers who, like Grandpa, were already widely known "in the business." They included Archie Campbell, another comedian as well as a singer, who helped found the program and who served as a writer. He was largely responsible for recruiting Grandpa, his longtime friend, to join the show. Other regulars included Minnie Pearl, Roy Clark, Buck Owens, Jeannie C. Riley, Junior Samples, and several more. The guests were even more impressive, including the likes of Dolly Parton, Roy Acuff, Porter Wagoner, Tom T. Hall, Billy Carter, Roy Rogers and Dale Evans, and Senator Robert Byrd of West Virginia, who as I write these lines is in the national spotlight daily in connection with the Senate's trial of President Clinton. Senator Byrd is not only a true old-time fiddler but also the most respected and scholarly Senator with regard to the history and understanding of the U. S. Senate and the United States Constitution.

There were other celebrities including Governor Lamar Alexander and President George Bush. Archie Campbell once asked me if I thought my friend, Alex Haley, would agree to be a guest on *Hee Haw*. At the time, Alex's book, *Roots*, had set records as the most popular book of the century, and around the world, and the subsequent television series by the same name was said to have been the most watched program in the history of television. At the time, Alex was staying in our house when he wasn't traveling, and while building a home adjacent to the Museum. I asked him if he would agree to appear on this country show, and he readily agreed; and he enjoyed it very much.

Relaxing between "shoots" of *Hee Haw*, Grandpa visits with Billy Carter, center, Archie Campbell at right, and the Haggard twins. Grandpa and Archie, both instrumental in starting *Hee Haw,* were non-drinkers; but Billy, they said, took their places. *Photo courtesy Grandpa Jones*

As Roy Clark once said, "Grandpa could be funny by just saying 'hello'." And I suggest that sometimes he could be funny without saying anything, with only his expression, as is the case here. He is shown in his Scottish kilt and bagpipes with Glen Campbell who became a national celebrity with his *Glen Campbell's Goodtime Hour*. The two are shown performing on *Hee Haw*, one of the longest running shows in television history. *Photo courtesy Grandpa Jones*

In addition to his comedy routine, Grandpa sang with the most popular Hee Haw Gospel Quartet, which consisted of Grandpa, Roy Clark, Kenny Price, and Buck Owens. When Tennessee Ernie Ford was in town, he would replace Kenny Price as the bass singer.

David Akeman was also a very popular comedian on *Hee Haw*, as well as on the *Grand Ole Opry*. He wore a shirt which extended to his knees where it met his pants, creating an appearance which gave rise to his name, Stringbean. He and Grandpa were closest friends. Grandpa called him "String." They each lived on farms north of Nashville near one another, and they hunted rabbits, squirrels, and quail, and in the summer they fished. When they weren't hunting or fishing, they searched the woodlands for ginseng. They would often take their wives on fishing trips, and cook their catch at the end of the day alongside the bank of the creek or river.

Grandpa arose early on November 11, 1973, and drove up the dirt lane to String's house. They had planned a hunting trip in Virginia that day, and they were to get an early start. A few hundred yards before Grandpa reached the home of Stringbean and his wife Estelle, he saw what appeared to be a coat lying near the house. When he came closer he found it to be the body of Estelle, shot twice. Grandpa rushed to the little house and found his dear friend Stringbean, lying in front of the fireplace, also murdered.

Just a few hours earlier Grandpa and Stringbean had performed on the *Grand Ole Opry*, and along with Ramona and Estelle, they had snacked and visited between shows. The impact of this tragedy on both Grandpa and Ramona was devastating. I think the effects of the tragedy never left them.

String was a true country man and was very parsimonious. It was common talk among his acquaintances and around town that he carried all his savings with him, and apparently this talk fell upon the ears of some local criminals who waylaid and killed both String and his wife as they returned home late that night. Ironically, String had only $104.00 on his person, which the murderers took. They overlooked the $2500 which Estelle concealed on her person, and they reportedly also overlooked a large sum of cash which String had hidden in a pocket of his clothing.

I think Grandpa never again tramped the fields and woods, nor fished the Harpeth and the Stones Rivers without thinking of String. The fields never appeared so warm and inviting, and the woodland and the fishing holes lost much of their charm for Grandpa—seeing them without his old friend. The old haunts brought sadness rather than joy. It also occurred to Grandpa and Ramona that there was always the danger that these murderers [unknown for a long time] would strike again. After all, the Jones' home was just over the ridge from where the murders took place.

So, for these and other reasons, Grandpa and Ramona were on the move again in 1979, this time to Mountain View, Arkansas, where the great Jimmy Driftwood had started the well-known Ozark Folk Center. Jimmy and his wife, Cleda, were friends and admirers of Grandpa and Ramona, and he on more than one occasion had invited the Joneses to come down and play at the Folk Center. (Jimmy Driftwood, one of the most interesting men I've known, started writing songs to motivate and inspire his history students, and he became an official "National Treasure." Among the many hundreds of songs he wrote were: "The Battle of New Orleans and "The Tennessee Stud.") Grandpa described Mountain View as being "way back up in the mountains, on the White River, and it was remote and unspoiled, and it was a great place to hunt and fish."

Grandpa and Ramona built a dinner theater there in Mountain View in 1980 which was operated by Ramona and their children, Alisa and Mark. Alisa is a fine singer and a great hammered dulcimer player, and Mark is a gifted musician and is especially adept at playing the banjo clawhammer style. When Grandpa wasn't performing around the country, he joined them for the evening shows.

The dinner theater in Mountain View was well received, and well attended. Elizabeth and I, along with Dr. Nat Winston and his wife, Martha, spent a couple of days with Grandpa and Ramona there, and we attended the "theater" in the mid-1980s. It was housed in a large wooden, rustic style building where good country food and traditional old-time music were both served.

Grandpa had to be in Nashville on the weekends for the *Grand Ole Opry*, and both he and Ramona taped shows for *Hee Haw* there; but the 800-mile round trip from Mountain View to Nashville became tiring. So in 1989, they leased the theater out, and Grandpa and Ramona moved back to their farm to which they had added several acres over the years.

Here he could resume raising a big garden, fruit trees, blackberries, and even some cattle. He had plenty of woodland from which to cut oak and hickory for the big fireplace. His older brother, Dr. Eugene Jones, a retired political science professor, would often join Grandpa in the cutting, splitting and stacking of firewood, just as they had done as boys nearly three quarters of a century before.

Grandpa enjoyed his isolated log cabin home where he and Ramona often entertained the "greats" of old-time country music. He continued to cut and split his own firewood until shortly before his death in February, 1998, at the age of 85. *Photo courtesy Grandpa Jones*

It was about this time that Elizabeth and I became acquainted more closely with the Joneses, and our friendship grew over the years. My first real involvement with the family was when I contracted with Grandpa to play for the annual Museum of Appalachia Tennessee Fall Homecoming in October, 1986. But even with my awareness of the respect and admiration he enjoyed, I had no idea how beloved and popular he was until he started performing for the many thousands of visitors who were, literally, from throughout the world.

I had stood in awe of the fabulous Grandpa Jones for many years, and once my band, called simply the Museum of Appalachia Band, had played on the same program with him at Cookeville, Tennessee. We did not play *with* him, mind you, nor did we even get to meet him, but we played on the same stage, the same night. Afterwards, my band members and I were wont to brag nonchalantly that, "Yeah, we played with Grandpa Jones down in Cookeville, for the American Fur Takers Association."

Ramona and Alisa also started playing at the Homecoming at the same time, but they usually played separately from Grandpa, who had his own act. They were joined by Ruth McLain Smith, Larry Sledge, Ron Wall, and sometimes by Mark Jones, their son. They are all great musicians and fine singers. Ramona would sometimes join Grandpa, especially for their cowbell playing act. But we have three stages running concurrently, and Ramona, Alisa, and her group were often not available when Grandpa performed.

Ramona, who plays the old-time fiddle as well as the mandolin, also sings, as does Alisa. Dr. Nat Winston, who serves as the master of ceremonies at the Homecoming, and I started calling Ramona "the first lady of old-time country music," and we always introduce her thusly [others may have given her this title earlier]. She not only plays the old-time, traditional music, but she also devotes a good bit of time and energy to the preservation of this type music. At the Uncle Dave Macon Days held in Murfreesboro, Tennessee, she was chosen in 1991 as the recipient of the annual Uncle Dave Macon Days Heritage Award. Previous winners have

included Roy Acuff, Curly Fox, Dr. Charles Wolfe, and Bashful Brother Oswald.

Eventually, Ramona bought a cabin near us in Norris, and she and Alisa play on weekends here at the Museum of Appalachia in summer months on the porch of the log smokehouse, and in winter months by the fire in the Homestead House. When visitors touring the Museum hear the beautiful sounds of the hammered dulcimer, the fiddle, and the beautiful singing, they are drawn from the meadow to the log homestead, the source of the music. When they come nearer, they are surprised to find that this old-time music, so synergized with the ambience of the rustic village setting, is indeed Ramona and her beautiful daughter Alisa Jones Wall.

Ramona's upbringing on a small, isolated farm in southern Indiana was almost as Spartan and hard as that of Grandpa's early years. She was raised by a devoted and giving mother and by a father who alternately worked on the farm, as a laborer, and occasionally in small coal mines. The home had no plumbing whatever, no electricity, and of course no telephone. Ramona has chronicled these hard childhood conditions, her love for old-time music, her desire to become a professional fiddler, and her career, first on her own and then with Grandpa, in her forthcoming autobiography, *Make Music While You Can*.

As noted earlier, it was in October, 1986, when Grandpa first played at the Museum of Appalachia in Norris for our annual Tennessee Fall Homecoming. (Seen on page 126) There were a hundred old-time activities ongoing, such as sheep herding, chairmaking, cooking on old iron stoves, hominy making, quilting, apple butter stirring in large copper kettles, and soap making. There was the cane grinding mill, powered by our old mule, and there was the boiling off of the molasses by Ed Disney and his family. The smoke rose lazily, for there was little breeze, but enough to carry the pungent and unmistakable aroma from the bubbling vat of hot molasses throughout the 60-acre farm village. The bright sun felt good against the chill of the autumn morning.

Grandpa and Ramona Jones pose for this 1990 picture on the porch of the Hall of Fame Building at the Museum of Appalachia in Norris, Tennessee. Both are included in the Hall of Fame which pays tribute to the people of the greater Southern Appalachian region. *Photo by Frank Hoffman*

Grandpa started performing at the annual Museum of Appalachia Tennessee Fall Homecoming in 1986, and continued to come every year for the four-day event until his death. His last performance here, in 1997, was also the last time he ever performed for an outdoor event. The great mandolin player Red Rector, in the background, is accompanying Grandpa. *Photo by Frank Hoffman*

There were, as one magazine writer averred, "the sights, sounds and smells of rural America," and of course Grandpa was familiar with them all, and all these things, blended together, quite literally "set the stage" for the performance of "Everybody's Grandpa."

Grandpa stood there and surveyed the crowd, as a good teacher sweeps over the classroom and gathers the attention of all. He struck the banjo with a vengeance, like he was swatting at a wasp. Then the songs began. The first one was about an old dog named Rattler. When Grandpa reared back and belted out with all his might: "Here! Here! Here Rattler, here," you knew that he was really calling that old dog from the barn. It was honest, and as the cliche goes, "from the heart." I was sitting on the stage with Dr. Nat Winston, and he turned and whispered to me: "See all those people out there—they believe that song. See them looking around," he said in pseudo-jest. "They're expecting that old hound dog to come loping through the crowd towards Grandpa any time." And the people, I thought, *were* looking around as if expecting to see old Rattler running toward Grandpa.

The crowd applauded with enthusiasm, and then they rose to their feet, still applauding. "Well, thank you so much," he was saying, in his slow, naturally country but articulate voice, with an air of sincerity and humility. "You're a mighty fine bunch of people, and I appreciate you all so much." Then he was interrupted by a woman who rushed up to the very edge of the stage with a camera—a Polaroid which spit out the image after each shot. Grandpa stopped his monolog, faced her, came to attention, and stood there stiff and solemn, much to the amusement of the crowd. Then he said: "I used to have a camera like that one time." Here he paused just long enough to build a bit of questioning anticipation, and then he said, "I never could get it to work right." He paused again, and then he said, "The only pictures I ever got from a pack of film was eight shots of me loading the thing." This brought much laughter, which continued until he started his next number.

Grandpa seemed to thoroughly enjoy playing at the Homecoming, and he returned every October for the next twelve years. He stayed for all four days except one year when he left a bit early for a show somewhere with Willie Nelson. His performance here in the fall of 1997 was the last time he ever performed for an outdoor festival, and the last show of any type except on the stage of the *Grand Ole Opry*, when he was stricken.

Tens of thousands of people attend the Homecoming each year, and generally they are scattered over the extended village and complex or at one of the three performance stages. Sometimes, though, the people who stroll hither and yon sense that something special is about to take place on the main stage and they drift quietly, but quickly, there. This has especially been observed when Alex Haley came out and talked to the people, and when Brooke Shields came by, and pretty much so when Bill Monroe, "the father of bluegrass" performed. But seldom has the crowd swelled faster, looked happier and applauded more enthusiastically than when Grandpa Jones performed.

Grandpa loved what he called old-time country cooking, and he and several other folks used to escape from the din of the crowd during our Tennessee Fall Homecoming and come to our residence at noontime for dinner. I remember once Alex Haley, Lamar Alexander, John Hartford, Cas Walker, and Grandpa were here at the same time. Grandpa was usually very quiet and rather shy in a group such as this, but he was encouraged by the others to talk a bit about his career. He sort of ignored their suggestions. But someone at the table passed him a baked sweet potato and he chuckled. Then he said:

"We took my old Aunt Suzie to town once there in Henderson, Kentucky, and we took her to one of them department stores, where they have them full length looking glasses—mirrors—where you can see yourself when you tried on a suit of clothes. Well, old Aunt Suzie, she had never seen one of these, and she walked up to that mirror, and she saw herself and said, 'Why, poor old soul, you look hungry. I'll go out in the truck and get you one of our baked sweet potatoes.'

"Well," Grandpa continued, "in a little while Aunt Suzie came back and walked over to that big looking glass, and she saw herself standing there with that potato in her hand, and she said: 'Oh, I see you've already got one—I'll just eat this one myself'."

Grandpa was the first to admit that he had a "sort of short fuse" and that he was often impatient, and some say a little cantankerous. But we certainly never observed any of the cantankerous side. He was always thoughtful and gracious. I vividly remember one time when we visited the Jones' home for an annual Christmas/New Year get together, and it was pouring rain. He was standing on the porch and saw us drive into the parking area a few hundred feet from the house. Here he came, trotting through the mud and rain with his umbrella, to escort us to the house, a courtesy he extended to other guests as well. It was this little Christmas get-together, in 1989 I believe, that proved to be somewhat historical. When Ramona and Grandpa invited a few close friends, they gave no thought as to who was important or famous, but they considered only whether or not they were old and cherished friends.

But nevertheless, the modest number attending on this particular night included virtually *all* of the greatest in old-time country music. There was, for example, Roy Acuff, the undisputed "king of country music," old and frail but who joined in the singing every time someone struck up an old Roy Acuff song. Chet Atkins, called "the world's best known guitar player," sat shyly on the couch, resting his guitar beside him, a little removed from those standing players in front of the fireplace. Earl Scruggs was there, also shy and quiet, giving no hint that he was the "country's best banjo player." Bashful Brother Oswald, "Mr. Dobro Player" himself, joined in both the singing and playing. John Hartford, whose eclectic attributes in old-time music are great but whose experience and style runs the gamut, was very much a part of the singing and fiddling, but also making sure that everyone, even the younger and less known people, got a chance to "join in." The colorful old-time national champion fiddler, Frazier Moss, never missed a chance to play with everyone. When Mac Wiseman wasn't in the kitchen sampling food from the large and fully laden table, he sang his old standards and everybody listened.

Every year around Christmas time, Grandpa and Ramona would have a party in their log cabin for a few of those who loved and/or played old-time music. The songwriter-musician John Hartford, left, plays an old tune with Ramona, and Frazier Moss, former world champion fiddler, is shown in the background. *Photo taken in the Jones' home by Les Leverett in 1989*

Then, of course, there were Grandpa and Ramona. An awesome group, I thought, and totally inspiring.

As these folks were preparing to go their separate ways, I turned to Grandpa and said something to the effect: "Grandpa, I hate to say it, but I think it's true. There'll never be another time when so many of the old-time greats in early country music will ever again be together on this earth in one room." And of course, that proved to be true.

Grandpa had undergone two heart by-passes, one in 1968 and another in 1977. His hearing deteriorated and he had other health problems as well. But his showmanship never waned, never wavered—when he took the stage, he literally took the audience.

I was at his home one Saturday afternoon, out in his little workshop, going through boxes of photographs and other memorabilia. Then we came out to his woodshed where he and his brother Eugene had been splitting wood. He had an old hickory mall, the same type that every old-time pioneer and country farmer had, and he had splitting wedges and axes, and we talked about the stacks of firewood, some split and some waiting to be split, or as he and I would say, "busted." We talked about how pretty and even the red oak would bust, and how the elm could not be torn open, even with dynamite. It must have been in August or September because I recall that we talked about how dry the summer had been, and Grandpa pointed out that some poke berries were not even maturing properly. We sampled some dwarfed and dried-up grapes from his make-shift arbor.

Grandpa patiently allows me (the author, John Rice Irwin) to go through his many scrapbooks, picture albums, and boxes of memorabilia at his home near the community of Ridge Top, some 20 miles north of Nashville. *Photo by Elizabeth Irwin on January 31, 1993*

I had spent such afternoons with hundreds of old men throughout the Southern Appalachian Mountains and beyond. Grandpa was so similar to those old timers—at peace with himself, observing his surroundings, and reminiscing about boyhood days in olden times, friendly, jovial, happy.

A few hours later, we went with him to the *Grand Ole Opry House*, and as it happened, Grandpa was the host that evening for the thirty-minute segment of the *Opry* which was televised nationally. Keith Bilbrey gave a big "build-up" for the "next guest," after which he said, "Folks, let's give a great big welcome to one of the *Grand Ole Opry*'s most beloved entertainers, Grandpa Jones!"

And when Grandpa came running out on the stage, dressed in his original Grandpa attire, carrying his banjo in one hand and waving the other at the packed house, there was much cheering and applause. This 82-year-old man whom I had visited a few hours earlier was gone, and here was a "young" vibrant entertainer, reared back, attacking the banjo, stomping his foot, and totally immersing himself in his act—just the way Bradley Kincaid had taught him to do nearly 60 years ago.

A trait which Grandpa had always emphasized was being prompt and never missing an engagement, whether it was playing at The Hollywood Bowl, Carnegie Hall, the Smithsonian Institute, Washington's Constitution Hall for President and Nancy Reagan or visiting them at the White House, or playing for a rural school in Tennessee. There is one exception, Ramona reminded me. They were scheduled to play in the town of State College in central Pennsylvania, and because of traffic conditions, detours, etc., they had to call in a "hundred miles down the road" and reschedule. "That's the first and only time that Grandpa ever missed a scheduled show in the 52 years I was married to him."

Over the years, Grandpa's hearing and his so-called "short-term" memory loss plagued him as it does most people his age. But here his true brilliance as an entertainer and as a shrewd observer of human behavior was employed. He used both of his frailties to his advantage, and they became assets rather than detriments.

When his hearing first became a problem, he would respond to questions with a polite, "What'd ye say?" He detected, I think, that others were, in a friendly way, using that phrase any time Grandpa's name was brought up: "What'd ye say?" So Grandpa started to respond to almost everyone, even when he understood them, with a questioned look, a cupped hand behind the ear, and a loud but most sincere, "What'd ye say?" Oftentimes he would add to the humor by turning to a person nearby and loudly asking "What'd *he* say?"

When we visited Grandpa and Ramona at their cabin in Arkansas, Grandpa had recently bought a new hearing aid, reputed to be a much improved device. I asked, "How do you like your new hearing aid?" With this serious, feigned blank and questioning look, he drew closer, cupped his hands over his ears, and in a loud voice said: "What'd ye say? I don't hear too good." I asked him again, although he had doubtless heard me the first time, and he said: "Oh, this thing is like all the rest of them hearing things. It picks up everything I don't want to hear, and the things I *do* want to hear it don't help out a bit."

During the 12 years Grandpa played at the Homecoming, Larry Sledge usually played with him. On a few occasions his son Mark also played with his father, and Ruth McLain of the famous McLain Family played bass for Grandpa and sort of "helped him along." She is a great musician, a beautiful lady, and a most kind and gentle person; and she apparently loved Grandpa as a father, or grandfather. If Grandpa introduced one song and started to sing another, or if he forgot the first line, or if he had to be reminded of the proper key, Ruth would subtly signal him, in a way that made it seem as if it were part of the act. Well, the people *did* think that it was part of the act, and Grandpa orchestrated his forgetfulness successfully into his act. He was that shrewd.

Like most celebrities, Grandpa's recognition came in two forms: the formal honors and awards, and then the recognition and tributes paid individually by the millions of admirers.

The granting of membership into the *Grand Ole Opry* in 1947 was certainly one of the highlights of his career; and his induction into the Country Music Hall of Fame by the County Music Association was a singular high honor for anyone associated with country or bluegrass music. Grandpa compared this honor to the Academy Award, the Emmy and the Pulitzer Prize all rolled into one. He received this prestigious award in 1978, and the ceremony was broadcast nationwide by CBS. The 4000-seat *Opry House*, where this and other awards were presented, had been sold out weeks in advance. In *Everybody's Grandpa*, the autobiography which Grandpa did in consultation with Dr. Charles Wolfe, the story starts with the particularities of his being chosen into the Country Music Hall of Fame.

Grandpa was the leading character in a video, titled "A Christmas Guest," which was filmed in and around one of the early log cabins here at the Museum. He played the role as professionally, naturally, and as believably as any Hollywood actor, and the video was warmly received nationally. It was shown several times on TNN and once in December, 1998, it was shown as part of the annual *Grand Ole Opry* Christmas party and Bill Anderson described it as "the greatest video ever made in this town (Nashville) or any other town."

There were many awards and accolades along the way, but as stated earlier, the soul of one's acceptance, popularity, and love lies within the hearts and minds of the people. And, of course, this adoration was widespread.

Dr. Nat Winston, the physician, psychiatrist, and a great proponent of old-time music has a cabin on a large tract of land in the wilds of western North Carolina, near Grandfather Mountain. Several years ago, Ramona and Grandpa were visiting there for the weekend, and Nat took them to see a legendary old man named Sam Coffee. They were welcomed into his tiny mountain cabin, and everyone noticed how sparse and austere the cabin was of ornaments, decorations, or pictures. They did notice, however, that there were two rather large photographs hanging on the otherwise barren walls of Sam Coffee's little abode. One was a photograph of President Franklin D. Roosevelt, and the other was of Grandpa Jones.

When my mother was very sick, drifting in and out of consciousness, I was not sure she recognized me when I visited her one day. I asked her. "Do you know who I am?" With a hint of mischief and an attempt to smile, she said: "Yeah, you're Grandpa Jones."

My grandson, Will, when he was five or six years old, became interested in his grandparents, great-grandparents, and other ancestors. One day he came over and said: "Pap Paw, I've got a question for you. Who was my great, great, great grandfather?" And before I could respond, he said, "Was it Grandpa Jones?" It's no wonder that he is called everybody's Grandpa.

The last personal appearance Grandpa ever made at a festival was at the annual Museum of Appalachia's Tennessee Fall Homecoming in 1997. This picture shows only a portion of those gathered to hear him, and the reader will note that every eye is on this 84-year-old master. *Photo at the Museum of Appalachia, Norris, Tennessee, by the author*

Chapter 6

Bashful Brother Oswald

"One of our true American legends"

It's a most fascinating and unlikely tale, the story of Bashful Brother Oswald, and it will no doubt never be repeated in the annals of country music history. It runs the gamut from the barefoot mountain boy—who as one of 10 children had to quit school before he could read, who started peddling his father's moonshine when he was only ten, and who literally rode a mule out of the mountains to see the world as a teenager—to the person who was to play the dominant role in creating a unique sound in country music.

We'll take a look at some of the unusual and colorful events in the life of Bashful Brother Oswald [Beecher (Pete) Kirby] which occurred after he rode that old white mule out of the mountains in 1929. But first we will leap forward some seven decades to see where Oswald went after he left his isolated home near Sevierville, Tennessee, and hitchhiked to Flint, Michigan.

It was Saturday night, January 21, 1995, and the *Grand Ole Opry* was being broadcast from Nashville, as it had been for 70 years. Some of the best-known purveyors of old-time country and bluegrass music in the business, and several modern-day country artists, were there that night for the show, a portion of which was televised nationally and broadcast across the country by radio as well. Among those performing during the two shows that evening were such personalities as Bill Anderson, Hank Snow, the Osborne Brothers, Little Jimmy Dickens, and Porter Wagoner. There was Connie Smith, Boxcar Willie, Marty Stuart, and legends such as Grandpa Jones and Bill Monroe, commonly known as the "father of bluegrass." Then there was Bashful Brother Oswald who was to be the star of "everything" that night.

Oswald had started playing on the *Opry* in 1939 as a member of Roy Acuff's band. Roy was known throughout much of the world as the "king of country music," and his famous Smoky Mountain Boys created a distinctive, even unique, style which characterized the Roy Acuff sound. More than anyone else, Oswald contributed to this sound with his Dobro guitar. This instrument is similar to the common Spanish-type guitar, but its distinctive sound results because it is corded with a steel bar, and in this respect is akin to the steel guitar.

Opposite page, top:
In this two-room log cabin, located in one of the most remote areas of the Great Smoky Mountains, Wesley and Barbara Ann Kirby reared Oswald and nine other children, five of whom are shown in this photograph. The addition to the back of the log structure was built there when the family outgrew the two-room cabin. *Photo courtesy Pete [Bashful Brother Oswald] and Euneta Kirby*

Opposite page, bottom:
When Bashful Brother Oswald became a bona fide member of the *Grand Ole Opry* on January 21, 1995, he was overwhelmed, and he remarked, accurately, that: "I am the 'youngest' and the oldest member of the Opry." He had played there for 56 years, and this was his special night—and he was the center of everything. Vice-President Gore wrote a congratulatory letter, as did President Clinton, who called Oswald a "true American legend." This photo was taken backstage at the *Grand Ole Opry* a few minutes after he made his first appearance after becoming a member of the august institution. Pictured from the left are Billy Walker, Grandpa Jones, Oswald, John Hartford, and the author. *Photo courtesy Pete [Bashful Brother Oswald] and Euneta Kirby*

Roy, who had passed on in November of 1992, had been a member of the *Opry* since 1938, and Oswald had joined him there one year later. It was not customary (unprecedented, I think) for a member of a band to be individually made a member of the *Opry*. So for 56 years the popular Bashful Brother Oswald played, sang, and did his comedy act on the *Opry*, but he was never invited to become a member.

This was to be the singular high point in Oswald's career, and nothing, absolutely nothing, in his life could have been a greater honor, as Oswald saw it, than to become a member of the *Grand Ole Opry*.

I was among several of Oswald's friends who had been invited to sit at the back of the large stage for his big night, the crowning jewel of his long career. As a prelude to introducing Oswald, Porter Wagoner sang some of the old songs which Roy and Oswald had sung so often, and for so many years: "The Wabash Cannonball"; "A Jewel Here on Earth"; and the ever popular, "Great Speckled Bird."

There was a moment of somber reflection, and then Porter Wagoner brought Oswald to the stage. Wagoner observed that Nashville's mayor had declared the day to be "Bashful Brother Oswald Day"; after which he read a long and complimentary letter to Oswald from Vice-President Al Gore. Gore's home had been a few miles "up the road" in Carthage, Tennessee. Wagoner then read a letter from President Clinton in which the President referred to Oswald as "one of our true American legends."

Oswald, dressed in his customary bib-overalls, floppy orange hat, and sporting his big watch chain, appeared with uncharacteristic trepidation, and the audience of thousands leapt to their feet and gave him a loud and protracted ovation.

Porter Wagoner reminded the audience that Oswald had been playing on the *Opry* since 1939, and Oswald responded by saying: "I'm the happiest man in the world. I've been auditioning for this honor for 65 years [from the time he first started playing, dating to 1930 or earlier]." Then he said, in a moment of genuine humility, and I made note of this line on the back of a program: "If it wasn't for you 'uns, I wouldn't be nothing." He observed that he was now the youngest and the oldest member of the *Grand Ole Opry*—the youngest (meaning the newest) and the oldest in terms of his birth years, which was 84.

He ended his portion of the program by singing "Good Old Mountain Dew" to another standing ovation; and no doubt the countless others who viewed the program on television felt the same nostalgic and reverential sentiments as those in the audience.

Jerry Strobel, the manager of the *Grand Ole Opry House*, had arranged for a celebration party back stage which was attended by many of Oswald's old friends, those who had known him for so many years. Some of those who attended the informal get-together backstage were members of the *Opry*, and they, along with the other guests, said that no one deserved the honor more than Oswald, and they universally commented that the honor was "long overdue."

Although Oswald first learned to play the standard flat-top guitar, it was the banjo, and especially the Dobro guitar, for which he became so well known. *Photo courtesy Pete [Bashful Brother Oswald] and Euneta Kirby*

Oswald has played at the Museum of Appalachia Tennessee Fall Homecoming for many years with Roy Acuff's Smoky Mountain Boys. He is shown at right with the author serving as Master of Ceremonies, and Charlie Collins at left, also a member of the Smoky Mountain Boys. *Photo taken by Frank Hoffman, 1987*

But back to that little two-room log cabin in the foothills of the Great Smoky Mountains, which reportedly had only a dirt floor when the Kirby parents started their family there. I remember listening to Bashful Brother Oswald on the radio as far back as the 1940s, and I have known him personally for some 15 years, during which time he has played here for our Museum of Appalachia Tennessee Fall Homecoming each October. He was joined by his longtime friend, Charlie Collins, a member of Roy Acuff's Smoky Mountain Boys and by other members of Roy's band, and by some 200 other old-time musicians and entertainers. I had, of course, talked and visited with Oswald and his wife Euneta numerous times, but it was during a rather long interview in their home in the Nashville suburb of Madison that I talked with him in a more substantive way about his childhood, and about his early years as an entertainer. It was on January 27, 1996, that I visited him and his wife, Euneta, in their comfortable, modern home near where Earl Scruggs, John Hartford, and several other old-time country music folks live.

Well, let's see, Oswald. Almost everybody knows something of your long career on radio, your record making business, the movies, and of course your many years on television, but I'd like to talk with you about

Beecher (Pete) Kirby—before you became known as Bashful Brother Oswald. Let's go back to where you were born—there in the Great Smoky Mountains in Sevier County, the same county where Dolly Parton was born. Tell me a little about your family—your people and your childhood.

(Oswald) "I was born there in Sevier County in a little log cabin, so far back that there wasn't no road to our place. I was born there on December 26, 1911."

What was the name of the place?

"Well, it wasn't close to anything—about seven miles to Pigeon Forge, the nearest little town. Back then, Pigeon Forge was just a wide place in the road, and now it's got to be a big place. Our home was on Walden's Creek. Sevierville was the county seat, and it was about 10 miles to the north."

And you were from a big family?

"There were 10 of us children, eight boys and two girls, and I was born about middle ways. My daddy's mother was a full-blooded Cherokee Indian, and I can remember her. [The Cherokee Indian Reservation Boundary was near their home.] I'd go out to her cabin when I was just a young kid, and I'd slip in and get sugar out of her sugar bowl to eat. One day she caught me, and she put me behind the door, and she poured a cup full of that sugar, and she said, 'Now eat all of it'." (Here Oswald bursts out with his famous horse laugh which has been his defining trademark.)

Euneta said in a voice a little above a whisper so as to avoid the tape recorder: "He still loves sweets."

And your mother's people?

"I remember my granddaddy on my mother's side, and his father also. They were Irish and they had great long white beards. But I took after my daddy when it came to hunting. He knowed all about hunting, him being half-Indian."

So you started hunting when you were very young?

"Yeah, I'd go out in the woods many a morning with the old shotgun before daylight and wait 'til the squirrels started stirring, and when I killed one, I'd skin him and run back to the house, and Mother would cook it and make gravy and biscuits for our breakfast. I've done that many a time. We's that low on food.

"Then we'd fox hunt. My dad had four foxhounds: Jay, Hunter, Storm and Old Hugh. Old Hugh was the fastest dog in Sevier County.

"We'd take a big piece of meat, some sweet potatoes, corn bread, and a jar of moonshine to keep us warm (Oswald chuckles), and we'd ride a mule way back into them mountains, build us up a fire, and set there and listen to them hounds run most of the night."

And the purpose was not to catch or kill the fox?

"Oh, no. We'd listen to the dogs on the trail, and we could tell how close each dog was to the fox, which dog was in front, which ridge or hollow they was in. . ."

You know that Bill Monroe, who lives not too far from here, has always been a great fox hunter, and still is, I understand.

"Oh, yes, he still likes to go out with his dogs. I used to 'possum hunt and fox hunt with him some when he lived out here on Dickerson Road. He's about my age—just three months difference in our ages." (Here Euneta softy adds: "September 13, 1911, is Bill's birth date and

Oswald's is December 26, 1911.")

We've talked earlier about the little farm your father had, and how steep and rocky it was. How big was it?

"There was about 80 acres, and it was all mountain land and full of rocks. All of us kids picked up rocks out of the garden and from the little corn patches, and we'd pile them up in the fence rows, trying to get it to where you could plow—improve the farm, you know. All of us kids, and Mother, too, spent most of our spare time picking up them rock. When my daddy sold the farm years later, for a few hundred dollars, the feller who bought the place sold them rock to a big restaurant there in Pigeon Forge, and I'll swear he got more for them rock than he paid my daddy for the whole place. He built a restaurant out of them." (Much laughter from Oswald.)

I assume that corn was the main crop?

"That was about the only crop; and we tried to raise enough corn to have roasting ears all summer, and to make meal for corn bread. Took it to the old water-powered grist mill and had it ground. We'd fatten a few hogs on corn; feed it to the chickens and the mules; and make a little corn liquor once in a while. We'd raise them whippoorwill peas, and we had a garden."

And the children had to help out?

"Oh, I started working before I can remember—just about. They said that my mother would take me up on the hill to the corn patch when I was just a baby, and that she'd tie me to a cornstalk with a blanket while she hoed the corn. She'd put me and some of the other little kids there on a blanket, tie us youngest ones to cornstalks so we couldn't crawl off and get in trouble. She hoed all the way to the end of the corn row and back, and she'd check on us. We'd set right there all day— 'til it was time to quit— before dark."

This beautiful lady, Barbara Ann Breeden Kirby, was the mother of Oswald and nine other children whom she largely raised in the crude mountain cabin, located about seven miles from the nearest village. Oswald recalled: "Mother would take her babies to the mountain fields at daylight, and work all day hoeing corn." *Photo courtesy Pete [Bashful Brother Oswald] and Euneta Kirby*

137

Roy Acuff, the undisputed "king of country music," is shown on the right with Oswald, and the author, in this 1988 photograph at the Museum of Appalachia in front of the old "log church in the wildwood." *Photo by Frank Hoffman*

And you started to work when you were old enough?

"Oh, yeah. Just as soon as we was big enough to hold a hoe handle, or a pitch fork. Soon as I was big enough to walk good, I was helping to hoe corn."

I take it that you never went to school very much.

"No, I never cared nothing about going to school. I'd druther hunt. I'd hunt all night, sometimes, and not even go home—just go on to the schoolhouse about daylight and build a fire in the stove, and be there sleeping on a bench when the teacher got there. It was just a little one-room school.

"I was left handed, and the teacher tried to get me to write with my right hand. I couldn't do no good that way. She started tying my left hand behind my back so I'd have to write and cipher with my right hand, and that embarrassed me in front of the other kids, you know.

"I didn't learn a thing. I'd go down to the spring with the water bucket and carry water, and I'd cut wood for the stove. A lot of times I'd hide out in the woods, and I'd just show up at recess in time to play with the other kids. And I'd nearly always have to go home at the last recess to pick beans, or peas, or to cut firewood. It took about all our time cutting firewood."

How long did you attend school?

"I stayed there off and on 'til about the third grade. There was a lot of things I'd druther do than go to school, so I soon quit."

When Oswald said he didn't learn a thing in school, he was remarkably close to the truth. It was commonly known that he could barely write his name and that he could read not one whit. When he joined Roy Acuff's band and started driving, he couldn't recognize such rudimentary words as: cafe; restaurant; hotel; winding road; slow; or danger ahead. After several weeks, Roy patiently taught Oswald to read, or at least to identify the words most necessary in their constant traveling.

After you quit school, when you were eight or nine years old, I suppose there was plenty to keep you busy around the home place.

"There was always something to do—carry water from the spring, help Mother make soap, and wash our clothes down in the creek. We'd fill them old bed ticks with straw, or shucks, or leaves to sleep on; make brooms from hickory saplings, and of course, take care of what little livestock we had."

I'm sure that you didn't get any allowance from your father or mother. Did you have a chance to make any money on your own?

"Back when I was eight or ten years old, me and my brothers would go back in the mountains and gather chestnuts; and we'd take them to a little store, "Fox and Benson" it was called, and we'd sell them for 10 cents a quart. And we'd pick blackberries for 15 cents a gallon."

Did you work any for other people, the neighbors, farmers . . .?

"I got a job working at a sawmill for Johnny Mack when I was 12 years old. You've heard of Johnny Mack; he had sawmills up there in that country.

"We'd work from daylight 'til dark, and in the summer time it didn't get dark 'til around nine o'clock. Long hours."

What was your specific job there, and how much did you get paid?

"Well, if I stayed there at the sawmill of a night, and they fed me, then I'd get 75 cents a day; but if I went home and didn't eat there, they'd pay me a dollar a day. I worked as an off-bearer."

The job of off-bearing was about the hardest job around a sawmill, wasn't it, carrying off those big, heavy, green slabs?

"Oh, mercy! Yes, sir. You do that all day long, and I'll guarantee that you won't have no trouble sleeping of a night. I was pretty stout back then, but I ain't so hot any more."

You didn't have any expenses; so were you able to save most of your money?

"When I got paid on the weekend, I'd take it and give it to Mother. She had all them children, and it took every penny she could get just to keep a few clothes on their backs."

How long did you work at the sawmill?

"I worked there with my brother for about a year. Then I got a job working on a farm that belonged to a fellow who ran a store. Worked a year or two there on his farm for 75 cents a day; then I went to Knoxville when I was 15 or 16 years old and got a job in a cotton mill— The Appalachian Cotton Mill."

Yeah, I remember that big plant, there on 16th or 17th Street. And how long were you there, what did you do, and the pay—I assume it was more than you made on the farm?

"Not much more pay—a little over a dollar a day, I think. My sister Allie was living there in Knoxville then, and I stayed with her. I run what they called a drawing machine, there in the cotton mill, and I did that for about two years, and I got homesick, and I quit and went back to the mountains."

It's interesting that so many musicians of your age started out working in the cotton mills—Mac Wiseman, Lester Flatt, Earl Scruggs . . .

"Yeah, back in them days, that's the only job you could get, and it was long hours, low pay."

I believe that you told me once that your father often had to go outside the area to find work—to help support the large family of 10 children.

"Back when my oldest brother Aldon and my sister Allie were little, Daddy went to Kentucky, around Hazard, I think, and dug coal. Then he taught singing schools—went around to the churches and schools and taught singing, and charged a little for each person to take part in the singing school.

"But he was having a hard time, and he was about to lose the little farm—couldn't even pay the taxes. He went down here to Sevierville and he told Sheriff Roberson that he's about to lose his farm, and he was afraid that his children would starve, and he wanted to put up a whiskey still and make a little liquor to help feed his family.

"The High Sheriff give him a still that he had confiscated and told him to go ahead, but to not let nobody catch him. So me and him set up a still and started making moonshine."

So you became a moonshiner at an early age.

"Yeah, I's just a boy, but I soon learned enough about it to help run it off, and to help sell it for the next seven years. We set up the still right up back of the house in a big patch of briars, and there was a good spring there where we got our water. You've got to have plenty of good water to make good liquor.

"When anybody complained to the sheriff that they suspected us of making whiskey, why the sheriff, he would come up and look around, but he always went up the wrong hollow. (Oswald laughs mischievously.) Sometimes the revenuers, the government [Federal] men, would come up there and look around; and they'd go all back in the mountains looking for our still, but they never thought of looking so close to the house. Of course we always kept a eye out all the time—to keep the law from catching us."

You didn't have any problem selling the moonshine, I assume?

"Well, we had a lot of competition. A lot of folks in them mountains made whiskey back then in them hard times, and we'd have to sell it in town—Sevierville. I'd go down there with two guitar cases. One would have an old guitar in it and one would be full of pint jars of whiskey. I'd ramble around back in the alleys and peddle it out."

What was moonshine selling for at that time?

"Ten dollars a gallon for the red whiskey and eight dollars for white whiskey. We'd put the regular whiskey in a keg and let it set a while and it would turn red, and it would bring more."

There wasn't any difference in it, was there?

"Not a bit of difference, except the color. Some people thought it was better—that it tasted better, but it was all the same except the color."

And your father later had a barbershop in Sevierville?

"He worked there cutting hair six days a week. He had him a little cot there in the back of the shop, and he worked every day except on Sunday. We'd ride the old mule down there to Sevierville and get him early Sunday morning and we'd let him ride the mule home, then take him back on Monday morning. Sometimes he'd take the day off on Monday to go fox hunting. Me and him would go fox hunting together.

"We'd go down there [to his barber shop] every once in a while in a wagon to take him a load of wood to heat the shop and to heat water for shaving people. Me and some of my brothers would cut and load the old wagon with wood one day, and the next morning at two o'clock, we'd start to Sevierville. It was about dinner time [noon] when we'd get there. We'd unload the wood at his shop, then we'd buy a few bales of hay and head back, and by the time we got back home it was getting close to two o'clock in the morning again."

It took you 24 hours to make the round trip, 20 miles, in the wagon?

"Yeah! See the mules was slow pulling that big load of wood, and the road was rough and rocky, sometimes muddy. Sometimes the wagon wheels would sink down in the mud to the hubs. Yeah, it was about a 24-hour trip."

Oswald, we've talked all this time and I haven't asked you a single question about your career in music. It would seem as though you wouldn't have had much leisure time to devote to things of that sort. When and how did you become interested in playing and singing?

"My daddy learned to read the old shape-note music, and like I was saying a while ago, he started going around the country teaching singing and my oldest sister Allie would go with him and she learned a lot of songs. She'd learn hymns, of course, but she learned a lot of other songs, too, and we learned them from her."

Did you learn any songs from the radio or record player?

"Oh, no! Didn't have no radio or record player at home—never did. Didn't have nothing. What songs we

learned, we learned from Allie. I don't know where in the world she learned all them, but she could sing all day and never sing the same song—the Carter Family songs and a lot of other old, old songs.

"All of us kids learned to play some instrument—just picked it up on our own. Our daddy had a guitar, banjo, and a fiddle, and when we had a chance, we'd grab one before somebody else got it, and play around with it—never had anybody to teach us anything. The guitar was the first thing I learned to play."

So you were very young when you started playing.

"Just a kid—just a young kid. I guess I was six or seven years old—started playing on my daddy's guitar, and later on I started playing the banjo."

Did your father play musical instruments?

"He played the banjar, guitar and the fiddle—just around the house. We'd have house parties nearly every Saturday night at our place, before my daddy started to work as a barber, and people would gather in there to listen to the music. The house would be full and running over—just two rooms, you know; but in the summer we'd play out in the yard. [As the family grew, a "lean to" was added to the back of the house.]

"Mother would go to bed while the music was going on, and then she'd get up about two o'clock in the morning and go out and catch some chickens and she'd fry them, make gravy and biscuits, and we'd all eat a big breakfast, and then we'd go back to playing.

"But we'd all go to church on Sunday morning. Mother would see to that. Yeah, stay up all night and play music, drink a little, and then we'd take off walking to church.

"My mother allowed no dancing, nor card playing. No sir! But she didn't mind us drinking a little moonshine. We could drink, but we couldn't dance or play cards."

Do you remember the first guitar you had of your own?

"I remember that well. I went down to Knoxville with some folks, and I bought a little pearl-necked Regal from a pawn shop there on Gay Street—paid $15.00 for it."

The circumstances surrounding the "how, why, and when" of Bashful Brother Oswald is remarkably similar to virtually every other old-time musician with whom I've talked. In general, the similarities are that: they had no encouragement to play music; they had no training; they all learned before they had their own instruments; and most had to grab a few minutes of practice here and there during the learning process, between times when they were not occupied with farm work and other chores. Interestingly, this phenomenon, it occurs to me, has generally held true for many (most) of those who have excelled in other professions as well. This seems to fly in the face of those who purport that youngsters have to be pampered, encouraged, guided, and otherwise presented with "all the opportunities." An "analytical analysis" of why some people become self-motivated and rise above all obstacles, while others who have many opportunities and much encouragement often accomplish little, would be interesting, and I think revealing.

I can certainly understand why parents of that era often did not encourage their children to play music—why they didn't want them "fooling around," wasting time, trying to play an instrument. I experienced the same attitude from my rural Appalachian parents, even at a much later time. I bought a guitar from my cousin Amos Stooksbury for $4.00 when I was a youngster, and a fiddle from Uncle Fate Butcher about the same time for $12.00—money I had earned from trapping and from working for neighbors. And although my parents were totally and lovingly devoted to the welfare of me and my brother David, they frowned on my attempts at playing, even after we had spent 12 hours in the fields and after all the milking and feeding had been completed. There were always other matters which needed attention.

Well, tell me about when you left your mountain home and headed North to Flint, Michigan.

"I had an uncle up there in Flint who was a boss in the Buick Motor Company, and he thought he could get me a job there. So I rode our old white mule down the creek, with my guitar and a little suitcase, down to the public road, and left the mule there for my brother to bring back home. Then I hitchhiked all the way to Flint, Michigan.

"But the Great Depression came on and when I got there, I coundn't find a job anywhere. That was in 1930, and I was 19 years old, and I was on my own.

"As I said, I had taken the old Regal guitar with me, and I just started playing anywhere I could find a place to play, for tips, like in nightclubs. I'd join other musicians sometimes and we'd play at what they called house parties. That was during Prohibition, and you couldn't buy alcohol in public places, and so they'd have house parties, sort of private parties, and that way they could serve bootlegged liquor and beer.

"I run into a boy named Rudy Wakakee, and he played the Dobro, Hawaiian style. I'd follow him around to where he was playing, and watch him and learn as much as I could. I'd go home and tune my regular guitar and use a pocket knife to cord, and that's how I learned to play the Dobro."

Well, after you joined up with Roy Acuff in later years, you certainly became the most popular Dobro player in the country, and you gave the band that unique and highly recognized sound—around the world. But I guess you weren't doing too well, financially, there in Flint.

"No, I didn't save a thing. I played for quite a while on the radio there, station WFDF. I'd been up there about two years when I got word that my mother had died, and my uncle sent me enough money for bus fare, and I come home."

Then you left again?

"I stayed around home for a couple of weeks and then went to Chicago in 1933 for the World's Fair [The Century of Progress Exposition]."

Did you play music there?

"I worked in the World's Fair in 1933 and 1934 as a fry cook at Wilson's Restaurant and I made music at night. I'd fry two or three cases of eggs every day and from 50-75 pounds of bacon. I'd play in beer joints around there at night, and sometimes I'd go down and play in Joliet, or go over and play in Hammond or Gary [Indiana]. They'd have crackers and what they called fish bologna for free on the bars, and that's mostly what I'd eat. All we'd get was tips—pass the hat, you know, and get a few nickels and dimes.

"I had a young boy who'd go with me and he danced and I played. We'd hitchhike wherever we went."

Do you remember Halstead Street—the Stockyard Inn, and all that area?

"I shore do. Played many a time on Halstead. I played all over the Chicago area, and I played in the theater where Dillinger was killed, just a couple of nights after he got shot up."

So you spent a couple of years there in Chicago, then where?

"I had met a boy named Ken Houtchens who lived in Champaign, Illinois, and we played together on a lot of radio stations, and on weekends we'd play on one of them excursion boats. We decided to hitchhike down to St. Louis one time, and try to hook up with Skeech Yancey who was playing on a big radio station there. He was a great yodeler and pretty popular, and we was trying to get a job with him.

"Well, he was in St. Louis and when we got there, we had to pay a nickel apiece to cross the river [Mississippi]—just to walk across the bridge—a toll bridge, you know. When we got over there, Skeech had left out on the road, and we was flat broke—didn't even have a nickel apiece to cross the bridge back over to East St. Louis. We played there for two days, just for tips, and made enough money to eat and get back across the river." (Oswald laughs heartily about those lean times.)

So you never found Skeech Yancey?

"No, never found Skeech, and we hitchhiked out of St. Louis with our instruments and our belongings. I come back to Tennessee and soon got a job at Kern's Bakery there in Knoxville."

Where did you first meet Roy Acuff?

"My brother owned a barber shop there in Knoxville, in the Fountain City area. Roy used to shine shoes in my brother's barber shop. Did you know that?"

No, no, I never heard that.

"Roy shined shoes in my brother's barber shop, and after they'd close up for the day, they'd set down and play their instruments at night. That's where I met him."

Were you playing the Dobro then?

"Just a very little, but I played the straight guitar and sung, and played the banjar. Roy liked what I did, and he told me that he'd call me if he ever needed me. And it wasn't long after that, that he got in touch with me. I was making $13.20 a week working at Kern's Bakery. Roy'd gone to Nashville after I'd met him in Knoxville, and some of his boys were leaving him. He told me that he'd pay me $25.00 a week, and I said, 'I'll shore go with you.' He came up to Knoxville and took me to Nashville with him, and we played on the *Opry* as soon as we got there."

It is to Roy Acuff's credit that he recognized that the style, talent, and demeanor of Oswald presented a unique and outstanding quality—different from hundreds of just good musicians. Oswald was not only adept at playing the guitar and banjo, but he apparently was impressed by the Dobro sound, almost totally foreign to old string bands. The Dobro proved to not only characterize the Roy Acuff sound, but scholars credit Oswald's Dobro for helping to shape the changing trend of country music in the 1940s and 1950s.

So, when did you join Roy and go to Nashville?

(Euneta answered) "In 1939. January the 8th, 1939, was the first time you appeared on the *Opry*."

So, he paid you a little more than Kern's Bakery?

"I never did get what he offered me. He offered me $25.00 a week, but he always paid me more. That's the kind of a feller he was—he'd always do more for you than he said he would. I played with Roy Acuff for 53 years, traveled all over the world with him, and we never had a cross word. He was just like a brother to me. He'd make sure that all his boys were taken care of before he took care of hisself. He'd never take a bed of a night before he made sure everybody else had one first. Me and him usually had the same room, and he'd teach me the words to new songs, and because I couldn't read, it'd take me a long time to learn a bunch of songs. But he was always very patient with me."

When you were playing on the *Opry*, you were traveling a lot, weren't you?

"Oh, yeah, we traveled seven days a week. And we worked every day when we first come down here. Every day. We'd play, like in Georgia or Alabama, Florida, somewhere, and come back here every Saturday night for the *Opry*, and go right back to playing Sunday—back down in Florida or somewhere."

How far would you go during the week?

"Well, North Carolina was our great big state to play in at that time. We traveled there a whole lot. And we's the first ones who ever went in Florida with a country band, and we's the first ones who went in to different countries. We went to Germany and all over in there. We's the first ones ever went over there with a string band, country band."

How did your name, Bashful Brother, come about?

"That comes about when Roy hired a farm girl banjo player named Rachel Veach from down here in Middle Tennessee to join the band—play the banjo, sing, and do comedy. We'd do comedy together, and it went off great. Then Roy started to get letters criticizing him for having a girl traveling around with all them men. Didn't look right, they said.

"So Roy started referring to me as Rachel's brother—Great Big Bashful Brother Oswald." [The criticism stopped, and the new name lived on, but few people remember the name Pete Kirby.]

I guess you'd travel all night sometimes, wouldn't you?

"Oh, yeah. A lot of times we'd go from Thursday 'til Tuesday and never take our shoes off. Just have one job after another. We played in lots of theaters then, little theaters. Many times they'd run us on the stage and they wouldn't run the picture at all, they'd just run us on for one show, clear the house out so the people waiting outside could get in. We'd play several shows a day a lot of times in one theater."

So that was a pretty hard, pretty rough way to make a living, wasn't it?

"It was rough. But we liked it. We rode along in the car many of a time and our clothes would get to smellin' so bad that we'd stop at a creek and wash our clothes and hang them out the window and let the wind dry them as we drove along. That's the way we done our laundry, there wasn't no such thing as a washing machine back then. I mean a . . ."

(Euneta interjected) "A laundry mat."

Do you think all these new boys that are getting so popular and making so much money, the modern country singers, would go through all that?

"I wish they would, just one time do what we done. Then they'd see the difference. You can't get them to work for you now."

(Euneta) "Also, a lot of times you all would come in to do the *Opry* and the wives would be there with a change of clothes for you and then you'd go out again."

(Oswald) "Yeah, they'd meet us at the *Opry House* with a change of clothes and we'd just put our clean clothes in the suitcase and take off again, from the *Opry House*. Never even got to go home a lot of times."

Hmmm. How long did that go on?

"That went on for quite a while, maybe two or three years."

In this early photo of Roy Acuff and The Smoky Mountain Boys singing on the *Grand Ole Opry*, Oswald is shown holding the Dobro, standing beside Roy. *Photo courtesy Pete [Bashful Brother Oswald] and Euneta Kirby*

Who did the driving?

"We all switched off, back and forth. Back then we had two cars most of the time."

(Euneta) "Tell him about driving through Virginia."

(Oswald, chuckling) "We'd go through Virginia—that's the worst place in the world where you'd get caught speeding; and Roy'd just take his pocketbook out, lay it on the seat. Say, 'I know we're gonna get caught, so I'll just lay my billfold down here.' And he'd pay off when they'd catch him."

(Euneta) "At that time, they wouldn't take you back to town, they'd have you pay a fine there where they stopped you."

How many movies did you all do?

(Oswald) "Made eight straight, half-hour films—movies."

(Euneta) "No, no, no. Eight one-hour movies."

(Oswald) "Eight one-hour movies, that's the way it was. And we made thirty-nine half-hour movies over in Australia for television."

Roy and the Smoky Mountain Boys made several movies in Hollywood, I remember. You took the great Uncle Dave Macon with you, I believe.

"Yeah, we's goin' to California one time to make this picture and Uncle Dave Macon took his meat, took a ham with him on the road." [Uncle Dave was one of the most popular and colorful old-time country entertainers in the nation at the time, and he has been called "the grandfather of country music."]

(Euneta) "And he'd take a bucket of molasses with him."

(Oswald) "Yeah, and a bucket of molasses, little bucket of molasses."

Molasses that he made on his farm down in Cannon County, I suppose?

"I guess so. Anyway, he asked Roy if he could haul that ham out there with him in the car. Roy says, 'Yeah, I'll take it for you.' And when we come to every state line, we'd have to take that ham out and let them see what was in it and unpack the whole car. They's lookin' fer bugs and things [to prevent infestation of insects from spreading across state lines]. And when we got out there, he had eat the ham up, and when we got ready to come home, everybody was glad that the ham was gone so we could get rid of that big old orange crate he carried it in. It took up so much room and crowded us up. But Uncle Dave went to Roy, says, 'Roy, boy, would you take this box back home for me? I'd like to make a hen's nest out of it.' (Laughing.) That's the truth if ever I told it. Said he wanted to make a hen's nest out of that wooden box and we had to lug it all the way back to Nashville, 2500 miles."

Who sliced the ham and cooked it for him?

"If we stopped at a little restaurant, he'd carry in that old moldy country ham and have them fry it."

Did he have to pay for it?

"Sometimes he would and sometimes he wouldn't."

(Euneta) "Os [Oswald] said Uncle Dave would get his big old handkerchief out, tie it on, you know, for a bib, and he'd clank his spoon on a glass and say, 'Come here, girlie.' And they'd come there and bring him a pat of butter and a biscuit to go with his ham. And he'd just get up and leave. . .pour them some molasses out in a cup as pay."

He figured that was the neighborly way of doing it.

"Oh, yeah."

(Euneta) "He'd say, 'I'm Uncle Dave Macon from the *Grand Ole Opry'*."

Did most of the people know him?

(Oswald) "Out in the country, the farmers and all would, but not so much in the cities. He thought they did. He thought everybody knowed who he was."

Whose car did you drive to California?

"On this one trip Roy bought us a brand new car, and we drove it out there, sold it when we got back. He knew we'd burn it up. (Laughing.) So he sold it when we got back."

How long did it take you to drive from here to California?

"Took thirty-six hours."

That's unbelievable!

"They wasn't no freeways then or nothing, just dirt roads lots of times. We never stopped, though, just long enough to get gas, and we'd grab a sandwich in the place where we got gas. Take turns about driving."

How fast would you go?

"We'd go seventy, eighty, ninety miles an hour."

In the 57 years you played on the *Opry*, and in making personal appearances all over the world, you've met and played for many celebrities and interesting people. Even presidents?

"I met six presidents, I believe. Nixon and Reagan, Jimmy Carter, and Ford. And Johnson. . ."

(Euneta) "And Bush."

(Oswald) "Yeah, that's right. Bush. He came down to the *Opry* and was on the stage with us"

Were they all friendly?

"Yeah, they's all nice. Every one of them. President Nixon had us to play for the soldiers who had been prisoners of war, there at the White House. That was the biggest thrill I ever had, to play for our boys who had been kept over there as prisoners in the war."

There were other celebrities there, too?

"John Wayne, Phyllis Dillard [Diller], Sammy Davis, Jr., Bob Hope, and James Stewart, and Roy's bunch. That's who went up there playing."

You were in high cotton then.

"Pickin' in pretty high cotton, yeah."

Did you meet all those folks?

"Oh, yeah. They was all real nice, every one of them."

How many states have you played in, do you know?

"Every one of them. Every state in the Union, including Alaska and Hawaii, and we played many times in most of them."

How many foreign countries?

"I got a list of them up there on the wall, you can see it. About every one except China and Russia, I haven't been there. And we always had big crowds. Roy drawed big crowds wherever he went. He was a big draw card.

"Hank Williams went with us once, the first trip, I believe, when we went overseas."

There was indeed a chart on the living room wall indicating the dozens of places Roy Acuff and the Smoky Mountain Boys had played outside the United States. There were the names of the countries which one would expect, such as: England, Germany, and Ireland, etc., but there were also the names of many unlikely places for an old-time Southern Appalachian band to perform, such as: Ethiopia, the Azores, Canton Island, Saudi Arabia, Jordan, Cuba, Morocco, Sicily, Cyprus, Libya, the Fiji Islands, and many more.

"During my 57 years of making music, I met, let's see, six presidents. There was Nixon, Reagan, Jimmy Carter, Ford, and Johnson—and oh, yeah, Bush." Oswald is shown here in Roy Acuff's dressing room when President Bush appeared on the *Grand Ole Opry* with Roy and the Smoky Mountain Boys. *Photo courtesy Pete [Bashful Brother Oswald] and Euneta Kirby*

One can hardly observe an Oswald photo of this sort without "hearing" his boisterous, resounding, and familiar horse-laugh with which he was so closely identified. *Photo by the author, spring 1990*

Japanese wouldn't ever clap their hands while we were playing, like people do in this country. They'd just set there right quiet like, but when we finished a number, man they would jump up and just keep clapping.

"Well, Shoji would come to our hotel nearly every night, and Howdy told him that if he'd come to the States that he'd learn him how to play the fiddle the old-time way—"The Mockingbird," and stuff. He really liked "The Mockingbird." Well, Shoji packed up and came over here right away."

We're jumping ahead a little, but since we're on the subject of Shoji, I remember that he bought two of Roy's fiddles at the estate auction, after Roy's death. I attended the auction, and you were there also, and Shoji paid some $57,000 for them. Remember that?

"I shore do. Me and Charlie [Collins] took them out to Branson to him, and he asked us to do a couple of our old songs on the stage, but we ended up doing eight numbers, and we got four standing ovations. Shoji's done awful well out there in Branson with his big theater. Every show he does, two or three times a day, he tells about how we caused him to switch from the violin to the fiddle."

When you were traveling all over the country, where were you playing mostly? In auditoriums, schools. . .?

"In auditoriums, theaters, schools. Wherever they had a room big enough to play in, we played it. A lot of times in Pennsylvania, we played parks. Had a lot of parks up through there."

Did you ever play at Hershey?

"Yes, sir. Played Hershey a many of a time. Sunset Park, Hershey."

How about Carnegie Hall?

"Yes, sir. Sure have. They had a big show up there one time; I don't know what it was all about. Lot of times we didn't know what we was doing."

Well, running night and day, I guess it was sometimes difficult to know much about where you were and who you were playing for?

"That's right. We had folks that done our booking—Ford Rush and Oscar Davis and Frankie Moore. They done the booking over in Australia, too."

What's the biggest crowd that you ever played for?

"I guess Baltimore, Maryland, was the biggest crowd we ever played to. They was over twenty thousand. Way over twenty thousand. I guess they's twenty-two or twenty-three thousand."

Our friend, Jim Clayton, flew us out to Branson, Missouri, and one of the most popular performers there was Shoji Tabuchi, the phenomenal fiddler. He told the story of how he turned from a classical musician to a country fiddler, and he gave total credit to Roy Acuff and the Smoky Mountain Boys. He said that he went down to hear you all when you were playing in Tokyo, and that he became totally hooked on that kind of music. You're familiar with him?

"Oh, yeah, Shoji. He beats all you ever heard when it comes to fiddling. We played a week at one big theater there in Tokyo one time, and the crowd got bigger every night; and Shoji would come to hear us every night. He liked to hear Howdy [Forrester] play the fiddle. Them

Oswald and his longtime friend and partner, Charlie Collins, are shown here in Roy Acuff's dressing room, backstage at the *Grand Ole Opry*. They played as members of Roy's Smoky Mountain Boys from the time Charlie joined the band in 1966, and they've continued entertaining after Roy's death in 1992. *Photo courtesy Pete [Bashful Brother Oswald] and Euneta Kirby*

During the 53 years Oswald was a member of Roy Acuff's band, he played to literally thousands of audiences, from the little schoolhouses throughout rural America to crowds in large banquet halls and municipal buildings around the world, such as the one shown here, ca. 1940s. *Photo courtesy Pete [Bashful Brother Oswald] and Euneta Kirby*

It must have been difficult at times, just finding the places and theaters you played throughout the 50 states, getting to the appointed locations in the largest cities in this country and in so many foreign countries.

"It was hard but we never missed a scheduled appearance in 53 years, and we was only late two or three times."

That's remarkable! Totally remarkable! Some of the newer folks could take a lesson from you all.

"Roy believed that if you told somebody that you'd do something, then you'd do it; no matter what."

We were talking a while ago about some of the movies that Roy and the Smoky Mountain Boys made in Hollywood, and I think I got you off the subject. How did you, Roy, and the boys like Hollywood—the movie business?

"I tell you, we didn't like it too well because we was used to going all the time and it [the movie business] was too slow. Man, sometimes you'd set in that makeup all day and not do a thing, and some days you'd work your head off. We went up to Big Bear Lake to film that one picture, "Night Train to Memphis," and I stayed

This photograph of Roy Acuff and his Smoky Mountain Boys (and Rachel) was taken in 1943 when the group was in Hollywood making the movie, "Hi Neighbor." When Oswald saw himself for the first time in a movie, he noticed the prominence of the space between his front teeth, accentuated on the screen, and he came back to Nashville to "have it fixed." He had to sell his horse, which Roy had given him, in order to pay the dental costs. Roy is shown here, front row center, with Oswald at right and Tommy Magness at left. Standing, from the left, are bass player Joe Zinkan, Rachel Veech, Jimmy Riddle and Jess Easterday.
Photo courtesy Pete [Bashful Brother Oswald] and Euneta Kirby

up there a week and never done a thing. Had that makeup on every day, never done nothing."

Roy didn't like that, did he?

"No, he didn't like that worth a dang."

(Euneta) "When they first went out there [to Hollywood], they wanted Roy and the boys to put on cowboy outfits. Finish telling it, Oswald."

(Oswald) "Roy said nobody wouldn't know him if he put on a cowboy outfit. Said he's a country boy and that he'd wear what he brought out there. Said, 'I'll go home before I put that cowboy outfit on.' Said, 'I didn't ask you

for us to come out here, and we can go home the same way we come out here.' They didn't say no more about us wearing them cowboy outfits—just went on with the filming."

How do you like the way country music has changed?

"I tell you, me being a country boy, I don't care much about it. I like country music. What I call country music is a fiddle, guitar, banjo, a mandolin and a bass fiddle."

WSM PHOTOGRAPH BY: LES LEVERETT

It's estimated that Oswald has appeared on the nationally broadcast and televised *Grand Ole Opry* some 3000 times, but each time he brings with him a fresh, enthusiastic, "I'm so tickled to be here" countenance. He is shown here singing and playing the five-string banjo. Charlie Collins, a member of Roy's band since 1966, and Oswald's close friend, is shown at right. *Photo courtesy Pete [Bashful Brother Oswald] and Euneta Kirby*

Oswald, at right, is shown here playing his ever popular Dobro with Roy Acuff and his band. The Roy Acuff "sound" was perhaps the most recognized in all country music for over half a century, and it was Oswald's Dobro, more than anything else, which was responsible for this defining sound. *Photo courtesy Pete [Bashful Brother Oswald] and Euneta Kirby*

None of the electric stuff, huh?

"No electric at all. I don't like electric. Now, they're pretty if anyone can play one right. Jerry Bird can play one real pretty. They's a lot of the boys play them pretty, if they want to. Most of them plays them too loud and too harsh. I just like the old country style, always will."

Oswald was always quick to totally credit Roy Acuff with his success in the music business; and he was, and is, always associated with Roy Acuff and the Smoky Mountain Boys. But it should be mentioned that Oswald made albums of his own, and he earned a Grammy award in 1995 for "The Great Dobro Sessions" album, featuring a number of artists.

The sacrifices which Oswald and the other band members endured certainly extended to their respective families. Oswald had married Lola Letner in Knoxville, shortly after he returned from Flint, Michigan. When they moved to Nashville in 1939, they rented a tiny apartment for $5.00 per month. They later lived in trailers and in small houses before moving to a modern ranch-style house in Madison, a Nashville suburb. Oswald and Lola had two children, a daughter, Linda, who died several years ago, and a son, Billy. Lola, who had been married to Oswald for 45 years, died in 1981 after an extended illness.

As previously inferred, the constant traveling left little time for family life, as illustrated by a humorous but revealing anecdotal story Oswald tells. His first wife, Lola, and the children, with Oswald's prior knowledge and approval, were moving from their home on Old Hickory Boulevard to a new home on Greycroft Street in Madison; but Oswald was not fully apprised as to when the move would take place.

He arrived in Nashville late one night and drove to the old Hickory Boulevard address, entered the house, undressed, and was ready for bed when he encountered strange people—in total fright and hysteria—until they recognized the intruder, whereupon they kindly informed him that his family had moved out a few days earlier!

The "take home" pay for the country musicians in that period, the 1940s and later, was very low—even for those who worked with a band as popular as Roy Acuff's. The following story by Oswald is aptly illustrious of this point.

(Oswald) "The first time I ever saw myself in a movie was the one we made in Hollywood called, "The Grand Ole Opry." I had a space between my teeth, and when I saw myself on the big screen, it looked like I had a tooth missing. It looked terrible, and I decided to go to a dentist and have it fixed.

"He put a bridge in and I didn't have the money to pay him so I had to sell the mare and colt that Roy had give me to pay the dentist. I sold them to Bill Monroe."

Oswald is shown here performing on the *Grand Ole Opry* during his early days as an entertainer. *Photo courtesy of Country Music Foundation, Nashville*

Oswald uses a team of Tennessee mules and an old-fashioned turning plow to break ground for the building of the colossal *Opryland USA* complex in Nashville in 1975. There was likely not an entertainer nor a political leader in the state or the region who would not have considered this to be a singular honor; and the fact that Oswald was chosen for this feat attests to the esteem in which he was (and is) held by his peers and by the officialdom of country music. Also, the first musical sound of this Grand Opening was that of Oswald's Dobro, "kicking off" the "Wabash Cannon Ball" for Roy Acuff. *Photo courtesy Charlie Collins*

Euneta Adams moved from her hometown of Cookeville, Tennessee, to Nashville in 1974 and went to see Oswald and Charlie Collins at Opryland every time she had a chance. In one summer alone, she calculated that she saw their performance 103 times. She had kept a scrapbook of clippings and photographs pertaining to Oswald for several years, thinking she might some day meet him.

They did meet and developed a close friendship, and in 1983 they were married in the historic Ryman Auditorium, the "mother church" of country music and the longtime home of the *Grand Ole Opry*, the place where Oswald first played 44 years previously. Although

they didn't bother to send invitations, several hundred of their "closest" friends attended. Since that time Euneta has been Oswald's constant companion on the road as well as at their home in Madison.

By pure happenstance, the television was tuned to TNN, as I read the evening paper recently, and the *Grand Ole Opry* program was about to begin. It was January 9, 1999, and it was announced that the program was to feature a person who started playing there in 1939, 60 years ago. I knew that this person had to be Bashful Brother Oswald.

Lorrie Morgan introduced, or more appropriately presented, Oswald to a packed *Opry* house, and to the nation. Lorrie, the daughter of an earlier *Grand Ole Opry* star, George Morgan, is a beautiful lady and has an incredibly beautiful voice; and she was most laudatory in praise of Oswald, and his longtime friend and accompanist, Charlie Collins.

Oswald played a slow tune on the Dobro which he had written for Euneta; then he played and Boxcar Willie sang "The Wabash Cannonball," in deference to the memory of Roy Acuff who made "The Cannonball" one of his signature songs. Oswald had had serious health problems, several operations, and was 87 years old at the time. (My wife, Elizabeth, and I had spent the evening with him only a week before at Ramona Jones' house, where he had to be helped to his feet at times. He was not the old Oswald we all knew.)

But when he and Boxcar Willie finished "The Wabash Cannonball" with the familiar Dobro sound which made both the song and Roy so famous, the entire audience gave him a protracted standing ovation. The camera panned those thousands of cheering people, and I thought that many of them were thinking that they may be hearing this legend for the last time.

The tears shed by some of his close friends and admirers were not so much out of sadness, I thought, but because of the genuine love, adoration and empathy they felt for old Oswald. It was good, I thought, that one of the very last of the real old-time *Opry* stars was treated with such cordiality and respect.

Roy Acuff's famous Smoky Mountain Boys are shown here not long after Roy's death in 1992. From the left is fiddler Dan Kelly, Larry McNeeley with banjo, Charlie Collins who played for Roy for over 30 years, and Oswald who provided the defining sound of Roy's band for 53 years. *Photo courtesy Charlie Collins*

A relaxed and out-of-costume Oswald is shown here on the porch of the Museum of Appalachia's Hall of Fame in which he is included. He is "fooling around" with a bi-centennial banjo made by Tut Taylor. *Photo by the author in the spring of 1990*

Mac Wiseman is shown here performing at the annual Tennessee Fall Homecoming at the Museum of Appalachia in Norris in 1996. His lusty yet clear and appealing voice, coupled with his masterful stage presence, may explain why he has been a popular American singer for over 50 years. *Photo by the author in October, 1996*

Chapter 7

Mac Wiseman of the Shenandoah Valley

Sixty years, six hundred recorded songs, and still going strong

Mac Wiseman's popularity as a singer has lasted more than half a century, and he continues to be a great favorite at festivals and concerts throughout the country. Mac was, and is, a part of the development and history of early country music, and his story is an exciting and somewhat incredible one. To know the life of Mac Wiseman is to likewise know and understand much of the history and development of the traditional, folk, old-time, bluegrass, and country music story in this century.

His fame and his widespread popularity, however, did not come easily for this poor Virginia farm boy who, though crippled as an infant with polio, did a man's work on the family farm when he was a mere lad. Later he would work full time in the cotton mills while attending high school full time, all the while finding scraps of time to devote to latent musical talents.

I've had the good fortune to know Mac for several years, and the more I've learned of his childhood, of his early years and of his remarkable career through this and other countries, the more fascinated I've become with this living legend. Additionally, he's a most articulate and expressive person, and his answers to my questions were substantive, factual, and often ladened with empirical philosophy and subtle strains of impromptu humor. This sequential memory of his childhood and his career is, I think, quite remarkable.

Even at the age of 15 months, Mac was posing for the camera. His mother noted on the back of this photo his age and that he weighed 25 pounds. It was not uncommon for boys to wear dresses in Southern Appalachia, and elsewhere, until they were three or four years of age. *Photo courtesy Mac Wiseman*

Mac, the Shenandoah Valley of Virginia is certainly one of the most pristine and beautiful valleys in America, and I understand that you were born and brought up there.

"I was born right in the heart of the Shenandoah Valley, on a farm near the little village of Crimora. That's about eight miles north of Waynesboro, and just a few miles east of Staunton."

Let's see, President Wilson lived in Staunton, and Thomas Jefferson lived down in Charlottesville, a few miles to the southeast?

"Yes, that was a very historic region, and my people had lived there for generations."

I assume that Wiseman is of German origin.

"Well, the German spelling was a little different. The German is Wiesman, and I understand that our people were English. Tex Ritter told me that it was an English name, but touring in Europe, I found a lot of Wisemans in Switzerland as well, so . . ."

Are you from a large family, and did any of the other children take up music?

"No, no. I have one brother, Kennie, and two sisters, Virginia and Naomi, but they weren't interested in music as a profession."

What about your parents? Did they have an interest in music?

"My mother had taken a few lessons from the singing school teachers who'd travel through the country setting up what they called 'Singing Schools', usually in churches or sometimes in schools."

You know this is most interesting. I learned that A. P. Carter also attended a singing school, and that this experience had a great influence on his career, and on the phenomenal success of The Carter Family. And Oswald [Bashful Brother Oswald of Roy Acuff and *Grand Ole Opry* fame] told me that his father also attended an old-fashioned singing school, traveled with one, and that's where Oswald's father, and sister as well, learned songs that were to inspire and influence Oswald.

"Well, I'll be derned. I never heard that about either one of them.

"My mother learned to read the old shape notes and she played the pump organ in the little church we attended."

What denomination?

"It was the Church of the Brethren, which I think was an offshoot of the Dunkers Church out of Pennsylvania. Pleasant Hill was the name of it. Still there, still open, and when I'm in the area, I still attend it."

Do you remember your grandparents?

"My mother's father died the same month I was born, and my mother's mother died when I was very young. I'd say I was just four or five years old and I have only the vaguest memory of her.

"My dad's mom used to make her home with us some, but I don't remember Dad's father. They've told me about little things he would do with me, and I've tried to visualize him, but honestly, I can't."

And none of your grandparents played music, as far as you know.

"No. No one in my family or background played anything, as far as I know—except my mother as we've discussed."

Who was it, then, who influenced you?

"Well, at the time I just liked all kinds of music; I liked Bing Crosby, Wilf Carter—Montana Slim, Bradley Kincaid, The Carters, and Jimmie Rodgers. Jimmie Rodgers was not my very, very favorite—as he was with a lot of people. I think his yodeling intimidated me.

"My dad had the first radio in our community when I was five, six years old. We'd gather in and listen to that on Saturday night, listen to the barn dances. Not just the [*Grand Ole*] *Opry*; there were others—Hopkinsville, Kentucky, I remember had a big Saturday night show. Jacksonville, Florida, had one and WLS out of Chicago. We'd listen to them 'til the wee hours of the morning.

"And we had, I guess, one of the first hand-wound phonographs, the table model. When I was six or seven years old my dad would give me the old scratchy, worn-out records that I couldn't damage much more, and he'd let me set it on the floor and wile away the hours with it."

Was your father a farmer?

"Yeah, he was raised on a farm, but my dad was quite an inventive fellow. When I was very young he worked as a tenant farmer. We lived in a little tenant house on a farm and he worked by the day.

"He later became a miller—operated flour mills in that area."

It took a very skilled and resourceful person to operate those complex flour mills.

"Indeed so. He took a lot of pride in it, and he and his brother and uncle did quite well. My dad would run the mill. His brother Luther was the salesman, and he would sell to small stores all down through Virginia and into the Carolinas. Then Uncle Sam Black would deliver the orders—sort of a family affair."

Do you remember the brand name of the flour?

"Red Mills is the one I remember."

This was in the 1930s, during the Depression?

"Right. My dad had bought a Ford T-Model truck and he was hauling rock for the state highway department. He was doing quite well, making $9.00 a day with his truck. Then the Depression hit, and he was out of work. We moved back to my mom's old place when I was six or seven years old, and that's where we stayed—for as long as I was at home.

"My dad couldn't afford to even buy licenses for his truck or car, and he just pulled them up in the barn shed where they sat and rusted into the ground; and that broke him—financially as well as spiritually. I remember that.

"He worked out on jobs and my mom and I ran the farm. It was just a little scratch farm—sixty-five acres.

My mom and her sister owned it, and they bought Mom's sister's interest in the place as the years went along. We raised chickens and pigs and we had a couple of cows."

You learned to milk?

"Oh, yeah. I learned how, but I never learned to like it." (Mac chuckled.)

Did you use mules and horses as draft animals, or did you have a tractor?

"Oh, no—no mechanized equipment. We had two horses and I started working them before I was really old enough. My dad would have to put the harness on for me, because I couldn't reach high enough to get them on."

How old were you when you helped run the farm?

"Oh, eight."

What kind of crops did you grow?

"We raised all kinds of garden stuff, and our field crops were mainly wheat, corn and hay. We'd rotate the crops: corn one year, wheat, and then hay the third. We'd put the wheat in the mill so we'd have a bank to draw from during the winter—get enough flour for our bread 'til the next crop came in. The corn and hay were not money crops; just kept to feed the hogs, chickens, cows, and the horses."

And in the winter, I suppose that there was firewood to cut? Did you have a fireplace, or a stove?

"Well, we had both. The old house, it had four rooms, was a hundred years old at the time. It's still standing. It didn't have any plumbing in it, no electricity, no telephone of course, and it was that way when I left home and went out on my own, when I was eighteen or so. That's the way I was raised.

"Yeah, I first recall going to the woods with my dad when I was eight years old, to cut wood with that old crosscut saw. I was so small that Dad would have to kneel down on the other side of the log so the saw would run level. When we wasn't turning the fields [with the turning plow], we were carrying water from the spring, feeding and tending the livestock, or getting wood to last 'til the next day so we'd have a fire."

We did the same, pulling that big saw all day—about the hardest work I ever did; and it took some know-how, to use a crosscut.

"Yeah, you can't ride one; you gotta let it do its own thing. Riding the saw is the worst thing you can do, and it makes it awful hard on your partner, you know."

Yeah, my father used to say that he didn't mind me riding the saw, but he didn't like me dragging my feet.

I assume that you made spending money picking wild berries, trapping and things of that sort.

"All the blackberries, as well as all the garden stuff, Mom would can. But I did trap some, and sold the fur hides. I'd use box traps to catch rabbits, and there was a fellow who ran a little service station near my grade school, and he'd buy rabbits—carcass and all. I'd jump off the bus with my rabbit, run in and sell it to him for 15 cents—or swap it for some luxuries—then I'd walk on to the school, which was nearby."

What other type varmints did you catch?

"I'd catch 'possums and skunks in traps, and the neighbor boy, Junior Parr, and me would hunt at night. On real still nights you could stand still in the woods and you could hear the polecat and the 'possum moving—scratching for grubs, I guess—moving the leaves. And we'd flash our light on them, you know, and we'd pick them up by the tail live, and put them in a sack. As long as—well, you know as long as a polecat can't brace his front feet, he can't spray you. And one of us would hold the sack open and we'd just drop him in there and we wouldn't get any of that odor on us, you see. One night my buddy, Junior, wasn't holding the sack quite wide enough and I got a face-full of it. Certainly will cleanse your eyes." (Mac laughs at the calamity.)

I could tell you a lot of stories about that from my trapping and hunting days, but I won't. Did you skin them yourself?

"No, I was going to come to that. We had an old gentleman, a Mr. Workman, who lived three, four miles away who dealt in hides, and he bought our fur hides. But he, after seeing a couple of my skinning jobs, let me know he'd rather for me to bring them to him, carcass and all, because I would botch up the skinning deal. He could get more out of the hides if he could skin them himself."

Your story about carrying the rabbits on the bus reminded me that I would sometimes carry a live 'possum onto the school bus, and sell it to old Bill Key, the bus driver. He paid me 10 cents for a 'possum, if it was fat enough. And like you, I hired an old man, Uncle Campbell Sharp, to skin my skunks, but in my case it was because the scent would keep me from going to school.

I started playing the guitar, too, when I was a youngster and it seems that we had a lot in common; but your musical career, it seems, turned out a little better than mine, and I've never figured out why.

(Laughter from Mac) "Well, you likely just didn't practice enough."

Did your trapping, your chores, and the farm work interfere with your schooling?

"I always enjoyed going to school and I wanted to get ahead and not miss out; so I'd get up at daylight and plow until seven or so, until time I had to catch the bus. And then I'd come home from school in the afternoon and change clothes and plow until dark, to keep from having to lay out of school. And on the weekends I'd do the same thing. When I was 13, I had two surgeries on my leg—the polio leg, and I was laid up for a year."

You had polio as an infant, I believe you told me.

"I was about six months old, I was told, and of course I don't ever remember being any other way."

Mac described the old home of his childhood in Virginia's Shenandoah Valley near Crimora: "The old house had four rooms, and it was a hundred years old at the time. It didn't have any plumbing, no electricity, no telephone, of course, and that's the way it was when I left home, when I was 18 or so." Mac's Aunt Ester and Uncle Jim Marshall are pictured on the stoop. The cane poles in the foreground stand ready for use as fishing poles—or are they "bean poles"? *Photo courtesy Mac Wiseman*

So you didn't have the corrective surgery until you were a teenager.

"No, they kept waiting until I reached my approximate maximum growth, before they would do it. And I had a couple of surgeries that summer. As a matter of fact, I finished my seventh grade on crutches."

Was it bothering you? Were you having problems before the surgery?

"Oh, bad, bad. Especially working that farm, it wasn't no fun. It was weak in the ankle. And it was also drawn up, the leader in the back of the leg where I walked on the toe. And each time I'd put my weight on it, it flopped over. The ankle was weak, and so, it was . . . wasn't much fun."

You had to have a special kind of shoe?

"No, I didn't then. After I had the surgery I wore a built-up shoe, 'cause it's still about an inch and a half shorter."

So you weren't able to walk at all for a while, after the surgery?

"No. In fact, they did the surgery as soon as school was out after the sixth grade. Then I was home a while with a cast; then they went back and did another operation. And the first time I had a shoe on was the following April, so it must've been a good ten months or so that I couldn't really walk on it, you know."

After not being able to walk for a year or so, you were able to resume the farm work.

"Well, let me think. I must've been about fourteen when I started working for other farmers."

Making a dollar a day?

"I was making a dollar and a half, for a ten-hour day. That was six days for nine bucks."

Hard work?

"Oh, you betcha. Again, no mechanized tractors, nothing like that. I remember that Will Bruce was the first farmer I worked for, and he had a couple of huge horses, beautiful horses, and I had the old turning plow. I was quite a scrawny little fellow, so at the corners I couldn't lift and turn that plow; so I'd make a complete circle to get the plow back in the furrow, and then I'd get going again. But I worked hard. The day after school was out, when I was in high school, the next day I'd be working. I'd work 'til the day before I was to go back to school. This went on for a couple of years. Back then you couldn't get a Social Security card 'til you were sixteen; and the day I turned sixteen I got a Social Security card and went to work at a textile plant. They did spinning and weaving and such as that."

That's interesting, because Earl Scruggs and Oswald both said they worked in the cotton-mill plant before they went into music—and so did Lester Flatt.

"I believe Earl told me that he worked in the cotton mills. Well, the only way they'd hire me was for me to say that I was gonna quit school. They didn't want you just working in the summer, then quitting and going back to school in the fall, you know. So I told them, 'Nah, I'm through with school; I want to work.'

"But then when the fall came along, of course I was back in school. I worked four or five months of my senior year. I worked the third shift at the factory and went to school, too."

Full shift, full-time in school?

"Yeah. I'd go back home at seven in the morning, after working the eight-hour night shift, change clothes and catch the school bus. But it was killing me so I finally quit [the job] around Christmas time."

You didn't get much sleep, did you?

"Whew, three or four hours a day."

But you finished high school—and made good grades, I bet.

"Yeah, I finished, and I was valedictorian in grade school, but I don't know exactly where I finished in high school standings—but it was pretty good."

Let's see, Mac, we're supposed to be talking about Mac Wiseman, the great singer, but so far (and this is all my doings) we've mainly talked about Mac Wiseman, the hard working Virginia farm boy. But this has been most interesting, even fascinating to me. I've never heard about that side of your life. But now, maybe we should get to the music part. You mentioned earlier that, as a youngster, you liked the singing of The Carter Family, Bradley Kincaid, and others. You certainly have a distinctive style, even a unique style, but your singing reminds me of Bradley Kincaid.

"I guess that's the first artist I was compared to. Do you remember Salt and Peanuts? Did you ever hear of that team out of Bluefield, West Virginia?"

Now, I'm not quite as old as you are, Mac.

(Laughing) "I thought maybe you'd read about 'em. But they were on the local station in Harrisonburg, Virginia, in the late '30s, and on the weekends; and on Saturdays, they'd have open mike, or an amateur program. I'd go in and sing sometimes, and that guy was the first to remark that I reminded him of a young Bradley Kincaid."

You mentioned earlier that your father had a little hand-cranked record player. Where did he acquire the records, and who were some of the singers you first remember?

"Well, I mentioned The Carters, and Jimmie Rodgers [called the Father of Country Music]. Then there was Charlie Poole, Gid Tanner, Gene Autry, and Vernon Dalhart.

"It seems to me, well, I'm sure of it, we got most of our records at the time through the mail-order catalogs—*Sears* and *Montgomery Ward*."

And you would be hard put to single out one or two, or three, people who had a dominant influence on you?

"Well, you know the names didn't mean a whole lot to me back then and I didn't pattern after anybody. I've never had the thought, well I'm gonna sing like him, or be like him. But in retrospect, Dalhart and Bradley, yeah, and the old ballads and things that The Carters did just blew me away. I've always liked the story-type songs."

When and how did you learn to play music?

"Well, I was about—I must've been ten years old before I got together the proverbial $3.95 for the mail-order guitar, which came in a cardboard box. But it took me another year to get it in tune; nobody in that community knew—honest to God I couldn't find anybody that knew—how to tune it. I got the instruction book and I'd try to go down to the fifth fret and get the second string to harmonize with the first one. But it had a neck on it like a wagon tongue, you know, and my ten-year-old fingers wouldn't reach around it very well."

I can certainly relate to what you're saying. I bought my first guitar, a used Stella, from my cousin Amos Stooksbury, and I had to take it across the mountain to get an old fiddler to tune it for me.

(Laughter) "Them were the good old days—I suppose. Well, there was a traveling minister that finally tuned mine. You know how the preacher would go to different people's houses and eat dinner, and he found out I had a guitar and he tuned that thing. Of course I tried to keep it in tune for a long time after. I'm sure by the time he got down the road, it was out of tune again." (More laughter)

And you didn't have anyone to show you the chords?

"Sure didn't. In another year, maybe by the time I was twelve, some boys in my grade school had already learned to play a little bit, and we compared notes. One of them, David Sullivan, played the mandolin a little bit and the other one, Homer Crickenburger, played the fiddle. We'd get together and boy, we'd make a lot of noise."

So you were playing by the time you were 12 or so?

"Well, I wasn't having much luck with it. First, I didn't have much of a guitar, plus I didn't have anybody to show me, as I mentioned. And really, I didn't have a lot of time to sit around and experiment with it, because I was always working and going to school.

"So I was very discouraged, but I'm a firm believer, always have been, that Fate has a big part in your life. I don't know, and I'm not sure to this day, whether I would ever have learned to play if I hadn't, when I was thirteen, had those two surgeries on my polio leg. I was laid up for the year, and that's when I learned to play the guitar."

That's interesting. That's the way Roy Acuff supposedly learned to play the fiddle. He had a sunstroke, you know, and while he recuperated, laying in bed mostly, he learned to play the fiddle, and that's why, he has said, that he became an entertainer.

So, did your mother or father encourage you to play the guitar?

"Oh, my mother, very much so. My dad liked it and never discouraged me, never! He knew that I had a great interest in it. But Mom had almost, I'd dare say even, a burning desire for me to succeed. And the people in the community, the same thing, because of the fact I had the polio leg. They knew that I worked quite hard, and they were glad that perhaps I could get into something that wouldn't require so much manual labor, you know.

"Yeah, I'd say when I was thirteen or fourteen, after I could play a little bit, why then they would pay attention to me, and as I said earlier, I had started playing a little with these other two boys.

"We'd play at lawn parties and pie suppers. Lawn parties, they called them. They were kind of like picnics at schools and at community affairs and they referred to them as lawn parties. Kind of like a covered-dish dinner except they'd charge for attending, maybe 15 cents. They'd give us a free dinner for our picking."

When was the first time you got paid, in money, for playing? Do you remember?

"Um-hum. . . I must've been about fourteen, and I entered a sort of talent contest at a place called McClanahan's Grove, near Mount Jackson, Virginia. I won first place in the singing division, and I received $1.50. I remember that well.

"And Buck Ryan, you remember the fiddler Buck Ryan, he won first place in the fiddle contest, and he went on to play with Reno and Smiley [Don Reno and Red Smiley] and with Jimmy Dean when he became so well known."

Was this contest held in a school building, or . . .?

"No, no, just out in a field, really, a little grove of trees. It was sponsored by those folks I mentioned earlier who had a radio program—Salt and Peanuts, they called themselves. They were a man and wife team."

Well, that must have been very exciting for you.

"Yeah, it was; very much so. That was the first taste of the big time for me." (Laughter from Mac)

And you got your start in McClanahan's Grove—such a beautiful name.

"McClanahan's Grove! Now I hadn't thought of that in years, until you asked me, but it all came back to me."

But for the next few years, all the way through high school, you worked on the farm and in the factory, and you didn't pursue your music and your singing too vigorously. It was moving a little slowly, I assume?

"Well, yeah, because I never once entertained the idea that I'd make a full-time career out of music. Quite honestly, I felt that I owed my parents more than that. At that time the music business wasn't the most reputable thing to do. People looked at it as though you were trying to get out of work, if you played music, you know.

"But I enjoyed it, and worked sometimes in the summer with local bands on the radio station. There was a factory nearby, Merck & Company, which is still very big today, the pharmaceutical place, and a lot of my relatives and friends worked there. It was the best place to work, I mean as far as advancement was concerned. And again, here's where Fate steps in, I think.

"I had my application in at that factory, and the day after graduation, I went down to try to get on and they turned me down on the physical. You talk about feeling so low that you could walk under a snake with a top hat on, that's how I felt. My world just collapsed, you know.

"So I went to Harrisonburg and I was sitting there wondering 'What am I gonna do now?' And this fellow I'd worked with was a regular on the radio station—Woody Williams was his name—came around the corner. He was going to his afternoon show, and he could tell I was upset.

"So I laid my story on him and he said, 'I'm fixin' to go up to do my program, come up and do a song.' So I went up and did a song or two. And then he said, 'Well, until you figure out what you're going to do, why don't you just work some this summer with me?' So I became a full-time member of his band for two or three months."

What was the radio station?

"WSVA in Harrisonburg, Virginia. But we played theaters. His work was curtailed some because of the shortage of gas and tires and such as that. That was in the midst of the War, about 1943, and everything was rationed.

"But I still didn't entertain the thought of being in the music full-time; so I went to work at a manganese mine, in the laboratory as a laboratory assistant, where they ran tests on the ore and such as that. I'd also work there as a night watchman on the weekends, and I'd save my money. I was very frugal.

"All the boys my age, and older, had gone off to war, and of course my polio leg prevented that. There was no one around to play music with; and I was a lost ball in high weeds.

"So, along in late fall [1943], I came up to the office one afternoon and they's a fella sitting there, wanted to know if he could give me a lift home. It was four or five miles to where I lived, and I thought it was a little bit odd, but he said, 'I need to talk to you.' So I got in and he said, 'I got a proposition for you.' Says, 'If you'd like to go to college, we'll match you dollar-for-dollar.'

"Apparently there was some fund set up through the infantile paralysis thing where they assisted deserving young men and women. So, at mid-term I took him up on his offer and went to the Conservatory of Music in Dayton, Virginia, a town near Harrisonburg."

I never heard of it.

"It's just a little Amish town more than anything else. But the Shenandoah Conservatory of Music was there, and the program director from radio station WSVA in Harrisonburg was teaching a course in fundamental radio at the college, and I took some commercial courses, thinking deep down I may become a CPA, an accountant. I had done quite well at taking typing and bookkeeping in high school.

"So I took a little bit of piano and a little speech, just enough to qualify for the Conservatory, and I took that general course in radio. Before the semester was out, they drafted one of his key men at the radio station and I'd shown enough aptitude, I guess, to where he said, 'I've never asked a man to do this, but, if you want to quit school, I'll give you a full-time job in radio.' So that's how I got into radio."

Where was that?

"In Harrisonburg again."

Same station?

"Yeah. WSVA in Harrisonburg, Virginia, the station that sponsored the amateur contest that I'd won a few years earlier."

So, were you on an early morning show or . . .?

"I did everything. I ran the board, I'd do announcing, I did the news."

Oh, you weren't just entertaining?

"No, no. Did very little of that. As a matter of fact, I was working sixty, seventy hours a week for eighteen, nineteen dollars a week.

"And I'd noticed all along that the program directors were driving Fords and the entertainers were driving Cadillacs. So, after a couple of years there, in the spring of 1945, I went up to Frederick, Maryland, and formed a little band, The Country Boys, whom I'd worked with in Harrisonburg. Denver Dan Spurrier played the accordion, Rusty Harp played bass (and sang like Gene Autry), and I played the guitar and sang. We did western trios like The Sons of the Pioneers."

So you had your own radio program during the day, and did you make personal appearances at night?

"Yeah. Every little town within the coverage area of our station had what they called a Firemen's Carnival, and that was their annual fund raising event. We played for these and, of course, at schools and at other gatherings—almost every night, and we got maybe $50 or $75."

A young Mac Wiseman started out in Northern Virginia as an announcer, newscaster, and program director working 60 or 70 hours a week for $18.00. He soon noticed that the program directors were driving Fords and that the entertainers were driving Cadillacs; and that's when he started a career in music. He is shown here in the early years. *Photo courtesy Country Music Foundation, Nashville*

And how long did you play there in Frederick?

"I left in December, 1945—for starvation reasons. The carnivals and things had closed down and it was pretty slim pickin's in the winter.

"I came back down the [Shenandoah] Valley to Harrisonburg and went to work at the same station WSVA with Lee Moore. This time I was working as an entertainer, rather than as an announcer. I worked there until Lee's contract expired in July, 1946, and there I was setting there without a job again."

And from Harrisonburg?

"In the fall of '46 I received a telegram from Lynn Davis and Molly O'Day who were playing there in Knoxville, on the *Mid-Day Merry-Go-Round*. Your friend Sunshine Slim Sweet had been their singer, and he was forming his own band with Archie Campbell, and Molly needed a solo singer and Leslie Keith had recommended me and that's what prompted the telegram."

So, you came down and joined the famous *Merry-Go-Round*. Everybody in East Tennessee and parts of three or four other states listened to that every day at noon—without fail. And there were many entertainers there who were destined for greater fame.

"Oh, yes. Charlie Monroe, Cliff and Bill Carlisle, Carl Story, Grandpappy [Archie Campbell] . . ."

Chet Atkins, and The Carters?

"They had just left. Well, Molly had always wanted to record, and on Thanksgiving weekend, 1946, we drove to Chicago and we recorded 16 sides for Columbia Records. I played bass for the sessions, and I'd never played bass in my life."

Where did you learn to play?

"I met a guy there at WNOX in Knoxville, and backstage he showed me the chords and the open string deals and I practiced on it, and it seemed to have gone off all right. Now, you'd think that we would have come here to Nashville to record, but there were no studios here at the time."

I have some of Molly's things here in the Museum—from Sunshine Slim, as a matter of fact. She was an outstanding entertainer, don't you think?

"She really was a tremendous entertainer, and she had such charisma. I've said many times that the best way I can think of to describe her is that she was a female Hank Williams."

You only stayed a few months at WNOX in Knoxville?

"That's right. The radio station in Bristol, WCYB, had a noon program sponsored by a furniture company that they called *Farm and Fun Time*. We played for two hours every day, five days a week. The Stanley Brothers were just starting out there. They needed to fill another slot; so I formed a band and went up there in the late spring of 1947."

Well, that's where it all started, there in Bristol, almost exactly 20 years earlier, with The Carters, Jimmie

Rodgers, and others. Was the station in Virginia or Tennessee?

"It was on the Virginia side, in the Shelby Hotel. I sold PI's—per inquiry, they called it."

Now what do you mean by that?

"I sold products over the radio on a percentage basis. You got a percentage of what you sold: baby chicks, Christmas tree ornaments, ladies' hose, tobacco plants—you name it.

"I was not aware of it, but Bill Monroe and his boys, I was told later, always tuned the radio in on this station when they were passing through this part of the country. I had a program from 6:00 until 7:00 every morning with just me and my guitar, singing. They said that Bill would say, 'Wake me up when we get close to Bristol. I want to hear that boy sing.'

"Well, I was not aware that they knew that I existed, but in the fall of 1947, Earl Scruggs got in touch with me and said that he and Chubby Wise [Bill Monroe's fiddle player] were thinking about leaving Monroe and were looking for a job—wanted to join my band."

Two of the greatest musicians in the business.

"Oh yes, and can you imagine how I would have loved to have had Earl Scruggs and Chubby Wise in my band? But the radio station was not paying anything to speak of and the only source of revenue was from a few square dances on Saturday nights and the tobacco warehouses. So I had to tell them that I couldn't even offer them a living. I said that I was going to have *myself* out of there that winter and go back to Virginia, and it wasn't long before I disbanded and went up to Waynesboro and worked in the produce business."

These were not good days for Mac Wiseman. Although he had been extremely well received everywhere he played, the competition was keen, the hours and the travel grueling, and pay was modest. He could not have known, or even dared to dream, of the phenomenal success that awaited him in this country and beyond. For those untold millions who were to enjoy his music, it is good that he held on during those lean years.

"In the spring of 1948 Earl [Scruggs] called and said, 'Well, Lester [Flatt] decided to leave Monroe also, and also Cedric Rainwater, the bass player, so we're going to organize together and we'd like you to be a member of the Foggy Mountain Boys.' So I joined them and we first started playing in Hickory, North Carolina."

And that was the beginning of the soon to be famous Lester Flatt, Earl Scruggs, and the Foggy Mountain Boys.

"Yeah, but we weren't getting much coverage there, and our personal appearances were pretty pitiful—twenty and thirty dollar shows. Our band was getting better because we spent a lot of time with it, and I suggested that we go back to Bristol in the spring of '48.

"I knew the territory there, and the band agreed. I did all the booking there and extra work, but they decided to put everybody on equal salary; so I decided that I didn't want to go that route and I declined that."

So you were on the move again.

"Bill Carlisle was down at WSB in Atlanta, so I called him and established contact, and I joined the *Atlanta Barn Dance*. James and Martha Carson were down there, the Sunshine Boys, Cotton Carrier . . ."

And in addition to performing on the *Barn Dance* on the weekends, you had a daytime program on WSB—a powerful station, I understand.

"It was a 50,000-watt, clear channel station. Yeah, I had my own program at noontime and one at nighttime, and I worked night shows on the weekends with Carlisle and his group all around the Atlanta area."

And how long did you play Atlanta?

"Well, the *Barn Dance* ran out on Easter of '49. Bill Monroe had offered me a job earlier, from listening to me on the Bristol station, and I called him from Atlanta and asked him if the offer still stood."

In his typical, decisive Bill Monroe fashion, he asked Mac to meet him in Huntsville, Alabama, on Friday of the same week where they were to play a show; and Saturday Mac played with Bill on the *Grand Ole Opry*, and on Easter Sunday they played in Indianapolis. Thence Mac played with Bill Monroe and his Blue Grass Boys for several weeks in Indiana, Illinois and surrounding states.

So, did you play the *Grand Ole Opry* every week, even as you toured throughout much of the country?

"Oh, yes. We came back every Saturday night for the *Opry*, had to be back —didn't matter if we were in Texas, Oklahoma, Kansas or wherever, we'd drive in for the *Opry*. If we played in Florida on Friday night and again on Sunday night, we'd drive to Nashville for the *Opry* on Saturday night, then head back for Florida as soon as the show was over, to perform there the next day. We did that a number of times. It was night and day, with a little sleep in the car, and I did most of the driving.

"We'd stop at service stations and gas up, eat sardines and Vienna sausages—bologna and cheese from a country store. To tell you the truth, that's why I joined up with Bill Monroe—to get on the *Opry*.

"I stayed with him, played the *Opry*, toured the country from Easter 1949 'til Christmas."

Early one morning, after having driven all night, Bill Monroe, shown at left, and his Blue Grass Boys heard a most captivating young singer as they passed near Bristol, Virginia/Tennessee. Monroe soon contacted Mac, whom he referred to "as that boy in Bristol," and Bill invited Mac to join his famous band in 1949. The two are shown here "on the road" at an unknown location. *Photo courtesy Country Music Foundation*

Every country entertainer that I've ever heard discuss the matter has said that their greatest single ambition was to play on the *Grand Ole Opry*, the "Mother Church of Country Music" and the oldest and perhaps most famous radio program in the world. These same entertainers seem to remember with vividness and clarity their first time on the *Opry*. I'm sure that you remember your first appearance—your first song?

(Mac, laughing) "Indeed I do—indeed I do. The first song I sang was 'Four Walls Around Me' and the Solemn Old Judge introduced me. I'd rather have him introduce me than . . ."

Than the Pope.

"You betcha. You can say that with emphasis."

It's quite well known among all early country musicians that Bill Monroe, the "Father of Bluegrass" had the reputation of being extremely difficult to work for—or with. He's had, I imagine, over a hundred Blue Grass Boys, all fine musicians. So what was it like for you, working with the great Bill Monroe?

"Well, truthfully, it was an enjoyable experience. We never had a cross word, we really didn't. I've seen him give other guys a lot of trouble, but I didn't provoke him or give him any reason to become upset. I didn't have to take any 'slack.' He treated me with respect and . . ."

Mac joined Bill Monroe's famous band in 1949, and he played on the *Opry* every Saturday night with the group and performed during the week with the band throughout the eastern United States. This picture of Bill Monroe and the Blue Grass Boys, taken at WSM radio station in 1949 includes, from the left: Jack Thompson, Chubby Wise, Bill Monroe, Mac, and Rudy Lyle. Mac is the only survivor of this group (1999). *Photo courtesy Mac Wiseman*

When Mac joined *The Louisiana Hayride* in 1951, he formed a band called Mac Wiseman and His Country Boys Band. The band was warmly embraced from "California to the East Coast," and made nightly appearances throughout several southern states. Shown in this picture, taken on May 3, 1941 (Mac Wiseman's birthday), are, from the left: Ted Mullins, mandolin player from Elkhorn City, Kentucky; Joe Medford, banjo player from Clyde, North Carolina; Ralph Mayo, the fiddler from Kingsport, Tennessee; and Mac with guitar, who is the only survivor of the group (1999). *Photo taken at radio station KWKH in Shreveport, Louisiana—courtesy of Mac Wiseman*

Yes, I noticed that he was friendly with you here at the Homecoming—the last time he played here for me. Now, let's see. You left Bill Monroe in the winter of 1950-51, and then what?

"Back to Bristol where I formed a band in early 1951 and worked there a while, and then after a few months, I joined the *Louisiana Hayride* in Shreveport."

The *Louisiana Hayride* was one of the Country's best known country music shows at the time, and KWKH in Shreveport was a powerful one, I understand.

"It was a 50,000-watt, clear channel station, and it went all over the country. My band, we called ourselves the Country Boys, regularly got mail from California to the East Coast. In addition to playing the *Hayride* on Saturday night, I had a show every morning at 5 o'clock, and it was very popular. We made a lot of appearances, especially in Florida, and when I had to be out of town, we'd record it."

How long were you in Shreveport?

"In May of 1951, I wrangled a recording contract with Dot Records, and did my first recordings with them on my birthday, on May 23, 1951. Back then they didn't like to release records in the summer; so they held them up until the first of September, and that's about the same time I left KWKH for Raleigh, North Carolina."

Dot was a pretty important recording company, was it not?

"Well, they were very small at the time, but of course they became one of the major companies. I was the first signed artist they had. This was before Pat Boone, The Hilltoppers, and other well known acts that came along."

What songs did you record and how did they do?

"'Tis Sweet to Be Remembered,' 'Are You Coming Back to Me?', and a couple of gospel songs: 'The Little White Church,' and 'I'm a Stranger Here.'

"The first one was a big hit, despite the fact that it was on a small label. It was played well, and sold well across the country, and then Cowboy Copus, Flatt and Scruggs, and others recorded it for the major labels."

Who wrote "'Tis Sweet to Be Remembered?"

"That was one of mine."

I didn't realize that you had written that popular song. Let's see now—why did you go to Raleigh?

"Clyde Moody had been on the *Hayride* at the same time I was there, and he had a home there in Raleigh and he enticed me into going over there with him on a radio station. He had an old agent who was supposed to book us for the nightly shows, but he didn't. I came the closest to starving to death there than I ever did, because I was depending on someone else. Up until that time, I booked my own shows.

"By October, November of '51, things had got so slim that I went to a station in Mt. Airy, WPAQ, where I worked the winter."

Mt. Airy of Andy Griffith and Barney Fife fame?

"Yeah, that's right. And I was back to just me and my guitar, and selling [via radio] Christmas tree ornaments and ladies' hose.

"By the spring of '52 the second record, 'Little White Church,' had been released, and it did exceedingly well, and it looked like I was on my way."

Back then, I assume that you pretty much had to keep moving around from one station to another, in order to get greater exposure.

"Yes, very true, and in the spring of '52 I went to Roanoke, advertising Dr. Pepper, on station WDBJ. After that I went back to Knoxville again on WNOX with Lowell Blanchard and *The Mid-Day Merry-Go-Round*."

Well, you were really moving around in those days. It didn't take long to work an area—all the little communities within driving distance.

"True. There were so many entertainers, so much competition, that the crowds would thin down."

So, from Knoxville?

"I went to Baltimore where a car dealer sponsored me, and for the first time I was paid some decent money. I did a morning show on station WBMD from a remote studio—'Johnny's Used Cars,' it was called, and it was located on Fayette Street, same as Highway 40 East, the main artery there in Baltimore."

How were your records doing by then?

"By that time 'Four Walls Around Me' and 'I Still Write Your Name in the Sand' were out, and they were big hits. My records were getting enough play that people were looking for me, and I got a good offer to join the *Old Dominion Barn Dance* in Richmond in the spring of 1953, and I went there for about five years. Those were the best five years I spent in the business—the most successful."

I remember that Professor Bill Malone, the country music scholar at Tulane University once stated that you and your band were averaging over 300 personal appearances a year during this time. This sounds like an incredible schedule. Is this accurate?

"Oh, I'd think so. We traveled constantly, day and night, and my records were selling well, too.

"But by the late 1950s rock-and-roll had pretty much taken over, brought the traditional and early country music to their knees, you know. So, I disbanded completely and went to California to run the Country and Western Department for Dot Records."

How did this come about, you being offered this important executive job in Los Angeles?

"Randy Wood had started Dot and he was located here in Gallatin [a suburb of Nashville]. Well, he had done well and some of the big companies were impressed with his financial returns, his growth, and they wanted to buy his company—the folks from New York and Los Angeles. Every time he was on the verge of making a deal, they'd say, 'How in the hell are we ever going to get anyone to go to Gallatin, Tennessee, to run the business?', and they'd back off.

"Well, Randy was a very astute businessman, and he sold everything here in Nashville [Gallatin] and moved out there [to Los Angeles] and that's when he asked me to go out there and help run the company. They paid him two million dollars more than he'd been asking for the company back here, and they gave him a contract to run the company for five years."

You had known Randy Wood quite well, I take it.

"Randy used to call me every Sunday night, discuss how my records were doing and such as that. And one night, out of the blue, he said, 'How'd you like to come out here [in California] and build me a Country and Western Department? Just take the department and run it, and continue to be at liberty to do what you want to do yourself with your career.'

"So I thought this was manna from Heaven, as far as I was concerned. I didn't have to drop anything I was doing, and at the same time I just learned a whole new facet of the business. It gave me so much more 'in' with people.

"When I started doing albums, it was sort of a new concept. By the time the major stars started doing albums, I had already recorded four or five albums.

While Mac Wiseman is best known for the more than 600 songs he has recorded, the many songs he has written, and for his personal performances before untold millions, he, unlike most entertainers, was also an executive in the music industry. He was one of the original founders of the now famous Country Music Association (CMA), and he was on the Board of Directors and served as the first secretary of the organization. He was also an executive with Dot Recording Co. Mac is shown here signing a contract. Standing at left is George W. Bland, General Sales Manager of radio station WWVA, and on the right is J. Ross Felton, General Manager of WWVA. *Photo courtesy Country Music Foundation, Nashville*

"But it was frustrating for the country and western music during this time—in 1956 and through that period when Cash and Presley became so big—just knocked the traditional country music folks out of the water. Virtually all radio stations just quit playing country."

So you had a big responsibility, deciding whom Dot would record, in both the country and western fields.

"That's right, but I had retained the right to continue performing, which I did—when it didn't interfere with my job with Dot. I'd come to Nashville on business, and I'd go into New York, Philadelphia, Cincinnati and other places to check with distributors, and I'd schedule some appearances along the way occasionally."

Of course everyone remembers how Elvis Presley just captivated the country, but Johnny Cash was also immensely popular—on network television as well as on radio and records.

"Oh, indeed. In fact, I think I'm correct on this, the first tour Johnny Cash ever did was the one he did with me in Florida."

Your offices in California were in Los Angeles?

"Yes, right in Hollywood, at Sunset and Vine. As a matter of fact, when Capitol built the tower, we moved into their old Capitol headquarters building. When I was there, I met a lot of people, and it was a most interesting experience."

When and why did you leave Hollywood?

"I had moved to Nashville while I was still working for Dot and opened up a branch, and I ran my department from here in Nashville—did my production here and sent the masters to California for release, much like Chet Atkins was doing for RCA, except he sent his masters to New York.

"I stayed with Dot until 1963, I guess, and then the Beatles just blew everything out of the water, country-wise I mean."

And the radio stations essentially stopped playing country music.

"There had been, I guess, 1500 radio stations that were devoted totally or in part to country music, but by 1958 the number was down to 150. Today there's in excess of 2500 that are playing country.

"I could sign anybody that I chose to record with Dot, but if you couldn't get the country air play, that's where it stopped.

"Buck Owens came to my office in Hollywood once, and wanted me to record him. I said, 'If I do, you'll be coming back in six months, mad at me because nothing happened'."

Mac, I understand that you were instrumental in establishing the most popular and successful Country Music Association [the trade organization for the industry and which most people will associate with its annual CMA Awards which are publicized nationally].

"In 1958 a group of us each tossed $100 in the hat and started the CMA. I was the first secretary, as well as being on the board of directors.

"Incidentally, the CMA had its 40th Anniversary in October, 1998, which I attended at the arena here in Nashville. During the evening a two-hour television special was taped for air on CBS November 28, 1998. At that time CMA recognized the five remaining members of the original board, namely Charlie Lamb, Dee Kilpatrick, Ken Nelson, Eddy Arnold and myself."

So after you gave up the executive job with Dot in 1963, what was the next phase of your career?

"Well, this Hootenanny thing was coming along, you know, and my country music repertoire from the '50s was being picked up and used again, so I had another ride out of it in the folk area. I was playing places like the Newport Folk Festival, the Philadelphia Folk Festival, Carnegie Hall, Marirosa Folk Festival in Toronto, the Hollywood Bowl, and Rice University in Houston. . ."

So you were playing to more and larger audiences than ever?

"Definitely!"

Was this about the time you started playing for the colleges?

"That started more in the late '60s and on into the '70s. Even before this started I had five or six albums and I wrote to every college bookstore and every radio station in the United States and offered them free albums, and a lot of them asked for my folk albums or my bluegrass albums.

"I went to Wheeling, West Virginia, in 1966 and ran the Wheeling Jamboree there until 1970, and my records with RCA were doing pretty good, and I decided to come back to Nashville."

So, during the 1960s you were making records and personal appearances. How many songs have you recorded?

"Well over six hundred. There's over fifty albums out and I don't know how many singles."

That's amazing. I thought I had all your recordings, but I can see that I have a long way to go. Your songs, more than almost anyone else's I know, have a lasting quality about them. I never tire of hearing them, especially the old ballads. They're like corn bread. I can have it every day, twice a day, and never get burned out on it. Now, enough of this. You've played the entire country, I believe.

"I've played in every state, except Hawaii, and of course many of the states I've played many, many times."

Then you made Alaska.

"Oh, yeah. Played Alaska many times."

And you played Europe?

"Back in the 1950s I played there a lot. They tell me that I had the first bluegrass record ever released in Europe: 'Footprints in the Snow.' They first released it in England; my version, not the Monroe version."

That's most interesting. Hugh Cross, an old friend of mine who lived down the road from me, wrote that song. He once told me the story of how he came to write "Footprints in the Snow." He left his home in the community of Oliver Springs, Tennessee, heading for a job he had in Hammond, maybe Gary, Indiana. Soon after he passed through Jellico and into Kentucky, his car stalled in a snow storm. As he sat there pining over his girl back home, as he watched the snow falling, piling higher and deeper, he wrote this classic song. That was one of Bill Monroe's most requested numbers, he told me, and I'm sure it was for you.

"Well, I sang it thousands of times, but I never knew the story behind it."

I wouldn't know how to characterize your music—folk, traditional, early country, bluegrass—which is it, or all the above?

"Well, I've recorded all different styles. I did a record with Woody Herman a few years ago, 'My Blue Heaven,' and it did pretty well in the charts, but a lot of stations wouldn't play it because they said I was a bluegrass singer, and they didn't play bluegrass music. I've done western swing, and one of my very biggest numbers was 'Love Letters in the Sand' and that was an old pop song."

This publicity photograph of Mac was widely released and distributed throughout the country by Mac Wiseman Enterprises of Nashville. *Photo courtesy Mac Wiseman*

Mac Wiseman is shown here singing for Bill Monroe's *Earlybird Bluegrass Show* during Nashville's popular Fan Fair in June, 1978. *Photo by and courtesy of Les Leverett*

Bill Malone characterized you as "the best solo singer in bluegrass," and he's considered to be "the authority." I totally agree. But even so, you've never considered yourself "only" a bluegrass singer. You've also been embraced by the folk music people, the traditional country folks, and, as you indicated earlier, you've delved over into other types of music. Maybe that's why you've managed to stay active and busy in the music business for over half a century, and you're still recording and have an active following. What has it been like for you the last several years? I know that I see your name in connection with the outdoor festivals

quite often. That's been a big thing for you over the past 20 or 25 years?

"Yeah, and actually the festival concept has been the preservation of the old-time music and bluegrass music, to be honest with you. Carlton Haney came up with this concept of the festivals in the early '60s. He used to call me, just bug me to death. He couldn't—he knew what he wanted but he couldn't put it in perspective. And the best way he could describe it was to compare it to the Boy Scouts Camporee that they had in Pennsylvania, you know? And that's what he was talking about. Said if we could just have three days of nothin' but bluegrass, where people could bring their campers and their trailers, and cook out and visit."

Where is he from?

"He's from Reidsville, North Carolina. And anyhow, he kept calling me, and he had the first festival in the fall of '65 at Fincastle, Virginia, just out of Roanoke, out on a horse farm. I was on it, and I think he only had fifteen trailers or something, campers or whatever.

"But he built it from that. And really, if it wasn't for that, a lot of people like me would be out of business, because that's about the majority—I'd say that's ninety-five percent—of my venues."

Are they still going strong, the festivals?

"Very good. It's just like the survival of the fittest of anything; the ones that are being treated like a business and promoted properly are doing well. A fellow called me yesterday from Oklahoma; this'll be my twentieth consecutive year with him. Yeah, and over twenty-five years in Myrtle Beach. I've been doing them in Myrtle Beach every Thanksgiving. This was the twenty-sixth year, last year was.

"I ran one in Renfro Valley for 13 years, just once a year—from 1970 until 1983."

Well, as you know, we have a very large attendance at the annual Museum of Appalachia Tennessee Fall Homecoming each year, 250 entertainers, and you consistently are among the top two or three most popular singers. If I brag on you enough maybe you'll reduce your fee. (Mac laughs boisterously.)

"I didn't know we could get much lower. Well, in all sincerity, the highlight of my year, every year, is playing for your Tennessee Fall Homecoming. I've said this so much that it's beginning to sound like a testimonial. With all the old-time activities, and the cross section of entertainers, it's so genuine, and I don't know of any place—there is no other place like it."

It was a bright October morning when Mac took the stage at the annual Tennessee Fall Homecoming in Norris, Tennessee; but the crowd started to gather quickly when they heard the smooth, robust, and distinctive voice of Mac Wiseman. *Photo by the author in 1993*

Well, you're an important part of Homecoming. We have tens of thousands of people who attend from all over, from every state and from some 50 or more foreign countries every year, and nobody has been more popular over the years than the great Mac Wiseman.

And you continue to be very active, don't you?

"At this time [November, 1998] I'm in good health, but I've reduced my touring schedule to approximately 35 concerts annually, but I'm still recording several packages each year to sell at my shows and by mail order. I'm on the board of directors for several charitable organizations here in Nashville, and I'm threatening to write my autobiography."

That would be great, because we've hardly touched the surface of your varied and fascinating life here. You've probably saved all the good stuff for your book. (Mac laughs, but doesn't respond.)

When I think of Mac Wiseman, the image which invariably comes to mind is that of a robust and rugged figure sitting on his special stool singing for an attentive audience of thousands of admiring fans. He always has that wide smile, really a grin, and a twinkle in his eyes; and his appearance suggests something of a cross between Burl Ives and Santa Claus. His stage presence and his charisma are inimitable.

Not only does Mac retain his "old" following, but he's constantly acquiring new fans. Although he's performed with some of the country's best known entertainers, such as Bill Monroe, Earl Scruggs, Elvis Presley, Johnny Cash, and a hundred more, Mac is somewhat of a loner, and that's likely the way it should be. I've heard him with many great bands, but what I remember, like, and savor the most is Mac Wiseman sitting there on his stool with his guitar, singing a timeless old ballad, with ten thousand people mesmerized by that simplistic combination.

It matters not whether one is in the mood for old-world ballads, early country, folk, traditional, waltzes, bluegrass, or even the blues—Mac can oblige.

Although he's not associated with the singing of gospel and old hymns, Mac has certainly been here also. When he sings "In the Sweet By and By," I'm taken back to the little country church at Robertsville, and I can see my venerable grandfather and the angelic face of Granny Irwin—gathered there with all our kith and kin. When he sings "Shall We Gather at the River?", I'm taken back to old-time Baptisms by mountain streams, and when I hear Mac sing "I Shall Not Be Moved," I always think of my mother and father singing that old song as we rode along a winding dirt road in our 1936 Chevrolet—on our way to have Sunday dinner with Granny and Grandpa Rice.

When we travel by automobile today, my wife Elizabeth may forget our luggage, but she's never failed to take a bag of Mac Wiseman's tapes because he is her very favorite singer. Mac has been our companion in song, hours on end, as we have driven through much of the country; and by listening to his songs, even the meadows, the mountains, and the villages look more beautiful.

Mac Wiseman is not just a great singer—he's a moving and inspirational purveyor of feeling—bringing forth the most cherished emotions from the inner souls of those upon whose ears his lusty, yet clear and inspiring voice may fall.

His singing is as beautiful as that picturesque region from whence he came—the great and beautiful Shenandoah Valley of Virginia. And the story of his rise against multitudinous obstacles as a poor crippled farm boy to a person of such prominence parallels the story of America, and it conveys much meaning and understanding not only in relation to music, but also relative to the residual of the pioneer spirit of our people and our country.

Earl Scruggs, at left, and Mac are shown here in 1996 in front of Grandpa Jones' fireplace playing and singing an old ballad as they did a half century earlier, when they started playing as The Foggy Mountain Boys. *Photo taken by the author*

This photograph of Earl Scruggs playing on the *Grand Ole Opry* shows the use of the thumb pick and the two finger picks used in the famous "three-finger style" of picking for which he became so famous. *Photo taken May 22, 1971, by and courtesy of Les Leverett*

Earl is shown at his desk at the two-room school he attended in Flint Hill, North Carolina. At this time, at age six, he was playing the guitar with his brothers for square dances every week. *Photo courtesy Earl and Louise Scruggs*

Chapter 8

Earl Scruggs—the Man,
the Musician, and the Folk Hero

**"Bluegrass music, as we know it today, started when Earl Scruggs
walked on the stage of the *Grand Ole Opry* with Bill Monroe."**

Earl Scruggs! Perhaps no person in bluegrass or country music is more revered and more respected than this quiet and totally unpretentious man from a small farm in the Piedmont area of western North Carolina. Bill Monroe, with whom Earl worked from December, 1945, until the last part of January, 1948, is called the "the father of bluegrass." But scholars on the subject, fellow musicians, and astute observers alike, agree that without Earl Scruggs there would have been no bluegrass music as we know it today.

It's likely that eighty to ninety percent of the people in America, either by design, or unwittingly, have heard the unique banjo playing of Earl Scruggs at one time or another. (We will address this claim later.) His phenomenal success in helping to establish the "bluegrass sound" and his important roll in ushering in the national folk music movement a quarter of a century later in the 1960s are legendary.

Much has been written about Earl Scruggs, the musician, but not so much is known about Earl Scruggs, the man—his childhood, his upbringing, and those stark conditions of which he was a part and by which he was to be so profoundly affected. How was it that this poor country farm boy would become a sort of national hero, first to those of an earlier generation who loved old-time music, and later to the youth and college students of America and abroad?

I had met Earl and his wife and manager, Louise, on several occasions, principally when we attended little get-togethers at the remote log home of Grandpa and Ramona Jones a few miles north of Nashville. We'd meet there, usually around Christmas, with a dozen or so couples, mostly musicians of present or past national fame, such as Roy Acuff, Chet Atkins, Bashful Brother Oswald, John Hartford, Mac Wiseman, and Marty Stuart. We'd sit around a big open fire, which Grandpa kept going, and listen to these old-time greats of country and bluegrass music converse. But that, of course, was not the time nor the place to try to interview anyone.

Dr. Nat Winston, the Nashville physician-psychiatrist and a great proponent of this type music, has for many years been one of Earl's closest friends, and for a long time they were next-door neighbors. Since Nat is one of our closest friends, and has been so for many years, he was able to arrange an interview with Earl.

We spent the night of January 20, 1995, with Nat and Martha, and on the following day Nat led Elizabeth and me across Nashville to Earl's large ranch-style home in Madison, a suburb north of Nashville. I knew that Earl and Louise seldom gave interviews anymore and that they had agreed to allow me to invade the serenity of their private lives largely because of their fondness for Nat. At first I felt the atmosphere was a little strained and formal. But this changed quickly once we started talking about Earl's boyhood days and his back-home memories of that rural, depression-plagued section of North Carolina. Earl talked freely and enthusiastically, and he seemed to delight in going back to his childhood. Those few hours of talking with Earl Scruggs were memorable, interesting, and revealing.

Earl, I understand that you are from a place in North Carolina called Flint Hill.

(Earl) "Yes, that was down in Cleveland County, not far from South Carolina. The only thing in Flint Hill was a church and a school, located on the hill, and the land actually had a lot of flint-type rock there, and I suppose that's how it got its name. We lived in the Flint Hill community, but our address was Shelby, Route 3. Flint Hill is approximately six miles from Shelby. We later moved to Boiling Springs. After I went to work at the Lily Thread Mill, I bought a house in Shelby, North Carolina."

You were born on a farm in what year?

"I was born on a little farm on January 6, 1924. My daddy died when I was only four years old, and I, of course, just barely remember him."

Your father was a farmer?

"He did a little bookkeeping work, but his first love was farming."

Tell me, who was the first person you ever heard play music?

"Well, I can't say that I remember it, but my brother Horace, who was two years older than me, always said that Daddy would come into our room every morning and wake us up by playing the banjo. So, I guess that he was the first person I ever heard play the banjo, though I can't say that I remember it."

Home' on the banjo, and I was so impressed that he could move his fingers so fast and note the banjo, him being blind like he was."

So you started playing when you were quite young?

"Well, members of my family said that I was playing when I was four or five years old. But we had to work on the farm most of the time, and I'd pick the banjo every time I had a chance. We would sometimes go to visit relatives or friends on Sunday. I would want to play the banjo and the lady at one of the places we visited said I should not play the banjo on Sunday. It probably got on her nerves and she did not want to hear it. So I told her I would just play hymns. That is what I did when I was in her presence."

On rainy days, when they couldn't work on the farm and especially on cold winter nights, Earl, at left, and his brother Horace would play music together for "hours on end." Earl recalls that: "We spent many happy hours picking away on the banjo and the guitar." *Photo courtesy Earl and Louise Scruggs*

Earl started playing his brother's banjo long before he could hold it, necessitating him to rest it on the floor or the ground, as is shown, at right. His older brother Horace is shown playing the guitar. *Photo courtesy Earl and Louise Scruggs*

Did other members of the family play?

"Yes, my mother played an organ, and my two sisters and two brothers all played the banjo and guitar. There was also an old autoharp at home that we played some."

I suppose that you listened to the radio as you were growing up, the *Grand Ole Opry* and such.

"No, we didn't have a radio or a record player when I was young. I think I was 15 years old before we ever got a radio, and I remember that one of us boys would have to go out in the yard and move the antenna around until we picked up a station."

Do you remember hearing any old-time musicians when you were a boy?

"I was over at my uncle's one time and I heard a blind man named Mack Woolbright play the banjo. I remember seeing him sitting there in a chair playing 'Home Sweet

It's always been interesting to me that virtually all successful musicians (and other successful people as well) seem to have been almost totally self-motivated. And conversely, those who were given lessons, educated, encouraged, and provided other opportunities often never acquired that obsessive drive and the perseverance necessary to succeed. I was interested in knowing what motivated Earl Scruggs, as a youngster, to play music. His comments were most interesting and revealing. Basically, no one seemed to have encouraged him to play, and he was just grateful and appreciative that no one stood in his way. This supposition is evidenced in Earl's comments relative to his mother, whom he obviously admired very much.

"My mother never said anything to discourage my picking. One day I was playing 'Step It Up and Go' and I got to playing it a little fancy, sort of jazzing it up, and my mother heard me. She said, 'Son, if you're going to pick, pick it where you can tell what the tune is.' [Many banjo players play in chords and concentrate on fancy and innovative styles and often do not emphasize the melody.]

"I've always remembered what my mother said, and all through the years, anywhere I was playing, I always tried to play any song so that my mother could have told what it was if she had heard it."

That one off-the-cuff passing comment made by Earl's mother, unlikely as it seems, apparently influenced his style throughout his career, and it strongly affected a whole style of music throughout the country.

I gathered that Earl's oldest brother, Junie, was a sort of father figure to him, and that Earl's desire, perhaps unconsciously, was to please and impress him, the way young boys often do with older brothers. But rural people are often not wont to pass out compliments, no matter how pleased they may be. My own father was like that.

During the course of our conversation, Earl casually alluded to his relationship with Junie: "Junie never gave me a compliment. One day he was coming up the road toward the house, and I was on the porch playing 'Reuben' on the banjo. This was on Saturday afternoon, the first weekend after I first learned I could play the three-finger style. I was really getting with it and I could see Junie was listening. He sort of cocked his head sideways, like he was trying to figure out how I was playing the way I was, but he never said anything about whether he liked it or not.

"Years later, after Junie had been hearing me play on radio and on records, I was over to his house and he asked me to show him how I played that three-finger roll."

Even at that late juncture, Earl seemed pleased and honored that his brother in his own non-demonstrative kind of way, had finally paid him a compliment.

I'm sure you expect me to ask you about your most famous style of playing the banjo—the three-finger roll, they call it.

"We had a cow that we kept tied out around the yard, and we'd move her from one place to another so she could eat the vines, weeds, and grass. It served two purposes. It got rid of all the undergrowth, and at the same time it provided food for her—made her give a little more milk. One day my brother Horace and I were arguing, not getting along too well, and Mother sent me, in order to separate us, out to untangle the old cow and move her down along the side of the road to where there was more weeds and stuff for her to eat. I was very young and that made me sorta mad, and when I came back in the house, I picked up the banjo—sort of pouting, and I just started playing without concentrating. I was playing 'Reuben' and all of a sudden I realized that I was playing with three fingers. I was afraid to stop, afraid I couldn't remember how to do it again. I must have played it for half an hour. But after I did stop, my brother, Horace, said I came running out of the room yelling, 'I've got it! I've got it! I can play with three fingers!' He remembers that he said, 'Let me get the guitar and we will see what you have got'."

You're given credit for "inventing" the three-finger roll and paving the way for bluegrass music, as we know it. Where did the idea come from?

"There was a fellow named Smith Hammett who lived near us, and he played a three-finger style. I heard him play when I was three or four years old, and I thought it was the prettiest playing I ever heard. Then later I heard a man named Snuffy Jenkins, a pretty well-known banjo player in the area, who played that three-finger style."

The three Scruggs brothers are shown here in front of their unpainted farm home near Flint Hill, North Carolina. Interestingly, Earl is shown, at left, playing the fiddle, while his brother Junie plays the banjo, and Horace, the guitar. *Photo courtesy Earl and Louise Scruggs*

According to Earl Scruggs, Smith Hammett, center, was perhaps the very first person to use the three-finger style of picking the banjo, and one who had much influence on the young Earl Scruggs. The father of nine children, Hammett was killed in 1930 at the age of 43. The fiddler in the picture is John Ross, and the jug player is Brooker Self. *Photo courtesy of Earl and Louise Scruggs*

After your father died, leaving your mother with five young children, I suppose that most of your time was spent working on the farm?

"Yeah, after my oldest brother and sisters left home, Horace and I did the farming. We had 40 acres and only one old mule to work it with."

Earl spoke kindly, almost reverently, when he recalled the faithful old mule of his boyhood days, and it prompted me to pursue the subject.

Earl, I realize that it's been well over half a century since you plowed that old mule, but do you remember her name?

He responded quickly and with amusement: "Maude! Old Maude! She saved my life many times. I remember once I was riding down a steep hill with her pulling the wagon. The belly band broke, the wagon was about to tumble off that hill with me in it, but Old Maude stopped immediately, and kept us from wrecking."

Two years after this interview, I was talking with Earl again in his home, and I mentioned Old Maude to him, whereupon he recalled that they had had a *team* of mules, and that one, Old Kate, foundered on young cane and died, leaving only the one mule, Old Maude.

I take it that most of the farming and gardening was devoted to raising food for the family, and that there was very little money coming in?

"That's right. We tried to keep two cows so that when one went dry, we'd have one that would still be giving milk. What little milk we could spare we'd separate for the cream. We had an old cream separator that we'd use. A truck would come by every two or three days and pick up that little bit of cream we had."

Once your family got a radio, who were some of the people whom you liked?

Earl answered forthrightly and spontaneously—almost as if he had been expecting my question: "Maybelle." [He didn't give her last name, and indeed he didn't need to. Everyone who knows anything about early country music knows that Maybelle is "Mother Maybelle Carter," a member of the famous Carter Family which, as I've noted in Chapter 2, was often suggested to have been the most influential musical family in the country.]

"Maybelle was just my hero. She had a great influence on me. I wanted to play some of Maybelle's songs, so I started playing the guitar some. But the banjo was always my first love. Horace played a good guitar, and he could back me up.

"Years later she worked with us, and we traveled around the country together, and she'd talk about how she got started, back in the country in Virginia."

When Mother Maybelle died in October, 1978, the family requested that Earl play one of the favorite old Carter Family songs at her funeral. The song was "You Are My Flower" and both Maybelle and the Foggy Mountain Boys had immortalized it on the guitar. When Maybelle's daughter, Helen, died in 1998, Johnny Cash, Maybelle's son-in-law by virtue of having married June Carter, asked Earl to play that same beautiful song on the guitar at Helen's funeral, which he did.

How old were you when you started playing on the radio—in Gastonia, North Carolina, I believe?

"I was 15 or 16 years old. I was playing with a group called The Carolina Wildcats."

It seems like you had to squeeze your banjo playing in between working on the farm and various household chores, and I know you started working in the thread mill at an early age. Tell me about that.

"I started working in the Lily Mill when I was around 18 years old, at 40 cents an hour. The mill made sewing thread. I worked 12 hours a day, six days a week—go in every night at six o'clock and get off at six o'clock the next morning. I'd work 'til midnight Saturday and then start back at midnight on Sunday night. That way, I got in 72 hours a week. I worked there for almost four years, and I left in 1945."

That didn't give you any time to practice the banjo, when you were working in the mill?

"No. After working 12 hours in the mill, you didn't feel much like playing."

If there were no Earl Scruggs today, who would be the most outstanding banjo player in the country? (Of course I knew Earl wouldn't give me an answer, but I was curious as to what his response would be.)

"I can't help you out there," he chuckled. "I don't know." Then after a moment of silence his wife, Louise, responded in a low, soft voice, almost as if she were talking to herself, something to the effect: "If there hadn't been an Earl Scruggs, there probably wouldn't be any banjo players today."

This reminded me of the oft-stated comment to the effect that musical instrument manufacturing companies in this country had stopped making five-string banjos before the era of Earl Scruggs. I asked him about this.

"I went to the Gibson factory in 1946 and they told me that they only made banjos for special orders."

At this time Earl was with Bill Monroe. Earl's banjo playing was gaining much notice, and the interest in banjo playing was beginning to increase dramatically. It wasn't long before virtually every music store in the country was selling five-string banjos. The Gibson Company alone now makes five Earl Scruggs models of banjos. Walter Carter, historian for Gibson, stated: "Earl's banjo is the only kind of banjo anyone wants to buy. Everybody who plays the banjo wants the kind that Earl Scruggs plays."

As stated earlier, this short treatise on Earl Scruggs is not intended as a chronicle of his long, productive and interesting professional career. Its purpose is to take a somewhat cursory look into the background, the boyhood

"I didn't have a banjo of my own [although he had played one since the age of five] until I was fourteen years old. I bought my first one for $10.95, and I will never forget the aroma when I opened the case." *Quote from Earl Scruggs, pictured here—photo courtesy Earl and Louise Scruggs*

and the heritage of this man, and hopefully to help understand some psychological and motivational aspects that steered him from a life of working in the lackluster cotton thread mill, to a life of national prominence.

But having said this, we should nevertheless look at some of the highlights of "life after the thread mill." Earl had played in public when he was only six years old, but he told me he never liked playing for square dances. "I like for people to want to hear what I play."

He bought his own banjo (for $10.95) when he was 13 from money he had earned and saved. He later played, in 1941, in Spartanburg, South Carolina, with Wiley and Zeke Morris, the Morris Brothers, before starting his four years in the Lily Thread Mill.

After leaving the thread mill in 1945, he came to Knoxville to work for "Lost John" Miller on station WROL. After a few months he was hired by the legendary Bill Monroe. The band was known as Bill Monroe and the Blue Grass Boys, named ostensibly in deference to Monroe's home state of Kentucky, the Bluegrass State. It was during Earl's two-year and two-month stint with Monroe that he made his first major contribution to the birth and rise of bluegrass.

Earl's friend and fellow banjoist, John Hartford, put it best when he said: "Bluegrass music as we know it today started when Earl Scruggs walked out on the stage of the *Grand Ole Opry* with Bill Monroe."

During 1946-47, Bill Monroe and the band made 28 recordings. It was during his association with Monroe that Earl Scruggs became so much more than just one of Bill Monroe's "boys."

This photograph of 21-year-old Earl Scruggs was taken soon after he joined Bill Monroe and the Blue Grass Boys in 1945. *Photo courtesy Les Leverett from his Earl Scruggs collection*

Uncle Dave Macon is referred to as being the "grandfather of country music," and he was likely the nation's foremost and most popular old-time banjo player, comedian, and interesting character of his time. A colorful showman, he was, in every sense of the word. When he first watched the youthful and much touted Earl Scruggs, Uncle Dave had already been a mainstay on the nationally broadcast *Grand Ole Opry* for over 20 years. He had made movies with Roy Acuff in California and in every way he was "king of the banjo." It was to be expected that the old master wouldn't be overly excited by this 21-year-old upstart, this Earl Scruggs fellow. Uncle Dave couldn't deny Earl's total mastery of the instrument, but Earl didn't "clown it up" like Uncle Dave did, and Uncle Dave likely viewed him as a threat. When asked what he thought of the youthful Earl's playing, Uncle Dave responded: "Well, he plays a pretty good banjo, but he ain't a damn bit funny."

Louise recalled a similar response when someone else asked Uncle Dave what he thought of Earl's playing. Uncle Dave responded: "He plays pretty good in a band but he don't sing a lick." [Earl did sing baritone in the band on trio and quartet vocals.]

In January, 1948, tired of traveling day and night from Canada to Mexico and other irritations that went with the job, Earl decided to leave Monroe, go home and get another job. Louise recalled that when Earl worked the last night with Monroe, Lester Flatt turned in his resignation, too. Earl had given a two-week's notice earlier in the month, required by the musicians' union, Louise told me, but he stayed on an additional two weeks at Monroe's request. Monroe was booked for the Prince Albert portion of the *Grand Ole Opry*'s network radio program two weeks after Earl had given his notice. He wanted Earl to stay on and work the Prince Albert network program with him. Earl stayed the additional two weeks.

Soon after Earl returned to his home in Shelby, North Carolina, Lester Flatt called with the suggestion that the two form their own band, which they soon did, with Jim Eanes on guitar and Howard Watts on bass.

First they went to a radio station in Danville, Virginia, known as the site of the "wreck of old '97 train"—the basis for the popular song by the same name. After three weeks in Danville, Jim Eanes informed them that Bill Monroe had called and offered him a job. Jim took the job with Monroe. Lester and Earl then moved to Hickory, North Carolina, where Jim Shumate, on fiddle, joined them. They had a radio program on a Hickory radio station, and it was there where the great singer, Mac Wiseman, joined them.

Mac had been on radio station WCYB in Bristol, Virginia, a few months earlier. He suggested it might be a good idea to audition for a radio program in Bristol. Show business was known to be good around that area. They went to Bristol, auditioned and were accepted with enthusiasm. The radio station management wanted them to wait a week to begin their programs. They were going to run promotional spots to peak the listener's curiosity, not telling them who was coming in, but encouraging the listeners to "tune in next week for a big surprise."

The name of the band became Lester Flatt, Earl Scruggs, and the Foggy Mountain Boys, after the old Carter Family song, "Foggy Mountain Top." This also became their theme song. [It is coincidental that Fiddlin' Bob Douglas, about whom Chapter 4 is devoted, had also called his group the Foggy Mountain Boys a quarter century earlier.]

Lester Flatt, who played guitar, was the principal singer for the band. His early life was remarkably similar to Earl's. He was one of nine children born to the family of a poor mountain sharecropper in the isolated county of Overton, in north Middle Tennessee, a few miles from the birthplace of Cordell Hull, considered by many, including this writer, to be the country's greatest statesman of this century. Sgt. Alvin C. York, this century's most celebrated War hero, was born and reared a few miles to the east.

Lester Flatt's family moved some 50 miles to the south to a rural, hilly area near the town of Sparta, Tennessee, when he was a lad. Like Earl, his family played stringed instruments, and Lester first learned to play the banjo. He also worked during his childhood days on the family farm and for several years thereafter in textile mills in Tennessee and in Virginia.

The band, which came to be known as Lester Flatt, Earl Scruggs, and the Foggy Mountain Boys, was formed in 1948. They first played on the small radio station WHKY in Hickory, North Carolina, but stayed only a few weeks, leaving for "financial reasons." Earl recalls that they played for a percentage of the gate receipt, and one night, after expenses, they made 17 cents each. The group, shown here in 1948, consists of Cedric Rainwater (Howard Watts), at left, Lester Flatt, Jim Shumate and Earl Scruggs. Mac Wiseman, a member of the original band, is not shown. *Photo courtesy Earl and Louise Scruggs*

In 1948, the Foggy Mountain Boys were playing on a radio station in Bristol, Tennessee-Virginia, often referred to as the birthplace of old-time country music, dating to the time in 1927 when Ralph Peer recorded the Carter Family, Jimmie Rodgers, the Stonemans, and others. In 1949, Mac Wiseman left the group to work on his own and the Foggy Mountain Boys went to Knoxville, on the popular WROL radio station.

For the next four years Lester and Earl played variously on radio stations in Kentucky, Florida, and in North Carolina. The same basic format of other country music groups of that era was followed. They would play early morning shows and noon-time shows, thus assuring themselves of a listening audience from the rural farm folk—before they left for the fields in the morning, and again when they came in for the noon meal. By keeping their radio schedule free in the evenings, they could make personal appearances throughout the broadcast area.

During the radio programs, they heavily promoted these personal appearances, or nightly bookings, mainly in school houses, at dances, and at public gatherings for as far away as the airwaves reached—often upwards to 100 miles. Like most all other string bands of this era and from this greater area, the band consisted of a fiddle, a banjo, a bass, and at least one guitar. Most other such bands had a mandolin, but Flatt and Scruggs did not feature a mandolin player in their band, possibly to avoid emulating Monroe's band. Many of the songs were the old Carter Family type, earlier ballads, and of course the old fiddle tunes.

The day after visiting with the legendary Earl Scruggs on January 21, 1995, I went to see my longtime friend, the inimitable John Hartford, in his large three-story house, which hangs on a rocky bluff over the historic Cumberland River. It, too, is located in the greater Nashville area—in Madison. I wanted to talk with him about Earl Scruggs, the man and his music.

John gained national fame appearing on television on the *Smothers Brothers Comedy Hour* and on the summer replacement, *The Glen Campbell Goodtime Hour,* in the mid-1960s when it became "the number one television show in the nation."

John's main interest is the banjo and fiddle, but he's played with various groups, and he's written hundreds, maybe thousands, of songs, including "Gentle on My Mind," one of the most recorded songs in U. S. history, having been recorded by some 300 artists and played countless millions of times throughout the world. John is an analytical man, and he is one of the greatest empirical scholars, in my opinion, of old-time, traditional, early country, and bluegrass music. I was anxious to talk with him about Earl Scruggs.

We built a fire in John's living room and while doing so we had a discussion about the importance of the proper back log, how big the fore-stick should be, and what type of wood "threw out" the most heat, and how important it is to have a charring and not a blazing fire. But we soon got to music. He talked at length about his fiddlin' grandfather from the country near St. Louis and the old-time banjo players and other musicians there in his childhood home of central Missouri.

John, I know that you were exposed to all types of music growing up—church music, jazz, and even classical. And your stay in Hollywood and all of your recordings and movies exposed you to an even broader spectrum of mainstream music. But you seem to have a great affinity for the banjo, and I think you told me once that you attribute much of that interest to Earl Scruggs.

"Well, I can tell you what he means to me. He's like a master. If I were a painter, Earl Scruggs would be the Rembrandt. He is my role model, and I wanted to be like him. If I'm a musician, I want to study Earl Scruggs. I think he is pivotal. What he brought into the music is, I think, tremendously important to it. I mean, it changed the face of traditional music."

Somebody said that Earl Scruggs was to the banjo what Paganini was to the violin. I believe that this comparison first appeared in *The New York Times*.

"Well, let me say this. Now, there's a lot of argument about who invented the three-finger style, and Earl Scruggs, if you talk to him, will tell you he didn't invent it, that it was here before him. But my contention is that if it hadn't been for Earl Scruggs, nobody would be worried about who invented it because no one would have ever heard of it, except a handful of people there where he grew up in North Carolina. It's the musicianship which he brought to whatever he decided to do, which happened to be the five-string banjo! He literally changed the face of what we call old-time music."

So you don't think that his contribution has been overestimated.

"No, not in the least, no! Bill Monroe was the greatest singer/songwriter we ever had. He was the composer. Earl Scruggs was the father of bluegrass music."

Earl Scruggs, left, and Lester Flatt are shown here playing on radio station WVLK in Lexington, Kentucky, in 1949, a year after they formed the Lester Flatt, Earl Scruggs, and the Foggy Mountain Boys Band. *Photo courtesy Les Leverett from his Earl Scruggs collection*

It might be noted here that John Hartford was a close friend to both Scruggs and Monroe, although Bill Monroe was a loner. John often visited him on his farm in his log house in the country north of Nashville. Not only did they play music together, but they often engaged in Bill's favorite sport—that of fox hunting. John and Earl are virtually neighbors, and of course their friendship has been a long and close one.

Almost all commentators and researchers on the subject agree with John Hartford's assessment of Earl Scruggs. The magazine *Bluegrass Unlimited* quotes Bill Evans, a banjo player and a student of European, African, and American banjo stylists. He calls Earl "the Mozart of American folk music." He pointed out that he was able to take the music which was around him in the community and crystallize it until it was perfect. He stated that, like Mozart's music, Earl's was never in excess. He played only that which was needed—not more, not less.

This same article, which appeared in the June, 1998, issue of *Bluegrass Unlimited*, referred to Earl as one of the world's great folk musicians, and in the acoustic world as a Johnny Cash and Mick Jagger rolled into one.

Do you think that the fact that Earl is so modest and unpretentious is one of the reasons that he did not get as much credit as the other fellow? [Referring to Bill Monroe without mentioning his name.]

"I think that Earl's statement, without him even saying anything, still speaks twice as loud as the other fellow's.

"He'll never have to say it, but eventually everybody else will say it for him. After Earl Scruggs came along, the banjo became the defining sound of what came to be called bluegrass music. You have the fiddle, of course, the mandolin, and the guitar and bass, but it was Earl's banjo style that gave it the defining sound, and I hadn't heard it before Earl Scruggs."

So the banjo was the centerpiece, the linch-pin, of the bluegrass band.

"I've always said that the bluegrass band was banjo band music. It was oriented around the banjo which is why Earl Scruggs should get the credit for the invention of it [bluegrass music]. In all the earlier string bands, the fiddler was the centerpiece. Everything was centered around the fiddle. The fiddle player was the main object of attraction and everybody else seconded the fiddler."

Earl Scruggs' career, though long and varied, may roughly be broken down into five or so segments. First, there were the early years when he played as a teenager on various local and regional radio stations; followed by the historic period in which he was a member of Bill

Monroe's band starting in 1945; then some reconnoitering before joining with Lester Flatt and Mac Wiseman to form the Foggy Mountain Boys in 1948, which we can call the third stage. The split with Lester Flatt in 1969 was followed by a different type of music, country-rock, played with his sons, and known as The Earl Scruggs Revue, which formed the fourth phase of his career. Then came the last phase, a self-imposed and semi-retirement from which Earl makes a *very* limited number of appearances.

The first phase, that of his early years before becoming a member of Bill Monroe's band, has been alluded to earlier. When Earl Scruggs, along with the great fiddler, Chubby Wise and singer/guitarist Lester Flatt, joined Bill Monroe in 1945, that group became the first recognized defining bluegrass band on the scene.

As has been noted, many credit Earl Scruggs as much as, or even more so than Bill Monroe for creating the bluegrass sound. He took the lead runs, and this crisp, new banjo style, along with the other great musicians, created a fast moving, hard driving exhilarating type of music. Old-timers remember that the first time Earl played the *Grand Ole Opry* the crowd went wild. Professor Charles Wolfe noted that Bill Monroe's Blue Grass Boys was soon the most influential string band in the country.

Their first recorded song was "Heavy Traffic Ahead," made in 1946. Other songs recorded during the same period included Scruggs' special "Molly and Tenbrooks," an old Kentucky folk song made popular by Bill Monroe, and "Bluegrass Breakdown."

As observed earlier, both Earl Scruggs and Lester Flatt left Bill Monroe the same time, in 1948, and formed the Foggy Mountain Boys. From 1948 and into the latter part of the 1950s, Flatt and Scruggs enjoyed widespread popularity, and the term "bluegrass" gradually crept into use, first among ardent followers, and then talked about in wider circles. Other bands, notably the Stanley Brothers, with similar styles appeared on the scene. Everybody was trying to figure out how Earl manipulated the complicated three-finger roll. Some, it is reported, even played the records on a slower than intended speed, i.e. a 78 RPM on a 45 RPM speed, in an attempt to emulate the popular Scruggs style.

While Bill Monroe did not take kindly to other bands taking "his" music and forming other bands, Ralph Stanley openly admired Earl Scruggs. Ralph Stanley and His Clinch Mountain Boys is now considered by many as the "replacement" for Bill Monroe and the Blue Grass Boys, as the premier old-style bluegrass band. When Stanley returned from the War in 1945, he said: "I really liked Earl's way of playing—still do—better than anybody I've ever heard." By 1950, Flatt and Scruggs were recording for Columbia Records and "Earl's Breakdown"

In 1952, the giant Martha White Mills of Nashville "discovered" Lester, Earl and the Foggy Mountain Boys, and thus began a long and mutually productive association. The group played seven radio programs each week for Martha White on WSM, and they later became even better known for their *Martha White Television Shows*. This 1964 photo was taken by Les Leverett while Flatt and Scruggs were taping their *Martha White Television Show* at WSM-TV studios in Nashville. From the left are: Paul Warren, Earl Scruggs, "Uncle" Josh Graves, Lester Flatt, and "Cousin" Jake Tullock. *Photo by and courtesy of Les Leverett*

recorded in October, 1951, and "Flint Hill Special," recorded in November, 1952, were very popular. These instrumentals were often used as theme songs on radio stations throughout the country.

In 1953, the Martha White Flour people in Nashville started sponsoring Flatt and Scruggs on an early morning show on WSM, and later they played on other radio stations, notably in Richmond, Virginia.

By this time, ominous clouds were on the horizon for traditional, old-time and even bluegrass music. It was the dawning of the rock-and-roll era, and it's ironic that the first record made by Elvis Presley was one he "borrowed" from the "father of bluegrass" himself, Bill Monroe. The song "Blue Moon of Kentucky," which Monroe is credited with writing and which he recorded,

was recorded by Presley and it became immensely popular. The story was reliably reported and oft repeated that Elvis, having sung "Blue Moon of Kentucky" on the *Opry* one night, encountered Bill Monroe back stage. Elvis apologized for using Bill's famous song, expecting a reprimand, or worse, from the famous Monroe who was known for his temper and his critical nature. Instead Monroe said: "Sonny, if it'll help you out, just go right ahead."

Rock-and-roll appealed to the youth of a new generation. While Flatt and Scruggs were singing to an older, more rural audience, "The Cabin on the Hill" and "I'm Crying My Heart Out Over You," Elvis was doing "I Wanna Play House With You," "Hound Dog," and "Good Rockin' Tonight."

By the 1960s, Lester Flatt and Earl Scruggs and the Foggy Mountain Boys were traveling an incredible 2500 miles each week, mostly on secondary highways. They literally drove night and day to make appearances. They slept in the bus and ate quick snacks along the way. This picture was taken by Nashville photographer Les Leverett in a roadside cafe in August, 1961, when the "boys" were on their way to play in Jumpertown, Mississippi. From the left are: Fiddler Paul Warren, Lester Flatt, Curly Seckler, and Earl Scruggs. *Photo by and courtesy of Les Leverett*

In 1955 Flatt and Scruggs fulfilled the dream of every country-bluegrass group when they became members of the *Grand Ole Opry*. In addition, they had attached themselves to an increasingly important media, television, and they had TV programs in Tennessee, West Virginia, Georgia, and South Carolina. I had read that during a two-year period in the early 1960s that the band traveled an incredible 2500 miles every week in their bus. I asked Louise about this, and she assured me that it was true, and that most of the traveling was over secondary roads.

Nashville was scrambling to stay abreast with more contemporary, urban-oriented music. Drums, pianos, and electric guitars were becoming the mode—and the banjo-fiddle band almost totally disappeared from the major record labels. Bluegrass was interpreted as old-fashioned and out-of-date.

However, this new rock-and-roll style did not appeal to everyone. There was evidence of a revival of the older style in the late 1950s. The New York-based Folkways Records released the first long-play record of bluegrass music called "American Banjo Scruggs Style." A revival of "folk" music was about to begin.

The banjo was being embraced by young and urban middle class and college type groups as an alternative to rock-and-roll, and among the first invited guests to the first Newport Folk Festival in 1959 was Earl Scruggs. Lester Flatt was *not* invited. The banjo came across as being consistent with folk music, but strict bluegrass was heard as whining, nasal, and hillbilly to the ears of this new group.

By 1955, Flatt and Scruggs were appearing every Saturday night on the *Grand Ole Opry* at prime time, and these Martha White television shows were being syndicated. Their records on Columbia were regularly on the rating charts, and the band was on the road constantly. In 1955, Louise started handling the bookings, and she also largely took charge of the publicity.

Perhaps through her leadership, Earl began to become even more popular with the folk groups. Flatt and Scruggs made albums to exploit this market, and they played at such places as Carnegie Hall and Vanderbilt University.

While playing at Ash Grove, a Los Angeles folk music coffee house, they were heard by Paul Henning, a television producer. He asked Flatt and Scruggs to play the theme song for *The Beverly Hillbillies*. The song was to be "The Ballad of Jed Clampett," but Louise did not immediately buy the idea. She was from a tiny rural farm community named Grant, some 50 miles east of Nashville, and within a few miles of the Senator Albert Gore, Sr., family home [Louise's father and Albert Gore, Sr., were the same age and attended the same country school], and her home was not far from where Cordell Hull lived. Louise resented what she felt would be a condescending portrayal of Southerners as dumb, unprincipled hillbillies, and she would not agree to being a part of what was to become one of the nation's most popular television shows.

I talked with Louise about this and she said that the producers emphasized that the Clampetts were to be portrayed as an honest, generous, mountain-smart family, howbeit unfamiliar with the ways of Beverly Hills. She said that the producers finally convinced her that the production would not portray this mountain family in an uncomplimentary light, and so it was that Flatt and

Scruggs came to perform the theme song for this situation comedy which ran during prime time from 1962 through the early 1970s. Louise, who keeps copious notes on such matters, said that the show was carried in 76 foreign countries, and it may even be seen today [1999] in syndication on various cable channels in this, and perhaps other countries. At one time, Louise recalled, the program could be seen on three different channels in the Nashville area. On December 8, 1962, "The Ballad of Jed Clampett" became the first bluegrass song in the country to become number one on *Billboard*'s country charts and was in the pop charts as well. In addition to being featured on the opening and closing of the program with the theme song, Lester and Earl also often appeared on the program with speaking (and playing) parts.

The success of Flatt and Scruggs continued unbridled throughout the 1960s. They were one of the busiest and most profitable of all country acts, and only the immensely popular Johnny Cash sold more records for Columbia. They were so popular in Japan that when they toured there in 1968 they were subjected to friendly mobs, reminiscent of The Beatles' concerts.

Earl Scruggs, at left, and Lester Flatt are shown here with Granny Clampett of the popular *Beverly Hillbillies* TV show for which Earl and Lester provided the music and singing for each episode; and they made periodic guest appearances on the show as well. One of the country's most popular prime-time TV shows in the 1960s and 1970s, it was carried in 76 foreign countries and continues on re-runs even today (in 1999). The song "The Ballad of Jed Clampett" by Flatt and Scruggs became the first bluegrass song in the nation to reach the number one rating on *Billboard's* Country Music Charts. *Photo courtesy Country Music Foundation, Nashville*

Lester, at left, and Earl are shown here in connection with the movie, *Bonnie and Clyde*, which Warren Beatty produced. Beatty was familiar with Earl's banjo playing and he convinced Earl to write the soundtrack which included "Foggy Mountain Breakdown" for which Earl received a Grammy Award in 1968. The movie became one of the most popular movies in the nation and much credit was given to Earl Scruggs for his most effective musical contributions. *Photo courtesy Country Music Foundation, Nashville*

In 1967 their popular "Foggy Mountain Breakdown," which Earl had written and which had been recorded 20 years earlier, was thrust into national prominence. It happened when Warren Beatty telephoned the Scruggs' office one afternoon and spoke to Louise Scruggs. She said:

"I answered the phone and he said, 'Hello. This is Warren Beatty. I would like to speak with Earl Scruggs.' I informed him I was Earl's booking agent and we chatted for a few moments. He mentioned some movies he had played in, etc. He then informed me he was producing and starring in a movie, *Bonnie and Clyde*, and would like for Earl to write and record the soundtrack for his movie. He had planned to be in Nashville the following week and wanted to discuss the possibility. He called back a few days later; his plans had changed and he had to go to New York and said he would be in Nashville in a few days.

"We spoke on several occasions about the music. Then, one day he called to say he had a collection of Earl's recordings and had been listening to 'Foggy Mountain Breakdown,' and he wanted to use it in the movie. Earl and Lester Flatt had previously recorded the instrumental for Mercury and for Columbia Records. They went into the studio and recorded it again for Columbia. A short time later they recorded an album titled 'The Story of Bonnie and Clyde.' Warren was very confident he had produced a hit movie. At one point he commented, 'I am going to get Earl a hit record with this instrumental.'

"He was not wrong. It did make a hit. It received a BMI [Broadcast Music, Inc.] Award, and was nominated for and won a Grammy Award in 1968. It has since won a BMI Millionaire Award for over one million performances in the United States and is well on its way to the second million."

Bonnie and Clyde became one of the most popular theater movies in the nation, and much credit for its phenomenal success was given to Earl Scruggs' banjo playing. True to Beatty's prediction, the song became popular and stayed on *Billboard's* "Pop Chart" longer than it did on the country-rating chart.

Even with all their success during the '60s, not all was well between Lester and Earl who had played together for over a quarter century. Lester was not happy with their drift into the folk-rock style, although their recordings had greatly increased in sales. Earl, however, continued to lean toward a wider audience and was likely influenced by Louise and their three sons who were also musicians of the country-rock and folk leanings.

So Lester Flatt and Earl Scruggs had a parting of the way, and one of the last major events they played together was in January, 1969, on the Tennessee float at the inauguration of President Nixon. At the time, they were not only considered to be one of the best known country acts in the nation, but they also were receiving considerable international acclaim.

To many of their fans it was inconceivable that Flatt and Scruggs would no longer play as a team. Flatt formed a new band, The Nashville Grass, mostly of the old Foggy Mountain Boys, with Dobro player Josh Graves and a young Marty Stuart, destined to achieve great popularity.

This formal portrait of Lester Flatt and Earl Scruggs was widely released with the three-word caption, "Lester and Earl," and that's all that was needed. *Photo courtesy Earl and Louise Scruggs*

[On the day of this writing, December 26, 1998, Marty co-hosted an hour-long program on Nashville's TNN, and he noted that "27,000,000 people" (his quote) were viewing this star-studded program.] Flatt and his band broadcast an early morning radio show in Nashville. He and Mac Wiseman, his longtime friend and former member of the Foggy Mountain Boys, did well with records they made for RCA. Flatt's fans were happy to hear the old sound, the old music, and the old traditional songs. His group played bluegrass festivals and college concerts until Lester's death in 1979 at age 65.

In the meantime Earl, along with his sons, Gary, Randy, and Steve, formed The Earl Scruggs Revue. The hard-core enthusiasts of bluegrass and old-time music were not pleased with the electrified guitar, electric bass, the piano and drums, even though Earl's five-string banjo remained an integral part of the band, howbeit sometimes diminished by all the electrified instruments. But the group appealed to the country-rock generation, and to some of the younger bluegrass fans. They were especially popular at college concerts and they continued to play at some bluegrass festivals.

The Earl Scruggs Revue became ever more popular during the 1970s, and an article which appeared in *Bluegrass Unlimited* (March, 1998) by Thomas Warlick stated that in one year during this period, The Earl Scruggs Revue ranked second to Elton John in the list of most popular college concert attractions. He further stated that this mix of bluegrass and rock helped to spawn other groups such as New Grass Revival. At one time, ninety percent of The Earl Scruggs Revue's performances were college concerts. At one point, Louise recalled, The Earl Scruggs Revue was rated as the number one college concert attraction for a one-year period.

Earl Scruggs is given primary credit for the idea to encourage the popular rock group, The Nitty Gritty Dirt Band, to come to Nashville in 1971 to record what has become an historic album.

The idea was planted one night in Boulder, Colorado, after an Earl Scruggs Revue performance. John McEuen had attended the Revue's performance. He had gone to the motel with the group after the show and they were all in Earl's room. Earl said to John, "I have done quite well with a young group of musicians. Have you ever considered recording an album with some of the older country music artists?" John said, "You are kidding." Earl said, "No. I am not kidding. I may kid about some things but not music."

John asked Earl if he would record with them and Earl said, "Sure," and he ". . . knew some other people who would likely be interested, too." The next week, Bill McEuen, the manager for The Nitty Gritty Dirt Band, called to talk to Earl about the project and ask him if he was serious about it. Earl contacted the band musicians who were to play on the album and helped Bill and John to arrange for the featured artists.

They recorded a three-disc album set entitled "Will the Circle Be Unbroken?", the epitome of early Carter Family-type and other well-known country songs. Featured on the recordings were Maybelle Carter, Merle Travis, Jimmy Martin, Doc Watson, Gary and Randy Scruggs, Earl, and the king of old-time country music himself, Roy Acuff. These remarkable recordings reached the pop charts and remained there for 32 weeks. They were embraced by rock music followers everywhere and by many bluegrass and country fans. It introduced The Nitty Gritty Dirt Band to country fans, and it introduced the country artists to a rock and pop audience. The album sold over one million copies, earning a platinum album.

While Louise and I were going over my rough draft of this chapter, Elizabeth and Earl were talking in the living room, and she asked him what he considered to be the most enjoyable and pleasant part of his long career. He answered unhesitatingly: "When I got together and played with my sons in The Earl Scruggs Revue band."

For whatever reasons, Earl went into a state of semi-retirement in the early 1980s, and has only infrequently engaged in public appearances. He has played on the *Opry* a few times and at one or two concerts, and efforts to "get him out" more frequently have been pretty much fruitless.

Earl's last major appearance was in June of 1998 when he, along with his sons Randy and Gary, Marty Stuart, Jerry Douglas and Glen Duncan appeared at the 27th Bluegrass Classic Festival in Columbus, Ohio. This historic appearance drew large crowds from various parts of the world and was greeted with great enthusiasm and warmth.

I acquired a "partial list" of the honors and awards which Earl had received over the years, and it consisted of more than thirty major entries. They include: the National Medal of Arts presented by President George Bush at the White House in 1992; induction into the Country Music Association Hall of Fame in 1985; an honorary Doctor of Humanities Degree from Gardner Webb College in North Carolina in 1986; nomination for eight Grammies; Grammy Award winner for "Foggy Mountain Breakdown" in 1969; starring role in the movie titled *The Banjo Man* in 1975; TV appearances on numerous national talk shows; and a number of guest appearances on national television shows too numerous to list.

Earl Scruggs is known not only for his modesty, but also for his taciturnity—his shyness and quietness. On the other hand, he is highly intelligent and is certainly quite colorful. He has a dry and droll sense of humor, which is often manifested in few words. I remember a classic example:

Several friends of Grandpa and Ramona Jones had gathered in the big living room of their log home during the 1997 Christmas season. Mac Wiseman was among the group, and as he swayed back and forth in his chair, in rhythm to the music of a spirited old song, the chair totally collapsed—shattered literally into dozens of small pieces—and Mac lay sprawled on his back in the middle of the floor, among the rungs and splintered parts of the flimsy chair. There was absolute and total silence in the room, and as Mac lay there, seemingly unable to move, everyone wondered if he was injured. How badly was he hurt?

Then Raymond McLain, who had been singing beside Mac, took his arm to help him to his feet, but none of us knew whether or not we should upright the great Mac Wiseman. Maybe his back was injured—even broken.

But as Raymond struggled with little success, I took Mac's other arm, and the two of us pulled mightily, but to no avail at first. Mac was of little help. Then with a second synchronized effort and with all our strength we had him on his feet, and the room full of people remained quiet; totally silent.

Mac looked across the room at Earl Scruggs, seated there with his banjo in his lap, and Mac said in a strong, serious voice: "Scruggs, you ain't going to say anything about this to anybody, are you?" And Earl, without the slightest change of expression or hint of a smile said: "I ain't making no promises."

Although this brief chapter offers only a few glimpses into the colorful, eventful, and celebrated life of Earl Scruggs, it may nevertheless convey important and substantive meaning, not only to those whose interest lies in the world of music, but also to those interested in the lives of "successful" people in general. Students of human behavior may derive understanding of why some people with most meager chance for success excel so admirably, while those with all the opportunities and expectations often achieve little, materially or otherwise.

In reading a bit about the lives of other musicians included in this book, a remarkable parallel and similarity can be noted. They succeeded in accomplishing their goals, not because of opportunities thrust in front of them, but rather in spite of obstacles and barriers set before them, and with scant assistance and encouragement from anyone.

Earl Scruggs is a good example of how a poor, fatherless lad, raised on a poor, rocky farm by a mother of five children achieved so much. First, he was largely responsible for the advent of a new style of music (bluegrass!) which became popular throughout the country, and beyond; and then he went on to play a major role in the popular return of folk music during the 1960s which swept through the country's colleges and universities. As John Hartford said, "He doesn't have to say anything about his accomplishments and contributions. Other people will say it for him." And indeed they have.

After Earl Scruggs and Lester Flatt had a "parting of the ways" in 1969, Earl formed The Earl Scruggs Revue with his sons. *Bluegrass Unlimited Magazine* stated that during a period in the 1970s, The Earl Scruggs Revue ranked second only to Elton John in the list of popular college concert attractions. A proud Earl is shown here with his sons, Gary at left, and Randy, the group which constituted The Earl Scruggs Revue. *Photo courtesy of and by Les Leverett*

Raymond is shown here playing his banjo in 1995 at the Tennessee Fall Homecoming. *Photo by the author*

Dr. Nathaniel Winston, at right, is a medical doctor, a psychiatrist, former Commissioner of Mental Health for Tennessee, as well as a player of the banjo, guitar, and bagpipe; and he is totally credited with discovering Raymond in a log cabin in the mountains of North Carolina. He invited Raymond to Nashville and arranged for him to debut on *The Grand Ole Opry*, and as they say, "the rest is history." *Photo courtesy Dr. Nat Winston*

Chapter 9

And Then There Is Raymond Fairchild
Farmer, Moonshiner, Stone Mason, Mountain Man, and Five-time World Champion Banjo Player

"I got a lot of good discouragement on playing the banjo."

There's a little two-room cabin at the very end of a dirt trail, far back in the hinterland at the foot of Dirty Britches Mountain a few miles east of Maggie Valley, North Carolina—and then there's the world famous *Grand Ole Opry House* in Nashville, Tennessee. It's a long distance from one to the other, but Raymond Fairchild has made the trip, figuratively and literally, and therein lies a truly exemplary American success story—pioneer and frontier in character, but late-20th century in its time frame.

We'll let Raymond pretty much tell his own remarkable story, about his childhood in those impoverished, isolated but beautiful mountains of western North Carolina, and how he attained his "impossible goal." But first we'll go with him to the *Grand Ole Opry*, the aspiration of every mountain, bluegrass, and country entertainer. Dr. Nat Winston, the Nashville psychiatrist, former Commissioner of Mental Health for the State of Tennessee, connoisseur of old-time music, and my longtime friend, was largely responsible for bringing Raymond to Nashville. On a recent visit with Nat and his wife Martha in their Nashville home, I asked Nat to retell his early involvement with the enigmatic and legendary Raymond Fairchild. That was enough to set Nat off.

(Nat) "Well, I have this cabin—you've been to it many times, John Rice—in North Carolina on Grandfather Mountain at the base of this 145-foot waterfall. And when I first started practicing medicine, I'd go up there every weekend, and the mountain people would come down to my cabin every Saturday night; and we'd go 'coon hunting until about midnight, come back and pick and sing until nearly daylight—drink a little moonshine.

"One night, about 1958 or 1959, Frank Buchannon came over from Asheville and he brought this old mountain boy with him. And I declare, he was the ugliest man I ever saw in my life—said his name was Raymond Fairchild. He had on this old dirty coat, an old floppy hat, and he had a banjo. I thought to myself, 'If that man can pick a banjo, I can be President of the United States'."

Raymond later told me that he was up in the mountains making liquor when one of his friends came up and said: "There's this here psychiatrist that's got a cabin up above Cary Flatts, and he knows people in Nashville, and we want you to come down and play the banjo for him." Raymond went on: "I just left the still with some other fellers, had slop all over me. Didn't have time to change clothes. Didn't have nothing to change into if I'd *had* time."

(Directed to Dr. Winston) **But you soon changed your mind about his ability to play, didn't you? You're a long-time banjo player, so you had a basis for judging?**

"Yeah; and he didn't say a word. And by Jove, he started to pick that thing, and the more he picked, the more astounded I became. I've never heard anybody play the banjo like he did. I said, 'Raymond, have you ever played at the *Opry*? Will you come to Nashville, and bring the Crowe Boys with you?' He was playing with the Crowe brothers then. 'You can stay at my house. I'm gonna get you on the *Opry*.' Well, he said that he'd come.

Roy Acuff, the "undisputed king of country music" always welcomed Raymond in Roy's dressing room before appearing on the *Grand Ole Opry* stage. [It was considered an honor for any old-time country musician to be invited to fine tune their instruments in Roy's dressing room before the show.] Shown here in the 1980 photograph are: the Crowe Brothers, Roy, Little Jimmy Dickens, Raymond, and Bashful Brother Oswald. *Photo courtesy Les Leverett*

"So, about two weeks later he came down. He doesn't drive, you know; and the Crowe Boys drove him, and they stayed in an apartment in my basement. I called up Bud Wendell, who was head of the *Grand Ole Opry*, you know, and I said, 'Bud, you gotta come over and hear this guy pick.' And I invited some other people, Bill Weaver, Jr., and his father who was head of National Life Insurance Company, the *Grand Ole Opry*, the whole thing. He and his father came over; they loved bluegrass. And well, Raymond dumbfounded everybody. Bud said, 'We gotta get this man on the *Opry*.' And he arranged for Raymond to come back, about a month later.

"I think he was on the *Hank Snow Show* first, and Hank didn't know anything about him, except a little I'd told him. Hank put him on in the usual way—something like, 'They say this is a fine banjo-picker, so give a warm welcome to Raymond Fairchild.' So when Raymond came on, well, he brought the house down. They wouldn't let him off the stage. He'd start off and Hank would say, 'Come on back and do one more verse of that'."

He got a standing ovation?

"Oh, yeah, four or five times. They say that he was the first entertainer on the *Opry* to get that many standing ovations. The audience went wild. That was a big mistake, because it ticked off all the other *Grand Ole Opry* performers that this old mountain boy was getting more applause than the most famous entertainers in the country. [Note: Raymond's recollection of this event was that he got *seven* encores.] He didn't come back for several months after that, but then he started coming back on a fairly regular basis, about every three months. And every time he came, he'd tear the house down."

As you know, Raymond was of the old school of mountain stock where it was considered to be the right, the duty, and obligation of every man to protect himself and his family from harm. And of course that meant going armed—always.

"Oh, yeah. Absolutely. One night Raymond started on the *Grand Ole Opry* stage, and one of the officials noticed this big bulge in his pocket, and he thought it was an apple or some sort of package and he politely suggested that Raymond remove it before going out for this nationally televised program. And Raymond just reached in his pocket and handed him his fully loaded 38 revolver and said, 'Here, you can hold this 'til I come off the stage.'

"So the exposure Raymond got from being on the *Opry* is how he became known outside of two or three mountain counties there in western North Carolina. After that, he started traveling around the country, playing at bluegrass festivals, all sorts of concerts; and he always did his own bookings."

Yes, Raymond has told me this story many times, and he gives you full credit for getting him started. Another tradition which Raymond acquired from his people, his ancestors, was the art of making moonshine. As you know, many of the Scots-Irish left Pennsylvania and other sections of the country during and after the so-called Whiskey Rebellion in 1794, and they came to these mountains so they could be free to practice the time-honored avocation, like their forefathers had done in Northern Ireland and in Scotland. A little whiskey served as medicine, and was used for snake bites, and such. Raymond is alleged to have continued this practice, at least there's a rumor to that effect. (Laughter from both John Rice and Nat)

"He had a 100-gallon copper still, with silver solder to prevent lead poisoning. He used to bring me a gallon or two every time he came to Nashville, and I'd have to buy it from him, whether I wanted it or not."

Yeah, I've had experience with that, too. During our annual Tennessee Fall Homecoming, he and the Crowe brothers, I heard, were selling it out of the back of their van—with ten thousand people, literally, roaming around. They thought they were unnoticed, sneaking around. When I found out about it, I got onto him.

"Raymond, you can't do that. I've got over 50 officers here—city police, county deputies, highway patrolmen, and I'm sure many federal law enforcement people. The governor will be here sometime today, and I know of at least three or four judges. You can't peddle moonshine in my parking lot! You'll get us both thrown in jail."

Raymond's response was short and simple, and to him, logical. "Hell, you know the Sheriff, don't you?"

It wasn't long after Raymond's occasional appearances on the *Grand Ole Opry* that he started playing for festivals, and this resulted in a kind of synergistic effect. Every place he played, other opportunities resulted, and soon he was playing in bluegrass festivals across the country. He won the world champion banjo playing contest five times consecutively, and as they say, "He was on his way."

We'll talk about this later; but presently we'll take a look at his unique, colorful, and frontier-like background—try to examine and understand those elements which blended together to produce such a prodigious talent. Or was it a matter of determination and sheer relentlessness and drive which resulted in the manifestation of this outstanding entertainer and musician?

Raymond has been described as a true unadulterated mountain man, farmer, bear hunter, moonshiner, philosopher, and as the world's best banjo player. He is rough, gruff, completely opinionated, and some think offensive. But underneath all this craggy, stern, severe countenance is a warm, empathetic soul—a description which those who know him only casually, or not at all, will likely strongly disagree. No attempt, by him or me, will be made to cover up his wayward years nor his uncomplimentary features—well, not much anyway.

I've talked with Raymond Fairchild many times, and on several occasions I've visited him in his home at a place called Beaver Dam, some 10 miles east of Maggie Valley, North Carolina. On more "formal" interviews, I've carried a tape recorder, and his answers are presented to the reader, pretty much intact.

Raymond, tell me about your people and your early childhood.

"Well, I was born way up in Big Cove on Bunch's Creek, about four miles up from Maggie Valley—in that little two-room house where I took you. That's where I was born, in 1939, and I lived there 'til I wandered off from home. I had three brothers and one sister."

Your mother was Indian, you've told me.

"She was a Cherokee Indian, and her name was Mary Ballew Fairchild, but she went by the name of Sant. Everybody called her Sant. My father, Joe Fairchild, he was Scottish, but I never hardly ever knowed him, I'll be honest with you. He was a military man and he was gone about all the time. He served 45 years in the Army and Navy."

Raymond and his wife Shirley are shown at the entrance to the thriving tourist town of Maggie Valley, North Carolina—in front of the sign proclaiming it to be the home of Raymond Fairchild. *Photo courtesy of Raymond Fairchild*

"My mother was a Cherokee Indian," Raymond proudly proclaims, "and her name was Mary Ballew Fairchild, but she went by the name of Sant. Everybody called her Sant." *Photo courtesy Raymond Fairchild*

Where was your father from?

"He came from over in Kentucky, over around Whitesburg in the coal mining country. His daddy was John Fairchild, and he was a doctor, and he was a good one. My granddaddy come from Kentucky to Yancey County, North Carolina, and I don't know whether my daddy was born in Kentucky or North Carolina."

You told me once that you didn't stay home too much, even as a child. What about schooling? Did you attend school very long?

"I went a few pieces of a year. I guess you could say that I got to the second or third grade."

And your mother didn't insist that you go to school?

"No, no, she said it was foolish. I'll tell you, John Rice, I never attended school enough to hurt me." (Laughter by Raymond)

And I suppose that your mother never attended school, either.

"Mother never did have no education, and my father was a military man, like I said, and he got his education by traveling around the world."

And you lived with your aunt and uncle part of the time?

"Yeah, they lived up in Yancey County and I'd go off up there and stay with them a lot. I'd stay there with my aunt Martha, my mother's sister, and my uncle Frank. Aunt Martha, she was Indian, too, you know, had an old, open-back banjar with a groundhog hide on it, and I liked the sound of it and I decided that that's what I wanted to do. But she played it left handed, backwards you see, and I couldn't catch on by watching her because everything was upside down. Uncle Frank and his brother, Uncle France, they both played music."

Dr. John Milton Fairchild, Raymond's grandfather, is shown here in suit and derby, in the only known formal family portrait of the Fairchild family. They are identified as follows, front row from left to right: Laura Bennet Fairchild holding baby John Milton Fairchild, Molly Kenchloe Fairchild, young Gibbs child, Dr. John Milton Fairchild, Joe Fairchild holding a baby, and a young Gibbs boy. On the back row, from left to right are: Thomas Nelson Fairchild, Mollie Florence, and Jane Gibbs. *Photo taken about 1912, courtesy Raymond Fairchild*

"Uncle France [shown here] lived up in the mountains of Yancey County, North Carolina, and he played a little music. I'd stay up there with him and my Uncle Frank and Aunt Martha a lot." *Quote from Raymond Fairchild, who furnished this photo*

On March 6, 1999, we drove a long distance through the mountains primeval, to the very end of the dirt trail, and then we walked to this little two-room house where Raymond was born and largely raised. He is shown here in front of his old home, looking toward Dirty Britches Mountain. *Photo by the author, March 6, 1999*

Did you know your grandparents?

"I knowed by mother's daddy, Grandpa Ballew. He was a Cherokee, and he never talked much. He was a very, very, very quiet man. If I'd get to set with him six years, he wouldn't speak six words. But a lot of times actions speak louder than words."

When you were at home, you said that you helped with the livestock, with the farming, and with the gardening. How much land did you have?

"We didn't have any land of our own. See, the Campbells owned that whole cove, and all them mountains—hundreds of acres. They just let us live up there at the head of the hollow. We raised cabbage, potatoes, squash, pumpkins, beans, peas, and of course corn. Corn was our main crop."

And you'd have to give part of what you raised to the people who owned the land.

"I guess we'd give a half or two-thirds to them—of the field crops and the hogs. But the Campbells were good people, and they let us keep our garden stuff— enough to get us through the winter. Sharecroppers is what we was. 'Lord have mercy on a sharecropper's son'." [Raymond quotes from Ralph Stanley's recording in 1977 of "Sharecropper's Son."]

So you kept busy, even as a youngster.

"Oh, as soon as I could walk good, they'd be something for me and the other kids to do—hoeing corn, slopping hogs, digging taters, putting up hay, stacking hay, gathering eggs. . . We'd have to hunt all over the place and out in the woods looking for hens' nests. Every time an old hen would cackle, we'd be off to try and find where she laid—her nest you know, to get that egg."

And you had none of the so-called modern conveniences—no electricity and such.

"No, no. We had running water, down at the creek, but none in the house. (Raymond chuckled.) People are always talking about having to use an outside toilet. We didn't even have that. We thought them outside toilets was for the rich folks. We just used the woods. Now I ain't kidding you."

No electricity, no water in the house, no telephone, no roads, except a trail through the woods and little or no money—a pretty hard existence, wasn't it, Raymond?

"John Rice, it was great! I wouldn't take nothing for being raised the way I was. We were free, and we didn't have to answer to nobody. We was happy."

Raymond, almost everyone knows something of the attempts of the United States Government to move all the Cherokees from here to Oklahoma, in the 1830s. The Trail of Tears, they called it, but some few hid out here in these wild mountains, and I suppose that your ancestors were in that group. Eventually they came out of hiding, I suppose, and they were given some land, on what came to be known as the Cherokee Indian Reservation. Did you live on the reservation—near it, or where?

"The place where I was raised was right on the edge of the reservation—not on it. From where I was raised, I could walk across the mountain and be on the Indian Reservation in ten minutes. A lot of my people lived there."

And the Indians and whites had intermarried, over a period of several generations.

"They got mixed up. Nearly any mountain man's got so much Indian blood in him, if he's a true mountain man. They ain't no difference in a Indian and in a mountain man. They've both got the same nature."

I think we should get back to your career in music: the why, how, when and so forth. You said that you wanted to learn to play the banjo from the first time you heard your Aunt Martha play that little groundhog-hide banjo, when you were a small child.

"I wanted to play the banjar from the first, but like I said, Aunt Martha played left handed and upside down, and I couldn't catch on how to do it, and I didn't have anybody to teach me—and no banjar, either."

So you first learned to play the guitar?

"My three brothers were older than me, and they had ordered a guitar from *Sears*—a Silvertone. I'd pick it up, you know, when I got a chance, and I soon learned. They showed me a few chords and I picked it up from there, when I was very young—seven or eight years old. Then later I sold garden seed around through the mountains and made enough money to buy an old guitar. But the banjar was always my first love. It was always on my mind."

What were the first songs that you learned to play on the guitar?

"Things like 'Wildwood Flower,' 'Under the Weeping Willow Tree'—old Carter Family songs. They had a whole lot to do with country music. To me, they's the pioneers of it."

You were telling me earlier that many of the people thought the fiddle and the banjo were evil instruments, and playing them was frowned upon.

"I got a lot of good discouragement when I first started playing the banjar. [Raymond was chuckling.] A lot of good discouragement. This is Bible Belt country and they said that the banjar was the devil's instrument— said I was hell bound if I kept up the banjo playing. Now a guitar and a piano was all right, I reckon, because they were played in the churches sometimes.

"Why, you could carry a banjar across the church lot, and if you lingered, they's liable to put you in jail for a month, and if you picked a tune there, they'd try to have you locked up for six months."

How old were you when you started on the banjo?

"I never could afford to get a banjar until I was about grown, sixteen or seventeen years old, and I ordered a Silvertone banjar from the *Sears and*

Roebuck catalog, and it cost, I believe, $28.00. A lot of people thought I was spending and wasting my time playing it so much. Said I ought to be raising tomatoes, or corn, or cutting acid wood for the tanneries; said I'd never amount to a hill of beans. I've heard that ten thousand times—never amount to a hill of beans. Well, I've noticed all them fellers who were telling me how to be successful, how to get ahead, every one of them was eating rhubarb and blackberries without any sugar on them; and when they died, they was still eating rhubarb and blackberries without any sugar and living in a one-room shack, but they shore knowed how to give out good advice. They could advise me what to do but they stayed as poor as Jobe's turkey all their lives."

So you didn't take the advice of all those people who gave you so much "good discouragement?"

"No, I decided early on that I was going to let that banjar make a living for me because I loved it. I don't pay attention to everything I hear."

After you learned to play the banjo, who were the people who influenced your style of playing?

"We didn't have electricity, of course, but we got an old battery operated radio, and we could pick up a station out of Asheville, and then we could get the *Grand Ole Opry* out of Nashville. They was four great banjo players that I'd listen to: Don Reno—man could he play the banjar; and Earl Scruggs and Ralph Stanley, and then there was an old feller in Hedgesville, West Virginia, by the name of Andy Borland. I'd put my style somewhere between Don Reno and Earl Scruggs."

All these people play the three-finger style incredibly fast. How could you learn this complicated style, get all those finger movements by just hearing them?

"See, you couldn't hear enough of a banjar when they was being played with several other instruments, to copy a note. I'd hear a little bit, and I'd hold it in my head 'til I could get to a banjar and just let my imagination do the rest. I'd go down here to Maggie Valley to some restaurant where they had a juke box, and I'd put every cent I had in there just to play Scruggs and Reno over and over, and I learned a lot from them. Earl would play 'Flint Hill Special' and 'Earl's Breakdown'; and Reno would play 'Banjo Blues' and 'Reno Blues.' It was two different styles and it was hard to tell which was the best."

When did you start playing in public?

"Ted Sutton was the man who give me my start. [Raymond answered spontaneously and with much conviction.] Ted Sutton had this little place he called Hillbilly Fun House where he sold crafts and stuff. It was on the main road there on Campbell's Creek, or some people called it Bunch's Creek, there in Maggie Valley, and he'd let me and some other boys come down and set in front of his place and play for tips.

A 23-year-old Raymond Fairchild is shown here in Yancey County, North Carolina, with two of his early picking buddies, Kent Wiseman, left, and Johnny Ray Barrier. *Photo courtesy of Raymond Fairchild.*

This is Ted Sutton of Maggie Valley, whom Raymond describes as "the only man who ever had any confidence in me, my hero, and the man who started my career." *Photo courtesy of Raymond Fairchild.*

"Ted Sutton was my hero. He was a highly uneducated man, but he knowed people. He could talk to a man for five seconds and he could size him up and he could tell you what kind of a feller he was.

"We played at his place, in the summer time, from early morning 'til about midnight, as long as them tourists was coming by. We played strictly for tips. We had a tip can and them tourists would throw money in that tip can. They loved that old mountain music. Sometimes they would block the road there was so many of them gathered around. Ted had two sons, Lloyd and Roe, and they'd play, and James Worley was a harp blower. Roy Mull played the rhythm guitar and Wilford Messer played the fiddle; and Frank Buchannon played with us. He was one of the original Maggie Valley Hillbillies. And Ted, he would play with us when he wasn't busy in his store. That's what we called ourselves, The Maggie Valley Hillbillies.

"I tell you, that practice made your picking perfect—12 to 16 hours a day, seven days a week. You'd get to where you couldn't mess up if you tried to. We'd all play together and at the end of the day, at night, we'd divvy up the tips."

After you played there all day, and half the night, you'd have to walk all the way up the creek to your home?

"Sometimes, many times, when we played late I'd stay there with Ted—eat his food, sleep in his bed."

You give Ted Sutton most of the credit for getting you started playing in public—playing for money.

"I give him *all* the credit. He was the first man who ever had any confidence in me. He was my hero." [Indeed, this old mountain man may have been the very first person to give any encouragement to Raymond, who was then about 17 years old. It's a wonder that he had continued his relentless practicing with all the "good discouragement" which he apparently received in abundance and unrelentingly.]

When you didn't stay with Ted, how did you get to and fro—seven or eight miles round trip up that hollow?

"There was just a trail up there that a mule could travel, but I just walked. I done most of my getting around on foot. The same way with Ted. He was raised up there on the top of that big mountain where Ghost Town is now. It used to be called Buck Mountain. It's almost straight up, and of course there was no road of any sort up there then. There was a little trail where you could walk, or maybe ride a mule—part of the way."

When did you start playing at the outdoor festivals—do you remember the first one?

"Yes, sir, it was for Carlton Haney up at Fincastle, Virginia. He had all the big guns there: Bill Monroe; Don Reno; Mac Wiseman; Clyde Moody. After that, I really started on the festival circuit, and played the *Grand Ole Opry* more, and a lot of nationwide TV shows."

How did you handle your engagements; did you have an agent?

"No, I never fooled with them—just handled my own bookings—Shirley [his wife] did. See, every time I did a

show, they'd be promoters there, from other places, and they'd sign me up for their shows.

"I just had some little cards I'd give out. Most of my publicity was just word of mouth. A lot of people remembered me from when I was a kid playing for Ted Sutton along side of the road, you know. A lot of people learnt me from there. I started doing festivals in the 1960s, but by the 1970s, after the Crowe Brothers joined me, why we really hit the road."

So, after you became known in the music circles, you were on the road, around the country. How did you travel?

"In the beginning, we traveled in cars, old Chevrolet cars, then we got a van, and now I have an extended van—the biggest you can get.

"Yeah, I've played in every state in the Union, in Canada, and Alaska—well, Alaska is a state. I spent a whole summer up there playing around Fairbanks—took Shirley and my young 'uns with me. We drove up the Alcan Highway. I've forgot how many hundreds of miles of dirt road there was. We played a big Air Force base there—the government hired us, and then we played at a place called Cripple Creek Resort, and at the Malamute Saloon. There's a picture of it hanging there on the wall.

"I flew a few times, but I ain't aiming to fly any more. We flew to California once, then another time to Denver. But we do all our traveling now in that van."

You just got back from California, I hear.

"Yeah, we all drove out there this time, and stopped off for some shows in Nebraska, and came back through Texas for a show after we left California, then did a festival in Georgia and went on to Summerville, West Virginia, to play.

During the time when you were traveling so much, who were the members of your band? I know you were billed for a long time as Raymond Fairchild and the Crowe Brothers.

"I had been hunting for the right sound for a long time and I never could find it 'til I heard the Crowe Brothers. I first heard them in a little barbecue place in South Carolina and I knowed that was the sound I'd been looking for all my life. That guitar and bass just fit my style; and they was on top of the beat. A lot of people won't understand what I'm saying, but . . . the bass, guitar, and banjar is all I ever used for years and years, 'til Zane [his son] came along and we hired him to play guitar. He's the greatest guitar picker in the world." [This is a claim Raymond often makes, even when introducing him from the stage, and Raymond sincerely believes it. Zane is truly an incredible guitarist, and he practices incessantly, several (many) hours each day. He can play various styles, including classical and he, like his father, is totally self-taught.]

What part of the country do you like best, or I should ask, what part of the country liked you best?

"Well, to tell you the truth, I seemed to go over better up north: Ohio, Pennsylvania, New York, and in Canada. They was plumb foolish about us in Canada."

One of Raymond's talents is that of a stone mason, as evidenced by his home he built from rock he gathered from a nearby creek. *Photo by the author in 1993*

Have you played in Nova Scotia? Their music reminds me of the old fiddle music we have here in Southern Appalachia.

"Nova Scotia, yeah. There's a lot of good musicians up there that nobody's ever heard of. There's some great fiddlers up there.

"And, well you were asking about our favorite place to play, and that's an easy question. It's at your Tennessee Fall Homecoming—the biggest crowds of any place I've ever played, and it reminds me of my childhood—the molassie making, apple drying, and all them old-time things—takes me back to my childhood."

Are you traveling as much as you once did?

"No, I'm slowing down a little. See, we have this Opry House here in Maggie Valley. Shirley runs it, and I'm playing there more. We opened it in 1988 and we're open from the spring of the year on into the fall, November."

In March of 1999, I visited Raymond at the stone house he built near Maggie Valley for the express purpose of going to see his boyhood home, about which I'd heard so much. My wife, Elizabeth, and Raymond's wife, Shirley, accompanied us. I drove my van and carried the recorder, and Raymond sat in the front seat beside me and talked. As we came into Maggie Valley, we decided to stop at what he proudly called The Raymond Fairchild Opry House, located on the main street, but mainly hidden from the thoroughfare by another building in the fore.

I had attended the Opry House a few years earlier during one of the shows, and I even played a tune with Raymond and his band on stage, but I had not noticed all the old posters, plaques, calendars, and photographs hanging randomly and without order on the walls. It was not surprising that the largest and most prominent picture displayed there was that of Raymond's mentor, old Ted Sutton.

Then I was amazed at what next I saw: two gold records; a plaque pronouncing that he was the winner of the outstanding banjo player of the year, for five consecutive years; a member of the Bluegrass Hall of Fame; and numerous other awards. (The gold records were respectively for the sale of over one million copies of "Mama Loves Bluegrass" and "Rural Rhythm," both banjo instrumental recordings.)

The Raymond Fairchild Opry House in Maggie Valley, North Carolina, is operated by his wife Shirley and features "old-time mountain music" from early spring until early winter. Raymond plays there when he is not touring. *Photo by the author, March 6, 1999*

We left the Opry House and turned off the main street in Maggie Valley, at the very spot where Ted Sutton's Hillbilly Fun House once stood; and we headed up Bunch's Creek, now more often called Campbell's Creek. Raymond kept worrying about whether or not we could drive to his old homeplace. The road was narrow, rough, and rocky, and we had to cross the creek two or three times.

Near the head of the hollow we encountered a large, well kept and most impressive old farm house, the kind you'd expect to find in a wide, rich valley, and not there hovered over by steep mountains. That was the home of the Campbells, who owned the land from there all the way to Raymond's old homeplace. While the graceful grandeur of the place belied its mountain setting, other aspects of the homeplace put it squarely and deeply in the remote Southern Appalachian Mountains: the many 'coon skins drying on the outside wall of the smokehouse, and the recently skinned coyote hides nailed to the barn.

Before starting the long trek up Campbell's Creek to Raymond's birthplace, we stopped at the Campbell homestead to get keys for the several gates we'd need to open. While Mrs. Campbell was hunting for them, Raymond played a tune on the old groundhog hide banjo which, when being played by his Aunt Martha, inspired him to become a banjo player. The 'coon hides drying on the Campbell smokehouse attest to the effectualness of the Campbell's several hounds—one of which is visible in the lower right corner of the photo. *Photo by the author, March 6, 1999*

As we came near Raymond's old homeplace, the cove opened up a bit, revealing some rolling, howbeit rocky, land where the corn and other crops were raised. Raymond decides to walk the last stretch of the road. A portion of Dirty Britches Mountain is visible in the background. *Photo by the author, March 6, 1999*

Raymond said that there were several gates along the way and that we'd need to get keys from the Campbells and maybe borrow a four-wheel drive vehicle for the trip. Mrs. Campbell and the whole family clan greeted Raymond, and all of us, warmly and in a most affable manner. As we traveled up the narrow wagon road, we generally followed the raging creek for what Raymond said was three or four miles, and at one point Shirley pointed to an old abandoned house on the side of the mountain and described it as being the place where she was raised.

We came to a little, flimsy bridge, not more than eight feet wide, and supported by three or four saplings. It was high above the roaring creek and it looked not at all sturdy. Raymond got out and jumped "up and down" on it and confidently pronounced it safe for us to cross, but we all noticed that he chose to cross it on foot rather than in the van.

Soon after crossing Campbell's Creek for the last time, we encountered some open land, old fields, and steep hillsides. I asked Raymond if they had once been cultivated and this brought back fond memories for him—one in particular. This strange and touching story has to do with an old mule Raymond had during his growing up

years, and he told of how he perpetuated its memory: "Old man Willis Harris give me a little mule when I was about seven years old and I named him Siron Slick. I plowed him to raise all our crops, and rode him, and hauled our corn, fodder, potatoes, and hay with him. He made a living for us—him and an old cow.

"My Uncle Frank delivered babies, and me and him would ride old Siron all over these mountains. I'd go with him a lot. He delivered, they figured, between 1,200 and 1,400 babies.

"One day old Siron just up and died. A lot of people don't understand how you can get so close to an old mule like that.

"We buried him and I guess it was several years before I went back there, and when I did I found that the varmints and dogs had dug up old Siron's bones. I saw his old skull a laying there and it made me kinda sad; and I took it home.

"I was talking to Paul Rice, a friend of mine, about old Siron Slick one day, and I kept talking about him. Paul finally said: 'If you thought that much of him, bring that old jawbone over and I'll make something out of it for you.'

Raymond is shown here playing the Jawbone Fiddle, made from the jawbone of his old mule Siron Slick. Raymond seems deep in thought—maybe about the tune he is playing, but more likely he's thinking about the faithful old mule with whom he spent much of his childhood. *Photo by the author*

Raymond was delighted to find that a young mountain couple had recently moved into his childhood homeplace at the head of Big Cove. It looked more natural, he said, to see people and dogs and chickens there—and to see smoke coming from the old rock chimney. *Photo by the author, March 6, 1999*

"Paul was just a small, little feller—lived over near Marshall, in Madison County—Bloody Madison they called it. I run into him a year or so later and he said, 'I've got your jawbone fixed,' and I went over there, expecting to see a picture frame or something like that; and there was this fiddle. He'd built a pretty fiddle out of old Siron's jawbones. And, I swear, it's not a bad sounding fiddle.

"Paul liked it so much that he wouldn't let me have it. Said I'd have to wait 'til after he died. Well, he kept it 'til he died: and not long after that, his wife called me up and told me to come and get my fiddle.

"Now that jawbone fiddle is right where it belongs *forever*, John Rice. Right there in your Museum."

I built a special case for this most unusual and much talked about "fiddle." The encasement allows it to be viewed from all sides.

Before I acquired it from Raymond, he carried it to various festivals and had many of his compatriots to sign on the jaw bone of Siron Slick. Those whose signatures are written thereon include: Buck Ryan; Jim McReynolds; Al Holderfield; Kenny Baker; James Monroe; Crickett Hill; Curly Ray Cline; Frank Buchmore; Jim Wiseman; Clyde Moody; Wade Hill; Birch Monroe; Mac Wiseman; Charlie Monroe; Bill Monroe; Ralph Stanley; Fiddlin' Tommy Cordell; Bill Harrell; Red Rector; Don Reno; Charlie Moore; Wallace Lee; Wilford Messer; Kent Setzer; Carl Tipton, WLAC Television; Curley Lambert; Polly; Pee Wee Davis; S. Wallens; Raymond Fairchild; Carl Need, Jr.; Earl White; Randall Collins; Zane Fairchild; Sheila Stanford; Leon Stanford; John Rice Irwin; O. A. Hayes, Asheville, NC; John Hartford; Jim Clayton, and others.

We continued on up the creek—Big Cove, Raymond said the place was called—and we came to another bridge, older and more suspect than the last one; and even Raymond opined that we should walk the remaining few hundred yards.

A more picturesque and serene setting I hardly recall than that little two-room house sitting there, embraced on three sides by towering mountains. We were greeted by barking dogs, cackling chickens, and a young couple who were in the midst of moving into the old house which for so long had no one to keep the hearthstone warm. The shy couple reminded me somewhat of how it may have been, with countless pioneers starting out so isolated and alone in the wilderness except for their dogs, their chickens and the bear and other wildlife abiding and abounding mysteriously in those lofty mountains and along the creek.

Raymond seemed equally surprised and pleased to see the old home once again serving as warmth and shelter, especially so for these young mountain folks. After talking with them, Raymond averred that he had "knowed most all of their kinfolks." They were most friendly and invited us inside where Raymond "toured" us through the two small [12' x 14'] rooms, divided by a large stone chimney. Then he took me upstairs, to an unfinished garret where he used to sleep. I could understand how this quaint and beautiful place could have served as inspiration and motivation for Raymond's musical dreams.

It was there as a youngster that Raymond got to wondering about "things," and he went out in the woods somewhere and sat there on a big stump, off and on for days, to figure things out. Raymond had discussed this with Nat at length, and Nat told me: "Raymond sat there in the mountains, all by himself, and he worked out in his own mind his beliefs; and he's never changed his thinking. He has all the questions answered, once and for all; and no one is going to change him on the things he worked out in his mind."

I took some pictures in and around the old homeplace, and Raymond seemed reluctant to leave. As we drove out of Big Cove and down the creek, he was in a nostalgic and talkative frame of mind. He continued to talk of the old times and of his thoughts on religion, philosophy, and myriad other subjects. On religion, he had this to say: "I believe in some kind of a supreme being. I don't know what he looks like, and nobody else does now. And I don't know what his purpose is, but I believe in a higher power. If you took a notion to be religious, which denomination are you going to listen to? They's hundreds of them, ever one of them preaching a different doctrine. Which doctrine you going to listen to?"

And all of them saying that they're right.

"Yeah. Ever one of them will say they're right. One'll come by and say, 'We're right, this is it.' Well, the next day here'll come another one, and say, 'He's wrong, this is right.' Here will come a third one the next day, and he'll say, 'Both of them's wrong, this is the way it is.' You have got to make up your own mind."

You've apparently spent time thinking these things through. You sit and study, don't you?

"Yeah, I study. I've read the Scriptures a lot. Burning forever in hell! That not in the Bible. Nowhere in the Bible does it teach you'll burn forever.

"They's a preacher who came to see me one time. He said, 'I'm Preacher So and So.' I could call his name right now, but I won't.

"We talked a while and he finally got around to his business. He said: 'You know you're going to hell, don't you?'

"I said, 'I don't believe that's left up to you, Preacher, where I'm going. I think somebody higher than you and me both has got a handle on that. Why would you think that I'm going to hell?' He said, 'Picking the banjar, down at them places where people are drinking and cussing—getting drunk.'

"I said, 'Well, let me ask you this, Preacher. If I quit going down there and playing the banjar, stayed at home, do you think all them fellers would quit their drinking—sober up, start going to church' ?"

I don't guess he was too impressed with your answer.

"No, he wandered off and he don't never come around any more. But now if I went down there to his church and throwed a crispy hundred dollar bill in the collection plate, I'm sure he'd love the banjar." (Raymond chuckles mischievously.)

You haven't always walked the "straight and narrow," have you?

"Oh, no, I've strayed a few times—a lot of times. (He chuckled.) See, I started making whiskey when I's just young and I started drinking it. I drunk a quart a day for years, and it got to bothering me—bad. I went to the doctor and he said that I's going to die if I didn't quit drinking—said I was the only one who could help myself, but said that he knowed I wouldn't quit. Alcoholics hardly ever do.

"'Well,' I said, 'here's one that can quit.' And I did. That's been 36 years ago, and I haven't had a drop since. If I took a good swoller out of a half-gallon jar, why I'd want to drink the whole thing. So I don't touch it 'cause I can't control it."

Did all those years of heavy drinking cause you problems, like fighting, shootings, and so forth?

"Oh, I reckon. Yeah, all kinds of troubles."

Tell me about the shooting that occurred in "The Friendly Cafe."

(Raymond chuckled as he responded.) "I went down to that place, 'The Friendly Cafe' they called it, near Asheville, to get a bite to eat. I got into a big argument with this feller. He was a regular smartass, and he come after me, and I pulled out my Smith and Wesson and shot him right there in the head."

But it didn't kill him?

"No, the bullet just made a circle around his head, under the skin, and come out the back and didn't even break the bone."

Raymond is immensely proud of his rough, earthy, and independent mountain ways, and of his Indian and his white heritage; and he's certainly a product of that frontier-imbued mountain culture. He's fiercely loyal to friends, and he can be counted on not to back down one whit in the face of adversity. It may be surprising to those who know him only casually that he has strong empathy and concern for others. There is a pretty close connection among the old-time country and bluegrass entertainers; and Raymond, more than anyone I know, keeps abreast of the health and welfare of many of them by means of the telephone which sits beside his chair, right next to his ever present spittoon.

He calls me rather frequently to either inquire or inform me of someone's health, or their death. "Have you heard from Grandpa Jones lately—in the last day or two?", he would say. Another time he would say, "I called down to check on old Oswald—talked to Euneta and she says he's doing better—may get to go home in a day or two."

My daughter Elaine, who is my "right hand" and the executive director of the Museum of Appalachia, recently suffered a broken neck and other serious injuries in an automobile accident; and even though Raymond barely knew her, he never calls but that he inquires of her progress. And he asks in such a manner, with follow-up questions, that one senses a genuineness on his part. Ramona Jones told me that Raymond called her regularly during Grandpa's long stay in the hospital.

Often he calls to inform me of the passing of some old friend. "Did you hear about our old buddy, Chubby Wise? Well he left us—died out. I shore hated to hear it. They wasn't a better fiddler ever born, I don't guess."

One day, after informing me of the death of another old friend, Raymond said: "Every time one of your friends dies, John Rice, a little bit of you dies with him." That was a statement Raymond was to repeat many times, and it reveals, I think, something of the man. "Every time an old friend dies, a little bit of you dies with him."

Whatever opinion one may form after having met Raymond Fairchild, it is quite certain that one will not forget him. Tom T. Hall, the noted Nashville singer and songwriter was so impressed after spending an evening with Raymond that he wrote and recorded a song entitle: "The World According to Raymond; and Raymond According to Me."

Later Raymond hired a professional crew and made an impressive 60-minute video in which Tom T. Hall appeared, along with Roy Acuff, David Holt, Dr. Nat Winston, this writer, and several others. (Raymond also designed a banjo, which he modestly called "The Cox/ Fairchild Banjo—The Banjo of the Future," and had some 200 built by one of the nation's best [some say *the* best] maker of banjos, Jimmy Cox of Topsham, Maine. Raymond touts these banjos with unwavering conviction as being the "world's best banjars, bar none.")

Raymond demonstrates for the author the quality of "The Cox/Fairchild Banjo," which he designed and which was built by the master banjo maker, Jimmy Cox of Topsham, Maine. *Photo by Berk Bryant at the Tennessee Fall Homecoming in 1991*

Roots author, the late Alex Haley, who said he was "mesmerized" by Raymond's banjo playing, is shown here on the stage with Raymond, along with Dr. Nat Winston, left, and the world-famous mandolin player Red Rector at right. *Photo taken on stage at the Museum of Appalachia's Tennessee Fall Homecoming in 1989, courtesy Raymond Fairchild*

Raymond's extraordinary banjo playing has brought untold pleasure to many millions of people, even to those who purport not to like banjo music or bluegrass music. (Although his career has been largely centered around bluegrass festivals, he doesn't like the term "bluegrass." "It's mountain music, back porch music," he insists, "and they've hurt it by calling it 'bluegrass'.")

There are those who contend that a musician, an entertainer, in order to be successful and well received before a live audience must also be a showman—go through gestures, smile broadly, move around the stage, make eye contact with the audience, and so on. Raymond does none of the above. He has played here at the Tennessee Fall Homecoming for a dozen years or so, before tens of thousands of people; and he always stands there like a craggy rock, with a singular consistent dour expression and with his hat half concealing his face. The only movements he makes are those of his hands, and yet he is the consummate crowd stopper. His playing is so exhilarating that it needs no augmentation, no extraneous frills. The Homecoming is not a bluegrass festival in the usual sense of the word, and the visitors

are more likely to be college professors, artists, executives, businessmen, lawyers, judges and doctors—people whose music of choice is often not bluegrass, or as Raymond would say, old-time mountain music. Yet all these folks seem totally drawn to his music, played so effortlessly yet so fast paced and exhilaratingly.

I remember finding Alex Haley sort of cornered by Raymond and his boys backstage at the Homecoming one year. Raymond was flying through his "Whoa, Mule Whoa," and while Alex seemed to be enjoying the serenade immensely, I knew that he, first of all was a jazz enthusiast, and second, I knew that he had been "played to" by other groups all day. I therefore thought I would rescue him. I approached the group briskly and said, in a voice loud enough for Raymond to hear: "Alex," I said, "the television folks are here and they seem to be in a bit of a hurry for your interview. Can you come and talk with them?" He sidled over to me and in a half-whisper said: "I know what you're trying to do, Brother—trying to rescue me. I appreciate it, but I don't want to leave; I want to stay right here and listen to Raymond."

At the time, Alex's book, *Roots*, was said to be the fastest selling book in the world [except the Bible]. It had been translated into over 45 different foreign languages, and it was reportedly selling at the rate of 40,000 copies per day, and the made-for-television mini-series had set all-time records for television viewers. So Raymond got to thinking that maybe Alex could help him. He called me one day and asked me the name of that famous Black writer whom he met over at the Homecoming. He said that he'd decided to let him write his life's story. He even had a title for the book: "The Life and Times of Raymond Fairchild."

I told this story to Alex, and he was much amused, and he laughed and laughed. (At the time, Alex was being inundated and beseeched by the largest and most prestigious publishing houses in the country.) Alex kept thinking about Raymond's inquiry as to the name of "that famous Black man." Then he said, with a wry smile: "Yeah, I bet he said 'Black man.' But I love Raymond anyway."

Raymond, left, and Bashful Brother Oswald, share remarkably similar backgrounds, although Raymond is 28 years younger. Both were born in the Great Smoky Mountains of Cherokee ancestry; both dropped out of school in "the second or third grade"; both started making moonshine as youngsters; and both developed an early and abiding love for old-time mountain music. They both learned to play before they owned any instruments, and they were both totally self-taught. Neither had any encouragement from their families, but they both gained remarkable success as musicians and as entertainers. They both became heavy drinkers, consuming a quart or more every day for decades. But when their drinking got totally out of hand, they quit—totally and for good. Oswald hasn't had a single drink since 1970, and Raymond quit a few years later and hasn't had a drink in over 20 years. *Photo by Les Leverett*

Chapter 10

There Were Others—Colorful, Unique, and Legendary

It is hoped, as previously stated, that the stories of the musicians and singers included in this volume will convey to the reader some understanding of the why and how this old-time music traveled from the back porches and the firesides of this mountainous region to the auditoriums, convention halls, and living rooms of America, and beyond. There are thousands of others whose lives, if studied, would likely have added to the portrayal of the country music story—and we've succumbed to the temptation to add just a few more here. Additionally, the incredible role of early radio will be briefly considered in this last chapter.

Here again, these persons are randomly chosen, without pretense that they are the "best" or most appropriate examples. It is maintained, however, that they each are good and valid examples of those who, in concert with so many others, were a part of one of the most interesting musical and entertainment stories in this country's history. Some became household names, and others were important but remained almost totally unknown to the general public.

Uncle Dave Macon
"The Grandfather of Country Music"

If there is a grandfather of country music, then surely Uncle Dave Macon is that person. Ralph Rinzler, the director of the Festival of American Folklife at the Smithsonian in Washington, D.C., aptly capsulized the legendary Uncle Dave when he said: "To fan, musician, historian, and folklorist alike, he stands a giant. No single country music figure will ever again dominate the field as he did."

As a child in the 1930s, I recall our rural neighbors gathering at our house on Saturday nights to "listen to Uncle Dave" on the *Grand Ole Opry*. We had no electricity, and the battery powered radio was of poor quality; but we sat in hushed silence as Uncle Dave whooped, hollered, and flailed mightily the five-string banjo as he sang lustily such songs as: "Keep the Skillet Good and Greasy," "Bully of the Town," and "Eleven-Cent Cotton and Forty-Cent Meat."

David Harrison Macon (Uncle Dave) was born of pioneer stock in 1870 on a farm at Smart Station, a rural community in Middle Tennessee. When he was 13, he moved to Nashville where his family ran a boardinghouse and where he heard various types of music, including Vaudeville acts.

Shown here in 1946 plowing corn at his farm, Uncle Dave illustrates his connection to rural America. He knew and related to the customs, philosophy, and lifestyle of the people; and he understood their likes in music and humor. *Photo courtesy David and Edna Macon*

When he married, he moved to Readyville, a community some 50 miles southeast of Nashville. He started farming, and he started a "freight hauling business." He used wagons and mules to transport produce, goods, and merchandise between Readyville and Nashville. He carried his banjo with him and sang along the way, whenever he stopped to rest, and at boarding and livery stations. It never occurred to him to charge for his performances until a local farmer paid him $15.00 for playing at a party. A talent scout heard him, offered him a one-night stand in Birmingham for $35.00, and these two events titillated him to develop the revolutionary idea of earning a livelihood by doing that which he enjoyed doing—playing, singing, and entertaining.

Uncle Dave turned the farming and freight business over to his wife Matilda and their nine children. In 1924, he started recording in New York on Vocalion Records. His early recordings became so popular that he was called back to New York repeatedly to record more of the old-time songs to satisfy an ever increasing demand. Many of the songs were old mountain ballads of the type Cecil

Sharp collected. But he tended to be eclectic in his choice of songs, including those with a tie to Vaudeville, the blues, and to old popular songs as well as hymns. In 1926 he joined the *Grand Ole Opry* and as more people acquired radios and could hear the *Opry* on the powerful WSM station, he became increasingly popular.

He recorded over 175 songs, and many of these are still available, after over nearly three quarters of a century. Although Uncle Dave had been an active farmer and teamster, he was considered to be the only professional on the *Opry* at the time. The other groups continued to make their living elsewhere, principally as farmers. He was also considered to be the first star of this, the longest running radio program in the history of broadcasting.

George D. Hay, known universally as the Solemn Old Judge and the founder of the *Grand Ole Opry*, wrote of Uncle Dave in 1937: "A troubadour of the Tennessee hills, Uncle Dave Macon, the Dixie Dewdrop, is one of the most colorful figures in the amusement world today." Dr. Charles Wolfe, the noted authority to whom I've previously referred in this book, said: "Uncle Dave must certainly be the Grandfather of Country Music." I agree.

Uncle Dave Macon, called the Grandfather of Country Music, is shown here warming his feet in his rural home in Cannon County, Tennessee. Standing beside him is George D. Hay, The Solemn Old Judge, founder of the *Grand Ole Opry* and the person who dubbed Uncle Dave, "The Dixie Dew Drop." *Photo courtesy David and Edna Macon*

The Courier, a magazine published by the Tennessee Historical Commission, recently stated that Uncle Dave had preserved more valuable American folklore than anyone except the Carter Family. Uncle Dave Macon was a fascinating, colorful, straight-from-the-country legend. Everybody who ever knew him, or who had any association with him, had a bag full of Uncle Dave stories. We've mentioned some of these in connection with the other folks we've included in the book. There are many more anecdotes, the following of which is a classic example: Someone asked Uncle Dave what he thought of the American superstar, a then young Bing Crosby. Uncle Dave responded, somewhat defensively: "He's a nice boy, I guess, but he'll never get anywhere until he learns to sing louder."

Uncle Dave died on March 22, 1952, at the age of 82, three weeks after he played his last show on the *Opry*. Although I never met him, I did become acquainted with his grandson, David Randolph Macon and his wife, Edna, from whom I was able to acquire some interesting Uncle Dave memorabilia, along with many great photographs. These are now a part of the Uncle Dave Macon exhibit in the Hall of Fame at the Museum of Appalachia.

I can't imagine anyone with the slightest interest in or exposure to old-time country music from the mid-1920s through the 1950s who was not familiar with and a fan of Uncle Dave Macon; and his influence certainly continues to this day. At our annual Homecoming, for example, we have two entertainers who dress, play, and sing like Uncle Dave. One is Leroy Troy, a popular entertainer, who makes his living replicating Uncle Dave. Then there's Dr. Hugh ("Uncle Doc") Wilhite of Calhoun, Kentucky, a family practitioner who emulates Uncle Dave in his dress, playing and rollicking singing.

Uncle Dave has been gone for almost 50 years, but his songs, his style, his wit and humor live on with an amazing familiarity, not only in the hearts and minds of those who remember seeing and hearing him, but also by many who were yet unborn when he passed on. As Dr. Charles Wolfe points out, Uncle Dave Macon, more than anyone else, took the 19th-century folk music and turned it into 20th-century country music.

Roy Acuff
The King of Country Music

We could, of course, have included Roy Acuff in an in-depth kind of way, for he **was** for several decades, the undisputed king of country music. We have mentioned him rather extensively in connection with the Bashful Brother Oswald story, and we could have devoted a full chapter to him; but we'll just add a bit more here.

He, like Chet Atkins (and the writer), came from Union County, a few miles north of Knoxville, one of the tiniest rural counties in the state. He was born in the hamlet of Maynardville in 1903, the son of Neil Acuff, a part-time farmer, postmaster, Baptist preacher, country fiddler, and later a Knoxville judge.

Roy learned to play the fiddle in bed by listening to old-time fiddlers on a hand-cranked phonograph as he was recovering from a sunstroke which occurred while he was playing baseball—his first love. He later toured with a medicine show, and in 1934 he formed a band and started playing on radio station WROL in Knoxville—for as little as 50 cents per show. In 1938 Roy Acuff and his Smoky Mountain Boys, then called the Crazy Tennesseans, joined the *Grand Ole Opry*, where Roy remained as a member for the next 54 years, until his death in 1992 at age 89.

I don't believe that it is an overstatement for one to assert that Roy Acuff was for a long time the most respected person in all country music. His down-home, old-time country style was what appealed to the people at that time. In addition to his unique, strained, and emotional singing which revolved around home, rural life, and family, often with religious references, Roy Acuff was well liked, not only by his fans, but also by his peers. Much of this is bound to be attributable to his modesty and lack of pretentiousness, and to his genuine love and concern for others. Once, when he learned that an old friend, a Union County farmer and fiddler named Bitt Rouse, had lost his arm in a corn picker, Roy dedicated the entire Saturday night *Grand Ole Opry* show to him. Bitt was so impressed, lying there in his hospital bed, that then and there he vowed to resume his fiddling, which he did; and he became known as "the one-armed fiddler from Union County."

I remember when our mutual friend Archie Campbell died. Many, maybe most, of those whom Archie had helped and had performed with over the years "couldn't" attend the funeral for various reasons. Just out of the hospital and almost blind from eye surgery, and enfeebled from another illness, Roy drove the 200 miles to Knoxville from Nashville and was one of the first persons to arrive at the funeral home. He never became so busy or important that he forgot his friends.

Some of those who started out playing and singing the old traditional music tried, some successfully, to change their style to suit the changing mood of the times. Roy never did. He essentially maintained the same band, and sang the same songs, such as "The Great Speckled Bird," "Wabash Cannonball," "Beautiful Brown Eyes," "The Glory Bound Train," and "Waiting for My Call to Glory," and literally hundreds of others, for some 54 years, even after most all other entertainers had "left" the old-time style.

One day while touring here at the Museum, he heard two old brothers, Stan and Otha Emert, singing from the porch of the Homestead House, and we could hardly pull him away. I recall that he said: "You just can't hear music like that in Nashville anymore."

The struggle endured by Roy Acuff in the early years, playing for nickels and dimes at school houses and local taverns, to his phenomenal success is a truly Horatio Alger type story. One writer wrote: "It is not an exaggeration to state that Roy alone transformed the *Grand Ole Opry* from just one of the many regional barn dances into a national institution." His was the first country music troupe to play on Broadway, and he played in every state, most of the Canadian provinces, and on every continent except South America and Antarctica.

There is an oft told story of a quickly and crudely made sign left by the Japanese during World War II, just before they retreated and as the Americans were approaching. The sign read: "To hell with F.D.R., Babe Ruth, and Roy Acuff."

One of his biographers, Elizabeth Schlappi in her book, *Roy Acuff—The Smoky Mountain Boy*, put it quite well when she wrote: "Brighter stars may shine here and there for a short time in the skies over country music, but not one is burning with a more enduring light than that of Roy Acuff."

When I took a framed enlargement of this picture to Roy in his dressing room one Saturday night, the inimitable Minnie Pearl was there, and she said: "Roy, you've had your picture taken a million times, but you've never had a better one taken than this one." Roy agreed. *Photo taken by Frank Hoffman at the Museum of Appalachia*

Redd Stewart
He wrote "The Tennessee Waltz" and over 400 other songs.

Henry E. (Redd) Stewart was born the son of a tenant farmer at the beginning of the Great Depression, in the late 1920s, near Ashland City, Tennessee. Even though his father supplemented his meager farm income by working as a cobbler, a barber, and as a cook (in nearby Nashville), he was forced to leave the farm during the Depression to search for a regular job in Louisville, Kentucky.

The father and mother, both part Cherokee, played music, and this doubtless influenced young Redd and his six brothers and sisters to take up music. "When I was nine or ten years old," Redd recalled, "I learned to play an old banjo that my daddy had made. Then it wasn't long before I was playing the fiddle."

At the age of 14, when he was in the seventh grade, Redd quit school, formed his own band, and was playing on radio station WGRC in Louisville. The group was called the Kentucky Wildcats.

His brother Bill, a great fiddler, was playing on the *Grand Ole Opry* when he was 16. He has a fine band today called The [Bill] Stewart Family Band. Their brother Gene also performed on the *Grand Ole Opry*, and another brother, Alvin, played on various radio stations before his death in the early 1970s. Brothers Eury (Slim) and Alvin started their musical career when they were ten and 13 years of age, respectively. They played guitar and banjo, instruments made by their father, and they were known as the Courier-Journal News Boys. Their two sisters, Juanita and Helen, were also musicians and were known as The Golden Girls.

In 1939 when he was 16, Redd Stewart joined the popular Pee Wee King and the Golden West Cowboys. He joined the Army in 1941 and served in the Pacific Theater. Influenced by the devastating scenes of war in the jungles, he wrote the song, "Soldier's Last Letter." Recorded first by Ernest Tubb, it became "an instant national hit." Redd rejoined Pee Wee King after the war

Redd Stewart is shown here at age 14 soon after he dropped out of school and formed his own band and started playing on radio station WGRC in Louisville, Kentucky. His straw hat and red bandana connoted his farm background, and the old-time country music he played. *Photo courtesy Redd and Bill Stewart*

and traveled throughout the world as a member of this popular band.

I once asked Redd how many songs he had written, and he answered: "I don't know exactly, but its over 400." He wrote "The Bonapart Retreat" and "Slowpoke," but "The Tennessee Waltz" was his best known and one of the most popular songs ever written. The following story of how "The Tennessee Waltz" came to be is based on a conversation I had with Redd during one of his visits with me here at the Museum in October of 1996.

On March 6, 1947, Redd Stewart and Pee Wee King were traveling by truck from a performance in Henderson, Texas. The radio was tuned to WSM's *Grand Ole Opry*. As they listened to Bill Monroe sing "The Kentucky Waltz," Pee Wee jokingly said to Redd, "Why haven't you written a song about your home state of Tennessee?"

At that moment, with pencil in hand and nothing but the cover from one of those large boxes of wooden matches on which to write, Redd began scribbling the words to "The Tennessee Waltz." Upon returning to his home in Nashville, he transcribed what he had written onto paper and penciled in the notes.

During this time in his life, Redd wrote and sold songs to various performers on the *Grand Ole Opry*. He offered to sell "The Tennessee Waltz" to a rising young singer, Cowboy Copas, for $25.00. Copas refused the offer, saying there were "too many waltzes already." So Redd put the song back in his guitar case where it remained for the next six months. He later sang it on a Louisville radio station in 1948, and it was recorded by others. It gained a good bit of popularity as a country song, and then it sort of faded away.

Several years later, the very popular Patti Page needed an additional song to complete a recording session she had planned. She agreed to add "The Tennessee Waltz" as the "B" side of the record. When it was released in May, 1950, Patti Page's recording of the song soon sold some 5,000,000 copies, and "it became the most popular song in the nation within six months." According to Dr. Bill Malone, a respected scholar on the subject, it became the biggest hit in modern popular music, and the top song ever licensed by Broadcast Music, Inc. (BMI). What started out as a country song, written by a country writer, became "an international pop standard."

The popularity of "The Tennessee Waltz" has continued through the years, and it reputedly has been played on radio and television more times than any country music song ever written. Several years ago the record sales were over 65,000,000, and I understand that it has now surpassed the 100,000,000 mark. It has been recorded by over 100 major artists, and it is a "Tennessee State Song." (Its popularity, of course, reached far beyond the boundary of country music, and it may be misleading to refer to it as a country song.)

Redd attended our Tennessee Fall Homecoming until his health forced him from the stage. His brother Bill, who also plays here every year, informed me recently that the

Redd Stewart at age 16 proudly poses with the members of his band, the Kentucky Wildcats. *Photo courtesy Redd and Bill Stewart*

very last time Redd ever sang "The Tennessee Waltz" was here at the Homecoming.

Although Redd was an entertainer, singer, and musician, his greatest gift to the development of country music was doubtless his songwriting. The fact that his early influence and inspiration was the old-time Carter-style music, and that his songs went beyond just "old time" and were enjoyed by those whose bent was for "progressive" country and even popular music, is an important part of the country music story.

Redd Stewart, shown seated on the right, wrote over 400 songs including "The Tennessee Waltz," which was first considered to be a country song, but which also became "the most popular song in the nation, and the biggest hit in modern popular music." Seated beside Redd is his brother Bill Stewart with fiddle, and on his left is Bill's wife Helen. Standing at left is Kent, son of Bill and Helen, and standing at right is the writer, John Rice Irwin. *Photo taken at the Museum of Appalachia in August, 1993*

When Jimmy Driftwood wrote songs to motivate his students in the mountains of northern Arkansas, he never imagined that these songs would go to "the top of the charts" in both the country and popular music fields, nor that he would be largely credited with the revival in America of folk music and other types of old-time music. He is shown here in this 1970s photo playing his guitar made from parts of a bedstead and an ox yoke, both of which his ancestors had brought to Arkansas when they migrated from Tennessee. *Photo courtesy Jimmy and Cleda Driftwood*

Jimmy Driftwood
A National Treasure

The story of Jimmy Driftwood from the Ozark Mountains in Arkansas is truly a remarkable and incredible one, and his influence on the revival of folk and old-time music borders on the amazing. He was born near the town of Mountain View in 1907, and he was named James Morris. Jimmy reputedly acquired the nickname of "Little Driftwood" shortly after his birth. As the story goes, a bell was rung at the farm to inform all within earshot, including the proud grandparents, of the baby's birth. Grandfather Elijah Morris arrived well in advance of his wife, and as a joke, he wrapped a piece of wood in a blanket; and when the out-of-breath grandmother eventually arrived, Elijah handed her the bundle. She assumed she was being given the newborn baby to hold, and she was quite surprised when she carefully took a look into the blanket, exclaiming: "Why, it's just a little chunk of driftwood."

At the age of ten, Jimmy learned to play a guitar which, he recalled, was made from parts of an old bedstead, an ox yoke, and a fence rail. (The ox yoke and the bedstead, Jimmy once told me, had been brought to Arkansas by his ancestors who migrated there from Tennessee.)

In 1923, at age 16, he walked for miles to teach in a one-room school, and he despaired that what he deemed a rich, colorful, exciting history, was not at all exciting to his students. He taught for several years and he, like all good teachers, sought ways to motivate his students. He later taught only the sixth grade and he started writing songs for that small rag-tag group of mountain boys and girls. In so doing, he did motivate them, and he also captured the fancy of untold millions of people and became a national celebrity and a folk hero in the process.

Jimmy was a farmer and a rancher as well as a teacher, and he developed an avid interest in history, even as a child. For example, he listened to the old folks talk about the famous Battle of New Orleans, one of the most one-sided battles in history from a casualty standpoint. The British suffered over 2,000 casualties, while the American losses under the command of Andrew Jackson of Tennessee numbered only 61.

When Jimmy wrote a song about this battle and sang it to his students to the accompaniment of his homemade guitar, the story they had read from the lackluster pages of history suddenly took on new meaning, and it became an exciting and meaningful adventure. When studying about the importance of horses on the frontier, he wrote about a famous racehorse which had been brought from Nashville to Arkansas called "The Tennessee Stud."

Over a period of time, Jimmy wrote over 1,000 songs, and his wife Cleda, a lovely lady and also a teacher who often sang with Jimmy, finally persuaded him to take 100 of his better songs to Nashville. They drove there in their old pickup and after a few days, they were ready to head back home to Arkansas in despair, because no one had expressed any interest in Jimmy's ballad-type songs— songs not in vogue at the time. But just as they were ready to leave Nashville, Cleda insisted that they make one last stop at a recording studio, and the company accepted some of the songs, one of which was "The Battle of New Orleans." It was recorded by Johnny Horton (and later by many other major artists), and it became an American classic. In addition to its phenomenal popularity in the country field, in 1959 it was rated number one on the "pop" charts and remained number one there for an incredible six weeks. This song and others, such as "Tennessee Stud" which was recorded by Eddy Arnold, are credited with helping to give birth to the national revival of historical ballads during that time. In 1959, six of Jimmy's songs were among the top 32 songs in the nation. They were Eddy Arnold's "Tennessee Stud," Johnny Horton's "Sal's Got a Sugar Lip," Hawkshaw Hawkins' "Soldier's Joy," Johnnie and Jack's "Sailor Man," Homer and Jethro's "Battle of Kookamonga," and, of course, Johnny Horton's "Battle of New Orleans."

He became recognized, not only as a songwriter and singer, but also as a lecturer on folk culture, history, and the like. He became a sort of national folk hero. He was made a permanent member of the *Grand Ole Opry*, and he was appointed by President Richard Nixon to the advisory board of the John F. Kennedy Center for Performing Arts. He played and sang for President Jimmy Carter's inauguration, and he was awarded three Grammys.

In recalling the story behind this picture, Jimmy Driftwood stated: "Jimmy Carter called and wanted me and Cleda to go to his inauguration, and we did. When he left the White House, he came by our farm and we killed and barbecued a big fat hog and everybody had a big time." *Photo courtesy Jimmy and Cleda Driftwood*

He performed and lectured at such places as Carnegie Hall, the Smithsonian Institute, the Newport Folk Festival, and the Berkley Folk Festival. His popular singing and talking lectures, extoling the culture and heritage of his native Arkansas and his nation were also received well in various other countries around the world, where he performed and lectured extensively. With the help of President Carter, Congressman Wilber Mills and others, he founded the Ozark Folk Center at Mountain View, near his home of Timbo, Arkansas. This center is often referred to as the Folk Capital of America.

When Jane Fonda was preparing herself for *The Doll Maker*, she spent a good bit of time with Jimmy and Cleda at their farm home near Timbo, learning country ways and speech from Jimmy in preparation for what came to be an important and widely acclaimed movie. Jane had visited us here at the Museum and she had told Jimmy, repeatedly he said, that he and Cleda ought to come and visit us, and that's "how come" I was able to have Jimmy and Cleda here for the October Homecoming for several years. He indeed was the kind of person who held the attention of everybody with his stories, his music, and his ballad singing.

When we later visited him at his home in Arkansas, I was impressed with his 1000-acre ranch and all his cattle. I said in jest, "Jimmy, like you, I was a teacher, a principal and a school superintendent, and I made very little money. How did you accumulate all this land and all these cattle on a school teacher's salary?"

As always, Jimmy had a quick, ready and most appropriate answer. "Old Andy Jackson bought all this for me," he said, with mischievous laughter, referring to the song he wrote about Jackson's Battle of New Orleans.

Jimmy's international fame did not infringe upon his neighborliness or his mountain hospitality one whit. He once told me: "Everywhere we've ever played, all over the world, I've invited people to visit us. If we're not home, they know to come in and make some coffee—find something to eat. We never lock the doors."

The reader will note that Jimmy's early involvement with old-time music was remarkably similar to that of all the other musicians we've observed. He was from a poor rural background, he developed an early interest in the traditional and old-time music, and he learned to play as a tyke of ten, on a homemade instrument. But unlike most of the others about whom I've written, he developed a profound and abiding interest in all aspects of his environment, and his enthusiastic interests were not confined to the subject of early music. He had, or acquired, what I call "a sense of history," a characteristic necessary for developing maximum potential in any and all fields of endeavor.

Perhaps this sense of history, along with his prolific songwriting, was at least partially responsible for his ability to endure so many tragedies. The same can be said for his dear wife Cleda. They lost their only daughter in her youth, and their other children, two sons, died in a most tragic manner, reportedly as a result of a murder/suicide, which occurred in the home while Jimmy and Cleda were away for the day. In later life, Jimmy and Cleda were involved in a devastating car wreck, leaving both of them critically injured and maimed for life.

Nevertheless Jimmy kept writing, kept singing, kept being totally thrilled when he learned another old fiddle tune, and especially exhilarated when he wrote his latest song. One night in 1997, he had Cleda call me from Timbo, the first time I'd heard from him in several months. Cleda said: "Hold on John Rice, here's Jimmy." And without saying a word, he started singing a song he had just written about Tennessee, the home of his forebears. When he finished singing the song, he said: "I wrote that for you and I'm sending it to you."

The last time he and Cleda drove the 600 miles from Timbo to perform at the Homecoming was in 1993. They were extremely well received during the three days they spent here, but Jimmy wasn't pleased with his performances. Several weeks later, it was brought to my attention, "Jimmy Driftwood has never cashed the check you sent him." And despite my repeated demands that he do so, he never did.

Cleda called me on July 12, 1998, to tell me of Jimmy's passing at the age of 91. Although he is gone, he lives on through the multitude of songs he wrote, and there are few festivals and old-time mountain music get-togethers in the country at which some of Jimmy's songs are not played and sung.

Dolly Parton
"She has probably done more for country music all over the world than any other person."

The oft-told story of Dolly Parton's dramatic life, from her childhood as a poor mountain girl to her rise as one of the country's most successful and long-lasting entertainers, has not been exaggerated. To understand this large but tight-knit and loving family provides insight and understanding into one of the country's most colorful success stories in the entertainment world. It also provides lessons relative to today's much touted importance of the family as a unit, and the comfort, love, and support it provides.

Dolly, the fourth of 12 children, was born January 19, 1946, in a one-room cabin to Lee and Avia Lee Parton in a rural and isolated section of Sevier County, some 40 miles southeast of Knoxville. Willadeene was the oldest child and even as a youngster, she served as a sort of mother figure to the other children. This was especially true with regard to her relationship with Dolly, who stated, "Willadeene was like a second mother to us all."

Volumes could be, and have been, written about the fabulous career of Dolly Parton, and these few pages cannot commence to chronicle her career as a singer, songwriter, movie star, entertainer, businesswoman, and philanthropist. I will, however, talk about that important aspect of her life which is often alluded to only in passing, but seldom revealed in a substantive and in-depth manner—her family, her childhood and her growing up years.

Much of the pioneer spirit, the love of family, the lore of old, the emphasis on total honesty, neighborliness, and an unwavering faith in God, and in oneself, which the Parton family possessed was undoubtedly a result of their local culture and their heritage. Severe poverty existed there much longer and more intensely than in other parts of the country.

The superficial image of an isolated cabin set in a hollow shadowed by those beautiful old mountains may first appear to be romantic and blissful, but there were hardships and repeated and relentless challenges; and the conquering of these adversities added strength, self-confidence, and an appreciation for life when these troubles were dealt with.

Lee Parton married Avia Lee Owens when she was 15 and he was 17 years of age. By the time Avia was 35, she had given birth to 12 children. Both the Parton and Owens families were well known and well respected but poor mountain folks, who had lived in that remote area of East Tennessee for as far back as anyone could remember. Interestingly and parenthetically, this area was near where Cecil Sharp, the English song collector, discovered more old English, Scottish, and Irish ballads than he had found in any of his travels in Europe or America. Perhaps this environment served to inspire and motivate all the children to develop a love for the music of the mountains; and every one of them, like their parents, learned to play one or more musical instruments. In addition to her singing, Willadeene is a poet and has written three books; and Stella, like Dolly, is a writer, musician, singer, and actress. Randy is a singer and musician, and Floyd, in addition to his singing and playing music, is also a songwriter. One of his songs, "Rocking Years," was a 1991 "song of the year." Frieda (Floyd's twin) is also a musician, writer, and singer; and Rachel, in addition to her musical and songwriting talents, is an actress. She played in the television version of *Nine to Five*. Cassie's a singer and part-time writer, and David, Denver, and Bobby are, according to Willadeene, all good singers but have not performed professionally.

Like most mountain families of the time and area, the Partons quickly learned the art of "make do" in conditions more primitive and stark than the poorest of the poor today. It is remarkable that they were able to provide for themselves and it is more remarkable that they were, as family members, apparently a most happy, loving and caring lot.

Willadeene remembers those early years more vividly than do some of the younger children. She recalls, for example, when there were only two chairs in the house, and two plank benches, one on each side of the kitchen table where the children ate. The girls' dresses were made from feed sacks, a practice which I remember my mother and all our neighbors following. Sometimes fertilizer sacks were used, but they were of a coarser, more scratchy and less supple fabric.

"We used bucket lids for plates and snuff cans for drinking glasses," Willadeene remembers. In the shank of the winter, as early as January or February, the children, under the tutelage of "Granny" Liddy Owens, gathered both dry land and water cresses. They picked poke, dandelions, dock, and many other kinds of "greens" for cooking; they gathered other plants for dyeing cloth; and various herbs were picked for medicinal purposes. During the summer months, Willadeene recalls, the children gathered, from the adjacent woodland, hazelnuts, walnuts, hickory nuts, and even beech nuts for the winter. They gathered pods from high in the honey locust trees. (I remember my hungry schoolmates doing the same.) Persimmons, haws, blackberries, pawpaws, and hackberries were gathered and eaten on the way to and from school. Wild berries and wild grapes were made into jam, jelly, and preserves; and apples were dried in the sun for winter use. Green beans likewise were dried over a period of days in the hot sun so they would last indefinitely, even for years. The Partons called these "shuck" beans because, I assume, they rattled like dry corn shucks. They were sometimes called "leather britches" or shucky beans.

Potatoes and turnips were stored in a hole dug in the ground and could be removed a few at a time during the winter months. Lee Parton, Dolly recalled, always carefully stored two bushels of his best potatoes in the "hole" for next year's planting. Seed potatoes, he called them. Bees were kept and the honey not consumed by the family was sold. Hogs were raised and butchered, and every part was utilized.

Lee worked as a laborer, when he had the chance, on local construction jobs, and he traded in horses and mules. He also trapped on the nearby creeks and branches for muskrat and mink, and in the mountainous area for 'possum, skunk, 'coon—all fur-bearing animals. He skinned them and sold the pelts or traded them for staples at George Franklin's store or to Greene's Rolling Store. Squirrels and rabbits were hunted or trapped for food, and the rabbit skins fetched 5 or 10 cents each. Willadeene stated, somewhat abashed, that the family sometimes ate turtles from the creeks and ponds. I can attest to the fact that "mud" turtle meat is indeed very tasty if cooked properly.

Molassie cane was raised for making sorghum which was eaten as a syrup and used as a substitute for sugar. Laundry starch was made from flour; and soap was made from hog skins and lye, which was also homemade, from the hardwood ashes in the fireplace.

The Partons first lived on land which belonged to a neighbor, "Aunt" Martha Williams, to whom the Parton family gave a share of their crops as rent. The Partons were, in other words, sharecroppers. Parenthetically, it just occurs to me that virtually every musician to whom we have introduced the reader was also from a sharecropping family. Mac Wiseman, Raymond Fairchild, Earl Scruggs, Redd Stewart, Bob Douglas, Jimmy Driftwood, and Grandpa Jones all farmed on land which they did not own.

Even in her early childhood, Dolly possessed an inquisitive mind and a zest for life. She was described by her sisters as an active, curious, mischievous little girl, always chasing kittens, butterflies, and June bugs; and gathering wildflowers. But it was apparent that Dolly Parton had grit and fortitude. Once she almost severed her toes on a half-buried iron object while playing barefoot near her home. Willadeene remembers that her mother poured kerosene on the wound and then sewed the dangling toes back in place with a common needle and thread. Her brothers held the foot in place, and there was no anesthetic whatever, but Dolly never cried.

She first exhibited an interest in music when, at the age of seven, she strung an old mandolin with strings she got from the remnants of a piano which had been left in an abandoned church. She soon learned to play, enough that she could accompany herself as she sang the old mountain ballads.

Much more attention could be paid to the grinding poverty and the periods of despair which befell the Parton family—the time, for example, when Avia and several of the children were gravely sick with influenza and little David had pneumonia and was given up to die. Avia, herself in danger of dying, would rally periodically and ask about her little boy, "Is he any better? Is he going to be all right?" She would pray to God to spare her little boy, until she lapsed back into a deep sleep. Lee's mother, Grandma Parton, came to help with the houseful of sick, and she, too, prayed, down on her knees, for their recovery. All the family did recover, but tragedy struck the Partons later on when little 18-month-old Margie died of pneumonia, preceded by the measles. The family children remember that their little sister died on a cold November night among family and neighbors. The church bell was tolled as was the custom when a person in the community died. The women in the neighborhood brought food; two uncles made a tiny coffin; some of the kind ladies made the child a burial dress; and others lined the coffin with their best cloth.

Grandma Cass and Grandma Tenny bathed their young grandchild with homemade camphor and dressed her for burial. Then Grandma Cass carefully laid the tiny body in her coffin, and the next day the men carried it a half mile in the cold rain to the graveyard where other neighbors had dug the grave. Her mother and father were greatly saddened with the death of their little girl, as if it had been their only child. A few days later they made a small headstone from a field rock, and they placed it on Margie's grave.

Who and what motivated Dolly to develop such an obsessive interest in singing and in music at such an early age? There appears not to be a simplistic answer to this question. She was, of course, introduced to hymn singing in the church, and her grandfather, "Uncle Jake Owens," had cherished and cared for the ancestral fiddle, and he loved music. He started preaching when he was 17 and later "taught" music in the neighborhood. He was the inspiration for the popular song Dolly co-wrote with her Aunt Dorothy: "Daddy Was An Old-time Preacher Man." It has often been observed that good and lasting things frequently result from sad, disappointing, and hurtful happenings, and this was certainly true in the case of the little coat Dolly's mother made for her. Winter was coming and Dolly had no coat, and for weeks Avia "pieced together" the many colorful scraps of cloth the neighbors had brought her. She, too, had saved pieces from worn out shirts, trousers, and coats. These scraps were intended to be used in making quilts, but Avia selected those most colorful for making Dolly's coat because she knew Dolly's affinity for such.

Each day after school Dolly would assess the progress her mother had made on the coat, and Dolly looked forward with great anticipation to the time the coat was finished and the weather was cold so she could wear it to school.

The time soon came, but instead of the approval and compliments she expected from her classmates, Dolly was confronted with laughter and ridicule and all manner of derisive comments; and she was totally devastated. This unpleasant incident inspired her, many years later, to write the song, "Coat of Many Colors" which became so popular that Dolly claims it as her signature song.

I once asked Willadeene if her mother ever sang, and she indicated that Avia "sang around the house" some. I was interested in learning the type songs she sang, and Willadeene graciously taped some for me to hear. The songs, not surprisingly, were from the old Carter Family, and Avia's plaintiff and lilting voice sounded remarkably like Mother Maybelle and Sara. Although Avia had never sung in public, I asked Willadeene if she would bring her to our Homecoming to sing with Willadeene and her group. At first it seemed that Mother Avia might do so, but then she became more anxious as the time neared and she decided not to "start her career" at her somewhat advanced age. Since she was an infant, Dolly had heard her mother sing these old songs, and the influence this had on Dolly can only be left to conjecture, but it may have been profound.

Soon after Dolly started singing around the house with her sisters, her Uncle Bill Owens took note. He had musical aspirations himself, and he became what Dolly described as her first and special agent.

It was he who was responsible for introducing her to the legendary Cas Walker, resulting in Cas hiring her for his early morning radio program in Knoxville. Cas was easily the region's most popular, interesting, loved, hated and talked about personality of his time in all the region. He, too, was from a poor mountain home near the Parton place in Sevier County, and he had become extremely wealthy through prodigious work and involvement in many ventures, the most successful of which was a chain of supermarkets, one of which was reputed to have been the world's largest at the time. He had several radio programs to promote his groceries, and "everybody" listened to "old Cas" and the many local singers of old-time music. It was natural, therefore, for all aspiring entertainers in East Tennessee and from surrounding states to try to "get on" one of Cas Walker's shows.

That's why Bill Owens took his precocious 10-year-old niece to see Cas Walker. She remembers the event as if it happened yesterday. As usual Cas was in a big rush, and Dolly hardly knew what to say, but she apparently impressed the enigmatic mountain man. She said: "Mr. Walker, I want to work for you." Cas responded forthwith, and said: "Well, you've got a job. A lot of people come to me and say they want a job, but you're the first person who ever said they wanted to work." Cas later said: "I put her on to see what she could do, and she went over like a house afire."

She sang her first song on one of Cas' programs, just the way she had practiced singing on the woodpile in the back yard. The people who had gathered to hear the live broadcast "exploded with approval" and Dolly knew for sure that entertaining was her calling. She soon became much talked about in the Knoxville area—that little girl from Sevier County with the sweet but gusty voice. She later appeared on Cas' television programs and received $5.00 for each show. Her parents were much impressed with the money she was paid, but they were unable to watch her because they had no television.

When she was 13, Dolly's Uncle Bill took her to Nashville, and she begged, pleaded and pushed herself until she was finally allowed to sing a song on the *Grand Ole Opry*, and she was stunned that none other than Johnny Cash was there to introduce her. She knew it was a live program, nationwide, and even Dolly, with her self-assurance and over-confident spirit, was challenged.

When she finished, 2,000 people applauded, and they would not stop until she returned for another song, and then another. Three encores and Dolly was ecstatic.

By day, Dolly and her Uncle Bill visited one recording studio after another, and they'd wait for hours to talk to anyone who might listen to this little girl from Locust Ridge. At night, they slept in Bill's old car, and they had little or no money for food. Dolly returned home to finish high school, and she continued to appear regularly on the Cas Walker early morning *Farm and Home Hour*, returning after her performance to her home 30 miles away in time for school.

When Dolly's graduation day came, parents and neighbors came to bid adieu to the little band of seniors, most of whom would likely leave their mountain homes forever. All the graduates were asked about future plans—where they would go and "what they wanted to be." Dolly, in her usual forward and self-confident way, gleefully said that she was going to go to Nashville and become a star. She expected smiles, nods of approval, even a light applause. But what she got was boisterous and derisive laughter. Dolly was stunned, and she slept little that night. But this, like many adversities, strengthened her resolve and hardened her ambition.

As the Parton family grew, Lee bought a few acres of land and built a larger house to replace the one-room cabin they had occupied. Both Lee and Avia, as well as all the children, worked hard, managed well, spent little, and sacrificed much, but by the time Dolly graduated from high school, the financial conditions of the Partons had worsened. A few days before Dolly left for Nashville, she found her usually composed and resolute mother softly crying. They had lost their little farm and the house for which they had worked so long and hard. Dolly told her mother not to worry, that as soon as she made enough money she would buy the farm back for the family. Slim chance of this happening, logic would suggest, because Nashville was full of talented and struggling young entertainers, most of whom would never meet with any success in the music world.

Early one morning Dolly took a Greyhound bus bound for Nashville, carrying all her possessions in three large paper bags. Dolly remembers that all the family gathered around to see her off, and they were all crying, and she admitted that she, too, cried all the way to Nashville. Although she got a job on an early morning television program, the money she received wasn't enough for rent and food. She stated that she would sometimes walk through corridors of the Nashville motels and find leftover food scraps set beside the doors of those who had had room service. She lost down to 90 pounds but she wrote her parents: "Don't worry about trying to send me any money. I've got a job on an early morning TV show, and I'll be making enough to get by on." She knew the hard times her parents were undergoing, and they likely could not have sent money even if Dolly had requested it.

True to her word, Dolly saved and skimped and as soon as she was financially able to do so, years later, she did buy the farm for her mother and father. Further, she had the house expanded, totally renovated and fully furnished it. She showered the family with other gifts, including new automobiles for her mother, who then

Dolly never failed to give credit to Cas Walker for starting her career on one of his early morning radio shows in Knoxville, when she was only 9 years old. This photo, taken in 1987 when Cas was 87 years old, was inscribed by Dolly: "To Cas—I love you—Thanks for a great start in life. Dolly 1987" *Photo courtesy Cas Walker*

learned to drive. Avia, liking a touch of affluence, gave up her snuff-dipping habit and started smoking cigarettes instead, which was at the time more stylish and acceptable.

Willadeene, who traveled with Dolly for years and who served as her helpmate, once said, "Dolly is truly the busiest and most generous person I have ever known."

Dolly started to gain recognition after she joined the popular Porter Wagoner Show in 1967 where she remained for the next seven years. Even as she gained national attention as an important member of Wagoner's band, she reportedly received only $300 for each show.

In 1974, to the surprise of the country music world, Dolly left Porter and went on her own. In 1975 she was voted by the Country Music Association as the outstanding female vocalist of the year, and that same year she became the first female country singer to have a syndicated television program, carried by 130 stations across the country.

For the next quarter century, her popularity continued as a singer and she distinguished herself as an important songwriter, prompting one country music scholar to declare that she was one of the most gifted writers in country music history. Both her singing and the songs she has written often were embraced by the popular music people as well as by country music fans. Her song "I'll Always Love You," which she wrote and sang and which was popularized by Whitney Houston, is an example.

Some have criticized Dolly, saying she abandoned the old-time country music, but others have hailed her for helping country music to expand so as to attract both country and popular music enthusiasts. Her historic albums with Emmylou Harris and Linda Ronstadt starting in 1987 represented a return to the poignant and simplistic songs and ballads of the Carter Family, and they became extremely popular across the country.

Her career broadened to include starring roles in movies, with the likes of Burt Reynolds, Jane Fonda, and Kenny Rogers. Additionally, she has proven to be an astute businesswoman, and she has made numerous important monetary contributions to the school children of her native Sevier County. Her entertainment and recreation park, Dollywood, attracts millions of people from throughout the country and the world.

No attempt will be made to even allude to her many and varied accomplishments, but it is significant, I think, to point out that her popularity, some 45 years after she started singing for Cas Walker on the Knoxville radio station, continues to remain remarkably strong. She is, even today, one of the most recognized figures on the American entertainment scene. The following anecdote adequately illustrates this observation.

As I was finishing this bit about Dolly, in longhand on yellow legal pads, I took a brief respite, and while doing so I read the *Knoxville News-Sentinel*. I had almost finished when I turned one of the last pages in the issue where my eyes fell upon a short, inconspicuous article titled: "Parton's All Over the Dial." The article chronicles three days of her then current schedule. On Thursday of that week she appeared on ABC's *Good Morning America* at 8:00 a.m. That night she was a guest on David Letterman's evening show on CBS. The next day she was back on ABC appearing on a talk show with Barbara Walters; and on Monday, she appeared on Rosie O'Donnell's show. A few days later, on June 17, 1999, Dolly's picture appeared prominently on the front page of *USA Today*, announcing that she had been inducted into the Country Music Hall of Fame. The article referred to her as "globally famous as a singer, songwriter and actor." Ed Benson, the executive director of the Country Music Hall of Fame, stated: "Dolly Parton has probably done more for country music all over the world than any other person."

The Radio and Early Country Music

Without the radio, the development of early country music would have been like the coal mines of Appalachia without freight trains, or the orange groves in Florida without trucks. In each case the product would have been of virtually no use without a delivery system, and old-time country music may have remained in the mountain enclaves and country villages had it not been for the radio as a delivery system.

The radio took early country music from the back porches, front yards, and community pie suppers to untold millions across the country. As if to justify this new and sometimes suspicioned "tool of the devil," several songs were written to represent the radio, not as the devil's device, but as an instrument of God. One of the old Carter Family songs, for example, was titled "Heaven's Radio":
There's a wonderful invention, it's called the radio
You can hear it everywhere you chance to go
But the static in the air sometimes makes it hard to hear
But it is not so with heaven's radio
Heaven's radio, on the other shore
For my Sacred Savior always listens in,
Listens in to Heaven's radio

A similar type song was titled "Turn Your Radio On." Some of the lines were: "Turn your lights down low and listen to the Master's radio. Get in touch with God; turn your radio on."

The reader will recall that virtually every early musician discussed in this book started on a small radio station. The importance of the radio in the development of this music can hardly be over estimated. For illustrative purposes we'll briefly take note of its role in one city, Knoxville, Tennessee.

Two men were especially important in the early recognition and distribution of early country music in Knoxville. One of these persons was Cas Walker, previously mentioned as the man who started Dolly Parton's career. He had radio programs on WROL and WIVK and other stations, and later he had a television program on WBIR. The other major radio station, WNOX, was for decades identified with Lowell Blanchard. These stations saturated the region with their broadcasts, and they were surprisingly instrumental in exerting influence on this early form of music across the country.

Knoxville, more than Nashville, had been known as a regional gathering place for the old-time fiddle conventions held there around the turn of the century, attracting noted regional fiddlers and audiences numbering in the thousands. These fiddlers, unlike their latter-day counterparts, tended to be men of some means, proud of the old-time music, and they often dressed in suits, white shirts, and ties.

Robert L. Taylor, for example, was one of those who played at these gatherings in Knoxville, and he was well

Knoxville was known as a regional center for old-time fiddle conventions and fiddle contests during the late 1800s, and during the first part of the 20th century. This was before the era when this type music and the musicians who played it came to be depicted in the foot stomping, toe tapping barefoot hillbilly kind of way.

Many of these old-time fiddlers, while playing the same old British tunes as the stereotypical ill-dressed mountain fiddler, often viewed themselves in a more formal, dignified, and classical manner, as this picture of Louis Wilson's band suggests. My great-uncle Lee Irwin, third from the right, was a full-time farmer and cattleman, but he was also known in several states as a champion old-time fiddler. His daughter, Lois Irwin, the only woman in the group, is shown with the cello. *Photo by Robin Thompson, Knoxville, Tennessee—Courtesy of Uncle Lee's grandson, Dr. Caulton Irwin of Morgantown, West Virginia*

known as an old-time fiddler. He defeated his brother Alf Taylor in the celebrated race for Governor of Tennessee in 1886, called "The War of the Roses." He served a total of three terms as governor, and he was later elected to the U. S. Senate.

It is not known to this writer whether Knoxville's notoriety as a center for old-time fiddlers' conventions and its early role in radio broadcasting is connected, but Knoxville certainly pioneered in this new medium.

Knoxville's WNOX came on the air in 1921, the first radio station in the state, and reputedly one of only eight radio stations in the nation at the time. Students of the subject still disagree as to why Nashville, rather than Knoxville, became "The Country Music Capitol" and the recording center of the nation. The point is often made that it was because some of the elite population of Knoxville looked down on what was derisively called "hillbilly" music, and thus they failed to support it. While this may have been a contributing factor, the more compelling reason probably lies in the fact that Nashville came on the air with its WSM radio station in 1925, backed by the giant National Life and Accident Insurance Company. WSM was infinitely more powerful than WNOX, and the *Grand Ole Opry* was started the same year, casting the die for Nashville's predominance in the industry.

The influence of WNOX on the development of early country music, however, is truly legendary. During the 1930s and 1940s, WNOX reportedly carried over 150 half-hour programs each week, most of them featuring "early" country music. But it was the *Mid-Day Merry-Go-Round*, started by Lowell Blanchard in 1935, that was the crown jewel of all those programs on WNOX. Farmers, factory workers, and indeed "just about everybody" listened to the popular program during their "dinner" (noon meal) hour.

The *Mid-Day Merry-Go-Round* has been described as the "stepping stone" to the *Grand Ole Opry*. Lowell hired the likes of Roy Acuff, Archie Campbell, Earl Scruggs, the Carter Family, Carl Story and The Rambling Mountaineers, Mac Wiseman, Kitty Wells, Homer and Jethro, Sunshine Slim Sweet, and a hundred more performers during the 30 years of the existence of the *Merry-Go-Round*. Many of these entertainers went on, not only to the *Grand Ole Opry*, but also to other powerful radio stations in various parts of the country.

Lowell Blanchard started Knoxville's legendary *Mid-Day Merry-Go-Round* on WNOX, the first radio station in Tennessee, and reputed to be one of the first eight stations in the nation. The *Merry-Go-Round* was often referred to as the stepping stone to the *Grand Ole Opry*. *Photo taken about 1940, courtesy Sunshine Slim Sweet*

One of those hired by Lowell was a teenager from nearby Union County who came to the station "dressed in a pair of overalls, a blue shirt, and carrying a $5.00 guitar." He was from a family so poor that he developed scurvy from lack of proper food, and he had left home to "wander around" in search of a job. His name was Chet Atkins, and he became one of the world's best known guitarists.

It's most coincidental, but the very evening I was writing this mite on Chet, I happened to see a documentary-type program on him, illustrating the style guitar he played when he started on WNOX. Asked about his poor upbringing, Chet quickly responded to the interviewer with one succinct sentence: "That's what made me."

A young Chet Atkins is shown here soon after he started his career on Knoxville's *Mid-Day Merry-Go-Round* radio program in the early 1940s. He came off the street in a pair of overalls with a $5.00 guitar, and Lowell Blanchard hired him for the *Merry-Go-Round*. After a few years, he went to Nashville, and according to one of his biographers, he "developed virtual domination of the country music world." *Photo from about 1945, courtesy Country Music Foundation*

He went on to say that if he had been exposed to other guitar players when he started playing as a child, he may not have developed his own distinctive style—or styles.

I remember listening to Chet soon after he started playing on the *Merry-Go-Round*, and I remember how Lowell encouraged him and bragged on him. He would always say that Chet's playing sounded like three guitars being played at the same time.

The narrator of the television program pointed out that Chet had received ten Grammy Awards and had sold over thirty million records. He also pointed out that Chet Atkins influenced a generation of musicians in the country, popular, and rock-and-roll sector as well.

Once when Chet visited the Museum, he took special note of a very old log house I had moved here from near his boyhood home in Union County, and I shall never forget his comment: "That old log house set close to where we lived, and my greatest ambition as a child was to someday have a house that fine." It's safe to assume that Chet's dream did indeed come true.

But then Chet Atkins was but one of dozens of important musicians to get their start from Lowell Blanchard and his ever popular *Mid-Day Merry-Go-Round*. If ever there was an institution which owed its whole being to one person, then the *Merry-Go-Round* owed such a debt to Lowell Blanchard. He initiated, nurtured, and developed it. He served as the Master of Ceremonies of the *Merry-Go-Round* from the beginning, and he was often called the most popular personality in all East Tennessee. (Others would reserve this title for WROL's Cas Walker.)

This photograph of a crowd waiting for the doors to open for the *Mid-Day Merry-Go-Round* is indicative of the popularity of this Knoxville based radio program. A spin-off of the *Merry-Go-Round* was the *Tennessee Barn Dance*, broadcast nationally on CBS. *Photo taken in the early 1940s, courtesy Sunshine Slim Sweet*

Lowell, a Midwesterner by birth, worked as program director for a small radio station in Iowa; and in that capacity, he hired a young Ronald Reagan as an announcer. During his years in Knoxville, he initiated many other radio programs including the *Tennessee Barn Dance*, a Saturday night radio program which was broadcast nationally on CBS. He was active in the total community, and he served on the city council and on numerous charitable boards. He was posthumously inducted into the Country Music Hall of Fame.

Cas Walker, many believe, helped to start and expand the careers of as many or more early country music folks than any other person. The contributions of the enigmatic, largely uneducated, mountain man are especially incredulous when one considers that he was not a musician himself, and arguably knew virtually nothing about the music industry.

He, like Dolly Parton, was born in a remote cabin in Sevier County, Tennessee, also one of 12 children. Cas left home at the age of 14, followed an Indian trail across the Great Smoky Mountains, sleeping in "overhanging caves" at night and foraging from the forest for three days. He joined a timber cutting crew on the North Carolina side of the mountains and even as a young teenager, he drew a man's wage as a lumberjack.

The legendary Cas Walker, standing second from left, is shown with his father and mother and eight of his 11 brothers and sisters. He was destined to become one of the most colorful men in all Southern Appalachia and he was a highly successful businessman, radio and TV personality, mayor of Knoxville, and a person who is credited with helping to start the music careers of Tennessee Ernie Ford, The Everly Brothers, Dolly Parton, the Louvin Brothers, and over 200 other entertainers. Members of his family shown in this picture include, from the left in the front row: Sallie, his father Tom Walker holding Dora, his mother Annie holding Ada, and Erma. Back row from the left are the Walker children: Hobert, Cas, Pearl, Lillie and Ambrose. *Photo courtesy Cas Walker.*

CAS WALKER---&--HOMER HARRIS ∟⨉
TRICK HORSE DOLLY. YR.
RIDIN' MY HORSE OO THE RADIO 1949

Cas Walker, at right, used thousands of gimmicks, many involving early country music entertainers, to sell groceries from his chain of supermarkets. He is shown in this 1949 photograph with the popular Homer Harris, mounted on his "Trick Horse Dolly," inside one of Cas' stores. *Photograph courtesy Homer Harris*

After three years in the log woods, he hoboed on a freight train to Kansas where he first worked in a grocery store and then threshed wheat throughout much of the state; then he was in Colorado harvesting sugar beets; thence to the hayfields of Wyoming. He herded "864 head of cattle" in Montana, and then he dug potatoes in Idaho. After two years of working in the West, he became homesick and came back to Tennessee to help his father tend the little mountain farm. Before long he and his brother Avis were off to eastern Kentucky to work in the coal mines. As usual, Cas worked longer and harder than anyone else.

He dug coal in a mine only 38 inches high for the Harlan Colliers Co. Several years ago, I asked my newspaper friend Vic Weals of Knoxville to check on Cas' claim that he had loaded more coal by hand than any miner in the company. Weals did, indeed, verify with the bookkeeper for the company that Cas was paid for having loaded an average of 13 ton of coal per day, by hand, a record which company documents indicated had never been broken.

Cas had saved enough money to buy a small grocery store in the poorest section of Knoxville which he opened in 1923 on his 21st birthday. He delivered turnips, potatoes, coffee, cabbage, and sugar in a little wagon, which he pulled through the streets, but which was later "powered" by a billy goat. By chance, Cas bought a "spot" on an early morning radio station, and he took a couple of local singers and guitar players with him. The early-rising farmers and cotton mill workers tuned in to listen to the old songs they loved to hear, and between songs, Cas sold groceries at a cut-rate price. In later years, he often said: "That old-time country music sold groceries."

It was a long and fascinating road, but the result was that Cas Walker eventually built a chain of supermarkets in Knoxville, East Tennessee, Kentucky, and in Virginia. One of his stores was reputed to have been the world's largest.

He became a dominant force in local politics; and he served on the Knoxville City Council for many years, as Vice-Mayor, and even as Mayor of Knoxville. He seemed to love to help those who needed help, and he was always raising funds for those whose homes had burned or were destroyed by floods. He started the Knoxville Milk Fund, a charitable organization which remains viable today, to provide milk for poor and destitute families. When I was starting the Tennessee Fall Homecoming, he worked tirelessly to promote it on his television shows, and he allowed my band to play on his program as often as we wished, to promote the event.

Cas, perhaps by accident and intuition, soon learned the magic which could be wrought by radio (and later television) combined with the singers and musicians of the old-time music which the people in Southern Appalachia were so eager to hear. And although his primary purpose in featuring these entertainers was to promote and advertise his wares, the by-product was the starting and nurturing of careers of many musicians.

We've already mentioned Dolly Parton, who has always credited Cas for her start. There was Tennessee Ernie Ford whom Cas hired as a bag boy for one of his stores, and as a singer on one of his early morning radio shows. Tennessee Ernie became popular with his country, gospel, and popular music. His own network radio program and prime-time appearances on national television made him one of the country's most popular entertainers in the late 1950s. Cas is credited with first calling Ernie "The Old Pea Picker," a nickname which he accepted, and kept all his life.

I asked Cas about the entertainers, as he called them, whom he had started on one of his several radio programs or in later years on one of his television programs. He kept mentioning so many familiar and famous names that I, apologetically, thought I should check on my old friend. I asked Curly Dan Bailey, a singer and musician who had played on Cas' programs for decades, if he would verify those whose music and singing careers Cas had helped to start. Curly Dan is a meticulous kind of person, very thorough and very reliable, and after a few weeks, he sent me the list, and it was, as they say, unbelievable. There was a total of 219 singers, musicians, and music groups who either started with Cas, or who had worked for him in the early days of their careers. Included in this group were the Everly Brothers, thereby providing fodder for the contention, made in pseudo-jest that Cas Walker was responsible for the birth of the Beatles. The story goes like this:

Ike Everly and his family lived in the coal mining section of eastern Kentucky, and they played "old-timey music." Cas liked their traditional style of playing and he hired the family to play on his shows in Knoxville. Cas liked the family's singing, but the two young boys, Don and Phil, started venturing off into a more modern and trendy style of music. Cas once told me that they wanted to do "that jumping up and down kind of music."

He kept warning them about their wayward ways, and finally he informed them that if they didn't quit that fancy, modern kind of stuff, he'd have to "get shed" of them. It wasn't long before there was a parting of the ways and the Everly Brothers left, and they eventually became one of the most popular acts in the country.

When the Beatles appeared on the scene, they created a truly world-wide phenomenon. It has been widely reported that the Beatles, on more than one occasion, had indicated that their major inspiration was the Everly Brothers. So, there. Cas was even responsible for circuitously starting the Beatles. . . maybe.

Others who appeared on Cas' radio programs include: Carl Story and The Rambling Mountaineers; The Masters Family; David West and the Cider Mountain Boys; and banjo player Larry Mathis. One of the early singers Cas hired was Hugh Cross who later teamed up with Roy Rogers and many of the leading country and western entertainers of the time. Hugh wrote many songs, ranging from those sung by Bill Monroe to those played by the popular swing bands of the era to those sung by the likes of Polly Bergen. For years Cas hired "Red and Fred," Red being Red Rector, the nationally renowned mandolin player. He had the Brewster Brothers, the Webster Brothers, and the Louvin Brothers, who the reader will recall were "discovered" by Bob Douglas. Charles and Danny Bailey played for Cas before going on the *Grand Ole Opry*. Then there was Honey Wilds of the "Jam Up and Honey" *Grand Ole Opry* fame. Some others include Carl and Pearl Butler, Carl Smith, Arthur Q. Smith, Tater Tate, Raymond Fairchild, Junior Husky, James Carson, Russ Jeffers, and a hundred more. Cas even claimed that Elvis Presley got his start with the Blackwood Brothers Quartet when they were singing on Cas' program.

The assistance which Cas Walker provided his entertainers was not limited to featuring them on his radio and television programs. He often accompanied them when they made "personal appearances" at night throughout much of Southern Appalachia—to little school houses, community centers, and small town theaters. David West started playing the banjo for Cas as a young man (at the same time he was driving a school bus for me when I was school superintendent). David became Cas' protege, and Cas was David's mentor, helping him not only in his music career, but in his successful business ventures.

While Lowell Blanchard and Cas Walker were introducing throngs of early country music entertainers to their rather extensive radio listening audiences, a similar pattern of broadcasting was commencing across much of the country. There has been a pretty direct correlation between the popularity of traditional country music and the number of radio stations which played it. The reader will recall that Mac Wiseman observed that the number of radio stations devoted wholly or in part to country music in the early 1950s numbered about 1500, and that when the Elvis and Beetle mania swept the nation in the late 1950s, the number of "country music stations" had dramatically dropped, by almost 90%, down to only 150. With the resurgence of contemporary and "modern" country music, however, the number of country stations had catapulted to some 2500 by the 1990s.

One may argue the "chicken or egg" question here. Was the up and down popularity of country music caused by the fluctuation of the number of radio stations playing this type music, or did the radio stations start, and stop, playing country music because of its popularity, or lack thereof, brought on by other important factors—records, tapes, television, person appearances, etc.?

A revealing incident concerning modern radio and old-time music occurred during the very last hours of my writing this book—even as Peter Schiffer, the publisher, called to "order" me to quit writing and send in the remainder of what I had.

It happened on Saturday night, June 26, 1999, in, appropriately, Knoxville, Tennessee. Garrison Keillor of *Prairie Home Companion* fame had come to Knoxville to broadcast his popular two-hour program carried by National Public Radio. It was held at the Knoxville Civic Auditorium, and tickets for the event had been sold out for weeks, even months, I'm informed. Scalpers were buying and selling them for in excess of $100 each. The event drew thousands of people of all ages and from all strata of society, from the old-time mountain folks, to largely professional people, as well as from the university and from academia in general.

Two of the three "special guests" for the evening were my dearest friends, both the epitome of old-time country musicians. One was fiddler Charlie Acuff who has been a member of my band for decades, and whom I've known and loved since my childhood. He's Roy Acuff's second cousin, and like Roy, Charlie is a native of Union County, Tennessee. The other featured musician was the beloved Bob Douglas, to which a chapter of this book is devoted.

Regrettably, I was not able to attend, but I did sit spellbound for those two hours, listening. And I'm informed that some 2.7 million other people also listened to this outstanding program.

Keillor introduced Bob Douglas, well into his 100th year. Bob, with his accompanist and benefactor Bobby Fulcher, first played "Polly Put the Kettle On," and the audience's response was wild. Keillor could not get them stopped.

Keillor talked with Bob, and Bob's quick and fitting wit was appreciated by the audience in the same manner as was his fiddling. Protracted laughter and applause followed all of Bob's quips.

After talking with Bob for several minutes, Keillor, cognizant of Bob's 99 years and of the fact that Bob had been standing, not only during his performance, but during the interview, said to Bob: "Mr. Douglas, why am I sitting down and you're standing up?" Bob responded dryly: "I's a wondering that myself."

When Charlie Acuff, with the Lantana Drifters, played "Cacklin' Hen," there was an instantaneous burst of applause which increased in intensity as it continued for several minutes. Keillor could hardly break in.

I listened to the two-hour program, and I was greatly moved, inspired and brought to tears. These two dear friends, totally unselfish, giving, caring, and empathetic souls, were being so well received in a day and age in which their type of music had been "out of style" for over a half century.

The tumultuous manner in which Charlie and Bob were accepted provided heart and hope that our old-time mountain music may after all possess a genuine and intrinsic quality which, while fading temporarily and periodically, will remain a part of our culture, our heritage and our being for generations to come.

Charlie Acuff is shown here at the annual Tennessee Fall Homecoming playing the fiddle his father made for him 66 years ago. *Photo taken at the Museum of Appalachia courtesy Charlie Acuff*

INDEX

Page numbers for photographs are in italics

W

Walker, Cas, 232, 239-242, *239*, *240*
WAPO Radio (Chattanooga, Tennessee), 83
WARL Radio (Arlington, Virginia), 114
Warmack, Paul, *17*
Warren, Paul, *190*
WBMD Radio (Baltimore, Maryland), 170
WBOW Radio (Terre Haute, Indiana), 70
WBZ Radio (Boston, Massachusetts), 106
WCHS Radio (Charleston, West Virginia), 111
WCYB Radio (Briston, Virginia), 166
WDBJ Radio (Roanoke, Virginia), 170
WDOD Radio (Chattanooga, Tennessee), 81
WFDF Radio (Flint, Michigan), 141
WFIW Radio (Hopkinsville, Kentucky), 70
WGRC Radio (Louisville, Kentucky), *224*
WHKY Radio (Hickory, North Carolina), 185
WPAQ Radio (Mr. Airy, North Carolina), 170
WSM Radio (Nashville, Tennessee), 60
Whitaker, Renda, *10*, 11
Whitesburg, Tennessee, *13*
Whilhite, Hugh, Dr. ("Uncle Doc"), 222

Winston, Nathaniel, Dr., *196*, 197, *217*
Wise, Chubby, *168*
Wiseman, Kent, *206*
Wiseman, Mac, *156*, 157-177, *158*, *165*, *167*, *168*, *169*, *171*, *173,174*, *175*, *177*, 184, 193-194
WJW Radio (Akron, Ohio), 104
WLAC Radio (Nashville, Tennessee), 65, 68
WLW Radio (Cincinnati, Ohio), 111
WNOX Radio (Knoxville, Tennessee), 46, 166, 235
Wolfe, Dr. Charles, 12, 41, 57, 60, 65, 68-69, 82, 94, 112, 124, 130, 188, 220, 222
WROL Radio (Knoxville, Tennessee), 183, 186
WSB Radio (Atlanta, Georgia), 167
WSM Radio (Nashville, Tennessee), *61*, 68, 69, *168*, 189, 235
WSVA Radio (Harrisonburg, Virginia), 164
WVLK Radio (Lexington, Kentucky), *187*
WWVA Radio (Wheeling, West Virginia), 110, *170*

X

XERA Radio (Villa Acuna, Mexico), 43